Lecture Notes in Computer Science 13622

Founding Editors

Gerhard Goos
Juris Hartmanis

The series Lecture Notes in Computer Science (LNCS), including its subseries Lecture Notes in Artificial Intelligence (LNAI) and Lecture Notes in Bioinformatics (LNBI), has established itself as a medium for the publication of new developments in computer science and information technology research, teaching, and education.

LNCS enjoys close cooperation with the computer science R & D community, the series counts many renowned academics among its volume editors and paper authors, and collaborates with prestigious societies. Its mission is to serve this international community by providing an invaluable service, mainly focused on the publication of conference and workshop proceedings and postproceedings. LNCS commenced publication in 1973.

Casper Harteveld · Steven Sutherland ·
Giovanni Troiano · Heide Lukosch ·
Sebastiaan Meijer

Editors

Simulation and Gaming for Social Impact

53rd International Simulation and Gaming
Association Conference, ISAGA 2022
Boston, MA, USA, July 11–14, 2022
Revised Selected Papers

 Springer

Editors
Casper Harteveld ⓘ
Northeastern University
Boston, MA, USA

Giovanni Troiano ⓘ
Northeastern University
Boston, MA, USA

Sebastiaan Meijer ⓘ
KTH Royal Institute of Technology
Stockholm, Sweden

Steven Sutherland ⓘ
University of Houston - Clear Lake
Houston, TX, USA

Heide Lukosch ⓘ
University of Canterbury
Christchurch, New Zealand

ISSN 0302-9743 ISSN 1611-3349 (electronic)
Lecture Notes in Computer Science
ISBN 978-3-031-37170-7 ISBN 978-3-031-37171-4 (eBook)
https://doi.org/10.1007/978-3-031-37171-4

This Springer imprint is published by the registered company Springer Nature Switzerland AG
The registered company address is: Gewerbestrasse 11, 6330 Cham, Switzerland

Preface

Welcome to the Lecture Notes in Computer Science (LNCS) ISAGA 2022 proceedings. The LNCS ISAGA 2022 proceedings are a result of selected full-paper contributions from the 53rd annual international conference of the International Simulation and Gaming Association (ISAGA).

Founded in the seventies, ISAGA is one of the oldest communities of people involved in the domain of gaming and simulation. Its members cover a vast knowledge and tradition in developing and using simulation, gaming, and related methods. Today, the community spans everything from traditional policy exercises to the latest in interactive technologies. ISAGA is highly relevant in this era of combining computer gaming, interactive media, serious gaming, new learning technologies, and much more in a powerful mix to solve many complex societal challenges. We celebrated this "powerful mix" for ISAGA 2022 with our main theme of "Simulation and Gaming for Social Impact" and the sub-themes of Education & Training, Resilience & Sustainability, Health, and Social Justice.

The 53rd ISAGA took place at the Interdisciplinary Science and Engineering Complex (ISEC) at Northeastern University in Boston, USA, from July 11 to 14, 2022. The hybrid conference program, with 70 in-person and 47 online attendees, included 14 workshops, 14 games/posters, 11 extended abstracts posters, and the following keynote speakers, each associated with one of the four sub-themes:

- **Constance M. Yowell**, Senior Vice Chancellor at Northeastern University, *Games, Simulations and the Future of Learning: Lessons Learned* [Education & Training]
- **Igor Mayer**, Professor at Breda University of Applied Sciences and Tilburg University, *Digital Twins for the Real World* [Resilience & Sustainability]
- **Kimberly Hieftje**, Assistant Professor at Yale University, *XR for Youth: Where Are We, and Where Are We Going?* [Health]
- **Kishonna Gray**, Associate Professor at the University of Kentucky, *Gaming by Another Name: The Racialization of Play in the Digital Era* [Social Justice]

In total, 24 full papers were submitted to ISAGA 2022. Each paper went through a double-blind review process with 2-3 reviewers and was revised and resubmitted prior to the conference. After the conference, we, as editors of the LNCS ISAGA 2022 proceedings, reviewed all revised submissions and independently determined whether a submission should be included. There was no predetermined percentage of submissions that we aimed to include. The aim was to consider submissions that were of sufficient quality and that did not require substantial revisions to be included. We considered in this process the ISAGA 2022 reviews and how these were addressed in the revision. In the case of disagreement, we would discuss the submission and do another review. Through this process, a natural selection emerged of which papers to include. In the end, we selected 15 papers, resulting in an acceptance rate of 62.5%.

These 15 selected papers make up the LNCS ISAGA 2022 proceedings and demonstrate the wide variety of simulation and gaming topics that the ISAGA community embraces, from using virtual reality (VR) to support chronic pain treatment to using physical cards for biosafety. Three papers stood out for their contributions to the ISAGA community and were awarded during the conference:

- **Best paper:** "Theory-based development of an inventory for the evaluation of simulation game lectures" by Friedrich Trautwein and Tobias Alf
- **Honorable Mention:** "Quantitative analysis of conflict-of-interest structures in the consensus building process" by Ibu Ueno and Shingo Takahashi
- **Honorable Mention:** "Feedback on a 'territory-responsive' participatory simulation on coastal flooding risk applied to two case studies in France" by Amélie Monfort, Nicolas Becu, and Marion Amalric

The proceedings are organized according to the four sub-themes of Education & Training, Resilience & Sustainability, Health, and Social Justice (in that order). While some contributions can fit multiple sub-themes, we see that the first three sub-themes happen to be somewhat evenly distributed (4–5 papers each). For Social Justice, however, we count only one paper. Therefore, the ISAGA community may want to consider focusing on this topic more.

ISAGA 2022 was made possible with the support of the ISAGA organization and the College of Arts, Media and Design (CAMD) at Northeastern University. In addition, the Center for Design at CAMD, the University of Houston-Clear Lake, and the Ghost Lab helped in organizing the conference. We thank these organizations for their support—as well as the authors, attendees, volunteers, staff, and everyone else that made ISAGA 2022 a possibility.

May 2023

Casper Harteveld
Steven Sutherland
Giovanni Troiano
Heide Lukosch
Sebastiaan Meijer

Organization

General Chair

Casper Harteveld   Northeastern University, USA

Program Committee Chairs

Steven Sutherland   University of Houston-Clear Lake, USA
Giovanni Troiano   Northeastern University, USA

Steering Committee

Heide Lukosch   University of Canterbury, New Zealand
Sebastiaan Meijer   KTH Royal Institute of Technology, Sweden

Website and Visual Designer

Mustafa Sonbudak   Northeastern University, USA

Program Committee

Ghada Alsebayel   Northeastern University, USA
Sandeep Athavale   TCS, India
Meike Belter   University of Canterbury, New Zealand
Rafael Bidarra   Delft University of Technology, The Netherlands
Malgorzata Cwil   Kozminski University, Poland
Upinder Dhar   Shri Vaishnav Vidyapeeth Vishwavidyalaya, India
Vinod Dumblekar   MANTIS, India
Pongchai Dumrongrojwatthana   Chulalongkorn University, Thailand
Maria Freese   Delft University of Technology, The Netherlands
Nadezhda Gerasimenko   Independent researcher, Russia
Shesh Narayan Gupta   Northeastern University, USA
Ryoju Hamada   National Institute of Technology, Japan
J. Tuomas Harviainen   Tampere University, Finland

Contents

Health

Social Justice

Education and Training

Theory-Based Development of an Inventory for the Evaluation of Simulation Game Lectures

Friedrich Trautwein[✉] and Tobias Alf

Centre for Management Simulation, Baden-Wuerttemberg Cooperative State University, Stuttgart, Germany
friedrich.trautwein@dhbw-stuttgart.de

Abstract. This article describes the theoretical and methodical procedure for the development of a standard questionnaire (inventory) for the evaluation of teaching with simulation games. Based on theoretical considerations, a starting model for the evaluation of lecturing with simulation games was created. To verify the initial model, surveys were conducted in eleven courses at the Centre for Management Simulation (ZMS) at the Baden-Wuerttemberg Cooperative State University/Germany (DHBW) using six different simulation games. Based on 182 data sets, exploratory and confirmatory factor analyses were used to test and improve the initial model for the evaluation of teaching with simulation games. This improved theoretically and empirically based model for the evaluation of teaching with simulation games forms the basis for the final questionnaire. Combined with different methodological approaches the inventory for the evaluation of teaching with simulation games offers a wide variety of opportunities for advanced research on teaching with simulation games. Between April and December 2021, the inventory has already been used in more than 75 simulation game courses and has been combined with other quantitative and qualitative research methods. In the meantime, roughly 3.000 students participating in over 150 Face-to-Face and Online simulation game courses with more than 30 different simulation games have filled in the questionnaire. First analysis on this broad empirical basis confirm that the questionnaire can be successfully used for a broad variety of simulation game based courses.

Keywords: Evaluation · Questionnaire · Empirical research · Factor Analysis · Simulation Game

1 Introduction

1.1 Background

Simulation games have become a standard part of teaching in many areas and are firmly anchored in the curricula of universities (cf. exemplary DHBW Stuttgart; Meßner et al. 2018). Similarly, simulation games are used in many ways in company training as well as in schools. At the same time, this creates the need for an evaluation of simulation game events in order to assess their quality and to improve them.

© The Author(s), under exclusive license to Springer Nature Switzerland AG 2023
C. Harteveld et al. (Eds.): ISAGA 2022, LNCS 13622, pp. 3–21, 2023.
https://doi.org/10.1007/978-3-031-37171-4_1

The evaluation of simulation game events has therefore been a much-discussed topic in science for years (Feinstein and Cannon 2002; Kriz and Hense 2006). In most cases, comprehensive and differentiated evaluation instruments were developed with the aim of gaining insights for a specific question or a specific simulation game (Cronan et al. 2012; Kriz and Hense 2006; Trautwein 2011). Unlike in classical course evaluation, there is no standard inventory for the evaluation of simulation game events. In practice, therefore, simulation game events are often evaluated, for example at the DHBW Stuttgart, with a standard questionnaire that is identical for all courses. However, in view of the characteristics of simulation game courses, which differ significantly from classic courses, such standard questionnaires are only suitable to a very limited extent and can only capture a section of the teaching/learning process in a simulation game. In particular, standard questionnaires do not contain any questions about the simulation game used. Furthermore, the importance of working in small groups, which is often central to simulation game events, is not adequately captured.

1.2 Objective

Due to this background, the aim of the ZMS research project was to design a (standard) questionnaire that makes it possible to evaluate a broad variety of different simulation games of all types at least from all areas of the social sciences and the simulation game events based on them.[1] This questionnaire allows to compare very different simulation games and to identify structural features for the successful use of simulation games. Furthermore, the questionnaire is intended to give teachers well-based feedback on their lectures and thus enable them to improve their seminar concepts.

In order to enable a broad use of the evaluation instruments, the focus was on developing a deliberately very short questionnaire that enables a low-threshold use without requiring changes to the conception or the time schedule of simulation-based classes. The questionnaire presented below can be completed in about five minutes and thus offers the possibility of being used on a broad scale without causing resistance.

This focus also means that limitations have to be accepted. Thus, no contribution can be made to solving questions that would require a more comprehensive, differentiated set of evaluation instruments. For example, learning success is not recorded in a differentiated way and not on an objective level, but as a self-assessment. Likewise, qualitative questions that could potentially contribute to a deeper understanding and explanation of quantitative results were omitted. Nevertheless, the inventory also offers opportunities to address research questions where it cannot itself make a direct contribution. The questionnaire makes it possible for additional survey instruments to be

---

[1] The only restriction is, that in case there are no teams in the simulation game course, these questions have to be ignored.

used with a sub-sample in order to pursue specific questions with, if necessary, much more complex and extensive survey designs, as it is currently done at the ZMS in several research projects (e.g. Hühn and Rausch 2022). Linking additional surveys with the standard questionnaire offers the opportunity to check the validity of the survey instruments. Furthermore, it can be checked whether a possibly quite small sample that was used for a specific question is representative of the population that is surveyed with the standard inventory. This offers the opportunity to critically reflect on research results based on small samples with regard to generalisability.

1.3 Procedure and Research Methodology

Based on the objective of the survey, a detailed initial questionnaire was first developed, which contains items from various teaching evaluation inventories in particular, but also questionnaires specific to simulation games (cf. Sect. 2). Based on an empirical study with data sets of 182 students from 11 simulation game courses with 6 different simulation games, this was condensed to a short version (cf. Sect. 3). Subsequently, Sect. 4 identifies restrictions and perspectives before the conclusion (Sect. 5) completes the article.

In essence, the empirical-quantitative study is based on the (self-)perception of the students, supplemented by the largely objective survey of the framework conditions by the facilitators. There are pragmatic reasons for this methodology, since an objective recording of success variables, group variables, etc. would be far more time-consuming and only feasible in a much smaller sample. However, there are other factors that speak in favour of focusing on the participants' self-assessment (cf. Trautwein 2004, 57ff.): First of all, the participants perceive themselves in a more differentiated way than is possible for observers. In addition, a connection between self-assessment and assessment by others has been empirically confirmed many times, even though self-assessment is certainly not an objective picture of reality. In addition, there is another important aspect: even if the self-assessment is objectively wrong, it would still be significant, as people's self-assessment is highly action-guiding (cf. Trautwein 2004, 58f.). With regard to the use of simulation games, Schwägele (cf. 2017, 59ff.) concludes that the subjective evaluation of each of the four key factors (consistency and closeness to reality, relevance and closeness to everyday life, requirements, social situation) is decisive for the success of simulation games. Therefore the subjective perception of simulation game events by the participants is a central element for the evaluation and further development of simulation game lectures.

2 Development of the Initial Questionnaire

First, an initial questionnaire was developed (see Fig. 1 for the structure of the initial questionnaire and the individual items and their origin). This questionnaire is based on the model of the Heidelberg Inventory for Course Evaluation (HILVE) (cf. Rindermann 2009) and the research results on the use of simulation games in industrial university studies by Trautwein (cf. 2011). From this, the relevant influencing factors for the success of courses in general emerged: students, facilitators and framework conditions (cf. Rindermann 2009, p. 66). In addition, Trautwein identified the simulation game and the group/team of a student as influencing factors specific to simulation game events (cf. Trautwein 2011, 124ff.). Due to the focus of current simulation game research on questions of facilitation and debriefing (cf. Leigh et al. 2021), specific questions were also asked about debriefing and interaction with simulation game instructors.

The dependent variables were differentiated between the learning success on the one hand and the overall satisfaction on the other. The model derived from this with the assigned questions is illustrated in Fig. 1.

Based on the theoretical model, items from various course inventories (cf. Knödler 2019; Rindermann 2009; Arbeitskreis "Lehrevaluation" im Fach Psychologie et al. 2002) as well as simulation-game-specific surveys (cf. Trautwein 2011) were considered and a questionnaire for students with 66 items was generated. This questionnaire was used to survey students from different business administration degree programmes at the DHBW Stuttgart in the period from 18.02.2021 to 19.03.2021, who took part in six different simulation games, all of which were conducted online. The survey resulted in a total of 182 data records, which were included in the evaluation[2] (cf. Fig. 2).

Based on the questionnaire by Trautwein (cf. 2011) and our own reflections, a questionnaire was also developed for the facilitators. In relation to the overall model, this mainly contains questions on the general conditions. This includes questions about the basic organisation of the simulation game (for example, the time frame and the form in which it was conducted, e.g. online or face-to-face), the didactics (for example, the scope of the debriefing), the students (for example, the size and formation of the groups) and the facilitators (for example, the number of facilitators and their experience). In addition, it was asked when the students completed the questionnaire and how satisfied the simulation leaders were with the course of the event. For quality assurance purposes, the questionnaire was discussed with several simulation game experts within the ZMS. In addition, it was subjected to a pre-test by four facilitators.

---

[2] A total of 197 students answered the questionnaire. 15 data sets were eliminated by the authors due to incompleteness, so that 182 are included in the further data analysis.

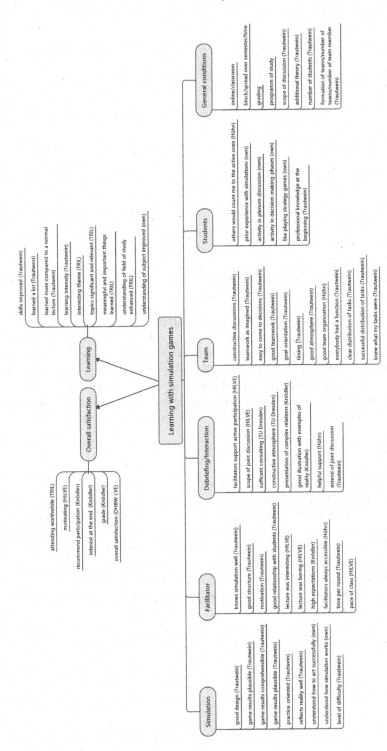

Fig. 1. Initial model for evaluating teaching with simulation games

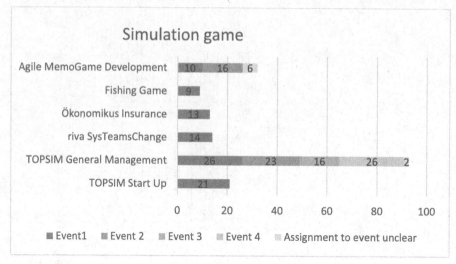

Fig. 2. Overview of the use of the initial questionnaire by simulation game and participants.

3 Development of the Short Questionnaire

Based on the quantitative evaluation of the initial questionnaire, the short questionnaire was developed (cf. ZMS Inventory Students). For this purpose, the results of the explorative factor analysis are first examined and discussed in Sect. 3.1, before the selection of the items for the short questionnaire is analysed and justified on the basis of the differentiated examination of the individual dimensions in the following chapters.

3.1 Exploratory Factor Analysis

On the basis of 55 items, which were answered by the students on a six-point Likert scale, an explorative factor analysis was carried out. The differentiated results of this factor analysis with all items included can be found in Table 1. Here, the theoretically assumed structure was confirmed, especially with regard to the different dimensions of the influencing factors. In the following, the results of the explorative factor analysis are examined in more detail. The analysis is based on the usual scientific conventions (Backhaus et al. 2016, p. 418). Variables are assigned to a factor if they load >0.5 on it. In the case of cross-loadings, a variable is only assigned to the factor with the higher loading if the difference is clear (>0.2).

The 14 items with the strongest loading on the first extracted component all relate to learning and the overall satisfaction. Contrary to theoretical assumptions, students do not differentiate between these two aspects. If students think they have learned something in a simulation game lecture, they are also satisfied with it. These items are therefore combined into one scale in the final inventory (cf. Sect. 3.7). The other items loading on this factor come from various other areas. What they have in common is that they load (significantly) weaker than the dominant items from the two areas of overall satisfaction and learning and are therefore less characteristic of this dimension.

With regard to the influencing factors, there was only one structural deviation from the theoretical model. The respondents see the facilitators (cf. Sect. 3.3) as one factor (component 3). This factor includes four items that were assigned to the area of debriefing/interaction and three items that were assigned to the facilitators in general. These two areas are therefore combined. The explorative factor analysis thus confirms Trautwein's model (cf. 2011, p. 124), which considers facilitation as one factor. The other dimensions can be confirmed structurally. Thus, all items from component 2 can be assigned to team/group work. Furthermore, the four items with the strongest loading on component 4 all relate to the simulation game used. In addition, three of the four items from the area of students included in the explorative factor analysis are found in component 6. The other extracted components refer to partial aspects of the theoretically assumed dimensions such as the distribution of tasks in the team/group (component 5) and the expectations of facilitators from students (component 7) or are individual items (components 8 to 11). The items "Like playing strategy games" and "Interest at the beginning" are so-called bias or control variables (cf. Rindermann 2009, p. 181ff.; Knödler 2019, p. 264). This means that they do not measure the quality of the simulation game event, but related topics, e.g. whether someone basically likes to play or is already interested in the event before it begins. This also becomes clear in the factor analysis. The two items are distinct from the dimensions determined by factor analysis, i.e. they are thematically different from them. This is an indication that, for example, component 6 with the three activity variables actually measures the students' engagement during the simulation game and not the possibly distorting effect of how much someone likes to play. The fact that "Interest at the beginning" differs significantly from the overall satisfaction in terms of factor analysis indicates that the questionnaire actually measures satisfaction with the event - and not the perception of the event distorted by the students' prior interest. The differentiating bias variables thus provide indications for a good validity of the questionnaire; the questionnaire measures what it claims to measure.

Table 1. Exploratory factor analysis

	1	2	3	4	5	6	7	8	9	10	11
Visit worthwhile	0,88	0,12	0,17	0,15	0,03	0,05	0,05	0,12	0,06	0,08	-0,01
Recommend participation	0,87	0,07	0,10	0,13	0,09	-0,02	0,04	0,02	0,06	0,24	0,01
Motivating simulation game	0,86	0,12	0,06	0,13	0,04	0,09	0,05	0,06	0,06	0,18	0,12
Meaningful and important things learned	0,84	0,07	0,22	0,19	0,06	0,05	0,08	0,08	0,11	-0,10	-0,05
Learned more compared to normal lecture	0,81	0,09	0,15	0,07	0,01	0,08	0,14	-0,04	-0,12	-0,18	-0,12
Overall satisfaction	0,81	0,22	0,16	0,18	0,01	0,02	-0,02	0,03	-0,06	0,22	0,04
grade (umcod)	0,81	0,12	0,16	0,17	0,02	-0,02	-0,06	0,06	-0,08	0,30	0,02
Understanding of field of study enhanced	0,80	0,11	0,17	-0,02	0,07	0,10	-0,06	0,01	0,19	-0,13	0,01
Interest at the end	0,80	0,12	0,10	0,18	0,07	0,10	0,03	0,00	-0,15	0,32	0,00
Understanding of subject improved	0,79	0,12	0,17	-0,02	0,04	0,06	0,00	-0,01	0,16	-0,12	0,04
Learned a lot	0,77	0,13	0,22	0,19	0,06	0,05	0,18	0,12	0,04	-0,10	-0,06
Learning intensity	0,77	0,15	0,15	0,08	0,03	-0,03	0,29	0,05	-0,13	-0,17	-0,05
Topics significant and relevant	0,76	0,02	0,19	0,10	0,05	0,13	0,07	0,05	0,22	-0,22	0,17
Skills improved	0,70	0,15	0,27	0,14	0,07	0,06	0,18	0,09	0,06	-0,15	-0,04
Interesting theme	0,64	0,10	0,10	0,18	0,01	0,18	0,06	0,11	0,39	-0,09	0,24
Lecture was interesting	0,62	0,11	0,38	0,06	0,08	0,13	0,09	0,09	-0,17	0,25	-0,10
Lecture was boring (umcod)	0,61	0,08	0,16	0,05	0,08	0,17	-0,06	0,11	-0,19	0,21	-0,20
Practise-oriented	0,60	0,13	0,17	0,16	0,11	-0,06	0,03	0,53	-0,09	0,00	0,14
Good design	0,48	0,12	0,18	0,39	0,13	0,00	0,07	0,01	0,06	0,44	0,10
Good structure	0,48	0,14	0,30	0,03	-0,20	0,18	0,14	0,30	-0,27	0,23	-0,34
Good illustration with examples of reality	0,45	0,10	0,45	0,09	0,00	0,16	0,03	0,07	-0,14	-0,31	0,12
Good teamwork	0,18	0,84	0,10	0,03	0,27	0,04	0,02	0,10	0,00	0,10	0,09
Good atmosphere in team	0,10	0,83	0,12	0,05	0,14	0,04	0,04	0,11	-0,03	0,13	0,05
Good team organisation	0,21	0,82	-0,02	0,03	0,16	0,07	0,02	0,03	-0,04	-0,02	0,00
Teamwork as imagined	0,19	0,78	0,13	-0,04	0,32	-0,06	-0,01	0,08	0,05	0,17	0,05
Easy to come to decisions	-0,01	0,75	0,06	0,11	-0,03	0,16	0,08	-0,22	0,02	-0,09	-0,13
Timing in group	0,13	0,73	0,06	0,11	-0,04	0,00	-0,12	0,04	-0,10	-0,09	-0,14
Goal-orientation	0,14	0,70	-0,03	0,25	0,13	-0,04	0,08	0,01	0,14	-0,14	0,12
Constructive discussions in team	0,21	0,66	0,21	-0,10	0,30	0,01	0,12	0,11	0,23	0,13	0,09
Constructive atmosphere with facilitator	0,21	0,15	0,85	0,10	-0,01	0,03	0,07	0,09	0,02	0,05	0,02
Sufficient consultation	0,12	0,18	0,76	0,17	0,03	-0,04	0,14	-0,12	0,00	-0,01	0,11
Helpful support	0,38	-0,07	0,75	-0,03	0,00	-0,06	0,06	0,21	-0,06	-0,09	-0,08
Motivation of facilitator	0,26	0,12	0,72	0,05	0,05	0,19	0,18	0,09	0,05	0,09	-0,17

(continued)

Table 1. (*continued*)

Good relationship facilitator and students	0,28	0,04	0,71	0,12	0,06	0,06	0,00	-0,04	0,13	0,08	-0,16
Facilitator always accessible	0,11	0,16	0,60	0,16	0,02	-0,10	-0,05	-0,16	-0,12	0,15	0,41
Presentation of complex relations	0,41	0,01	0,57	-0,05	0,10	-0,09	-0,05	0,16	-0,27	-0,28	-0,05
Scope of joint discussion	0,24	-0,06	0,55	0,15	0,12	0,15	0,29	0,17	-0,07	0,03	-0,04
Game results comprehensible	0,20	0,08	0,24	0,78	0,14	0,02	0,01	0,05	0,00	-0,11	-0,08
Game results plausible	0,26	0,07	0,22	0,75	0,15	0,10	0,00	0,16	0,03	-0,08	-0,03
Understood how simulation works	0,32	0,10	0,06	0,63	0,00	0,21	0,03	-0,07	-0,08	0,26	0,11
Understand how to act successfully	0,49	0,09	-0,06	0,53	0,10	0,12	0,12	-0,01	-0,03	0,16	0,10
Game results plausible	0,25	0,27	0,14	0,51	-0,05	0,02	-0,03	0,33	0,02	0,08	-0,02
Clear distribution of tasks	0,05	0,24	0,05	0,08	0,86	0,13	0,07	-0,01	-0,01	-0,04	0,06
Everybody had a function	0,09	0,38	0,05	0,06	0,81	0,01	-0,03	0,05	0,00	0,04	0,06
Successful distribution of tasks	0,12	0,49	0,03	0,13	0,74	-0,01	0,01	0,02	0,00	0,03	-0,02
Knew what my tasks were	0,13	0,12	0,12	0,16	0,55	0,43	0,17	-0,06	0,23	-0,01	-0,04
Others would count me to the active ones	0,17	-0,02	0,04	0,01	0,09	0,87	-0,11	-0,01	0,02	0,00	0,06
Activity in decision-making-phases	0,24	0,17	0,08	0,12	0,06	0,81	0,01	-0,10	-0,03	0,11	0,05
Activity in plenum discussion	-0,02	-0,01	-0,01	0,18	0,07	0,53	0,14	0,35	0,05	-0,13	0,15
Facilitators support active participation	0,19	0,04	0,27	0,29	0,09	0,05	0,66	-0,06	-0,02	-0,05	-0,04
High expectations	0,21	0,06	0,19	-0,29	0,07	-0,08	0,63	0,03	-0,06	0,05	0,19
Facilitator knows simulation well	0,18	0,08	0,33	0,15	-0,10	0,09	0,41	0,31	0,04	0,30	-0,35
Reflects reality well	0,46	0,18	0,19	0,24	-0,01	0,02	-0,05	0,60	-0,03	0,00	0,07
Interest at the beginning	0,12	0,07	-0,07	-0,03	0,05	0,02	-0,06	-0,03	0,82	0,02	0,03
Like playing strategy games	0,05	0,02	-0,07	0,01	0,04	0,22	0,07	0,11	0,06	0,01	0,75

3.2 Simulation Game

If we only examine the items on the topic of simulation games in a factor analysis, two components emerge that can also be interpreted very well in terms of content (cf. Table 2). The three items of component 1 express the extent to which the students consider the simulation to be logical and comprehensible. Component 2, on the other hand, expresses whether the students consider the simulation to be close to reality. If a reliability analysis is carried out for the two components determined, the values for Cronbach's alpha[3] are 0.783 for component 1 and 0.863 for component 2. If all five items are combined into one scale, Cronbach's alpha is 0.806.

---

[3] In accordance with scientific practice, Cronbach's alpha values from 0.7 are considered acceptable, from 0.8 good (cf. Hossiep 2021).

Table 2. Items Simulation game

Rotated component matrix[a]: Items Simulation game

	Component	
	1	2
The results of the simulation are very comprehensible[b]	**,882**	,069
The results of the simulation are plausible	**,825**	,186
I understood how the simulation works	**,652**	,346
I know what I have to do in order to act successfully in the simulation	,561	,463
The written information provided is easy to understand	,495	,418
The simulation has a close practical orientation	,157	**,889**
The simulation game is a good representation of reality	,204	**,867**
The simulation game is attractively designed	,508	,516

Extraction method: Principal component analysis.
Rotation method: Varimax with Kaiser normalisation.
[a]The rotation has converged in 3 iterations.
[b]Items used in the final questionnaire are always marked in bold.

3.3 Facilitator

As described in the results of the explorative factor analysis of all items, the differentiation into more general aspects of the facilitation and the debriefing/interaction phase in particular was not confirmed. However, if we look at the facilitation items in isolation, a different picture emerges (cf. Table 3).

If the items of the two theoretically derived dimensions are combined in a factor analysis, two factors emerge that tend to represent the two theoretically derived dimensions. Thus, all four items of component 2 belong to the area of facilitator in general of the initial questionnaire. Of the eleven items in component 1, seven belong to the area of debriefing and interaction. For the short questionnaire, the three items that loaded most heavily on the first factor were selected from the total of 15 items ("There was sufficient opportunity to consult with the facilitator.", "Consultation with the facilitator took place in a constructive atmosphere.", "Support of the facilitator was professionally helpful."). As an alternative, it would be worth considering using the item "The instructor was always available to answer questions.". Although this item has a somewhat weaker loading on factor 1, it does not have a double loading, but the explorative factor analysis speaks against this approach. From factor 2, the factor with the highest loading, "The seminar was well structured.", was selected, as well as the additional item "The instructor is very familiar with the simulation.", which is clearly assigned to factor 2. Taking all five items together results in a scale with an alpha value of 0.803. The two subscales have Cronbach's alpha values of 0.823 (factor 1) and 0.744 (factor 2).

Table 3. Items Facilitator

Rotated component matrix[a]: Items Facilitator and Debriefing/Interaction

	Component	
	1	2
There was sufficient opportunity to consult with the facilitator	**,852**	,052
Consultation with the facilitator took place in a constructive atmosphere	**,834**	,277
Support of the facilitator was professionally helpful	**,649**	,492
The instructor was motivated	,638	,473
The relationship between instructor and students was good	,630	,384
The instructor was always available to answer questions	,617	,035
The facilitator presented complex contexts instead of superficial factual knowledge	,589	,328
Discussions were well guided (stimulating contributions, responding to contributions, time management, stopping of frequent speakers)	,544	,454
The facilitator clarifies content with examples from practice	,504	,421
The facilitator encouraged questions and active participation	,434	,306
The facilitator set a high level of expectations for the students	,357	,061
The seminar was well structured	,156	**,839**
The lecture was boring (umcod.)	,086	,771
The seminar was held in an interesting format	,361	,731
The instructor is very familiar with the simulation	,172	**,696**

Extraction method: Principal component analysis.
Rotation method: Varimax with Kaiser normalisation.
[a]The rotation has converged in 3 iterations.

3.4 Team

Based on the twelve items of the category team/group, SPSS extracts two factors that can be interpreted very well. Factor 1 focuses on cooperation in the team, while the items assigned to factor 2 deal specifically with the distribution of tasks in the team. Since all items are basically suitable in terms of content and assignment to one of the components, when selecting the items for the short questionnaire, the main focus was on which items had only low double loadings. The items included at the end express a broad spectrum of group-related perceptions. The reliability (Cronbach's alpha) for the total scale with the seven selected items is 0.825, while the values for subscale 1 and 2 are 0.833 and 0.819 (Table 4).

Table 4. Items Team

Rotated component matrix^a: Items Team/group

	Component	
	1	2
I would say that our team was well organised	**,826**	,243
We worked well together in the group	,824	,377
The atmosphere in the group was good	**,812**	,261
The cooperation in the group was as I imagine it to be	,775	,402
The timing in the group worked well	**,748**	-,005
We found it easy to come to decisions as a group	**,734**	,109
We have taken a targeted approach	,720	,235
The discussion in the group was constructive	,641	,396
There was a clear distribution of tasks in the group	,147	**,886**
Everyone in the group had a function	,291	**,841**
The distribution of tasks in the group worked out well for us	,421	,789
I knew what my tasks were	,094	**,728**

Extraction method: Principal component analysis.
Rotation method: Varimax with Kaiser normalisation.
^{a}The rotation has converged in 3 iterations.

3.5 Students

Four questions to be answered on a 6-point scale were asked about the student activity (Table 5).

Table 5. Items Students

Component matrix^a: Items Students

	Component
	1
When others look at my role, they would count me as one of the more active participants	**,883**
I actively participated in the decision-making phases (work in small groups)	**,836**
I actively participated in the evaluation phases (joint discussion of the game results in the plenum)	**,622**
I like playing strategy games (e.g. chess, Risk, Settlers of Catan)	,453

Extraction method: Principal component analysis.
^{a}1 components extracted.

The factor analysis shows only one factor for this dimension. The low loading of the bias item "I like playing strategy games (e.g. chess, Risk, Settlers of Catan)" is immediately striking. Looking more closely at the reliability of the scale, the scale with all four items would have a Cronbach's alpha of only 0.627. If the item is eliminated, Cronbach's alpha rises to 0.690. The reliability increases significantly again (Cronbach's alpha of 0.835) if the item "I actively participated in the evaluation phases" is also omitted. However, since this item is interesting in terms of content and may allow a more differentiated view of student behaviour and its effects on the success of the game, it is included in the short questionnaire.

3.6 General Conditions

The general conditions are only collected from the facilitators and are not combined into scales. Since there is always one data set per simulation game event, the available data sets would not be sufficient for multivariate quantitative evaluations.

In the questionnaire for the facilitators (cf. ZMS Inventory Facilitator), the main aim of the present study was to check whether the questions were comprehensible. In addition, the respondents were asked to give feedback on whether they felt there were any issues missing. On this basis, the questionnaire was minimally revised.

3.7 Overall Satisfaction and Learning

What was already indicated by the explorative factor analysis with all items is confirmed by a closer look at the items "overall satisfaction" and "learning". Although there is a large number of 15 items, the factor analysis extracts only one component.

Due to this fact, the selection of items for the final questionnaire was based not only on factor loading but also on the importance of the content of the questions. In addition they should come from both underlying areas "overall satisfaction" and "learning". The question "How satisfied are you with the seminar overall?" was included because it is the only item that is also present in the standard evaluation instruments of the DHBW and thus a connection to this survey could be established if necessary. In addition, the overall satisfaction is covered by the item "All in all, attending the seminar was worth it for me". Furthermore, questions were selected that refer to the quantity "I learned a lot in the simulation game" and the quality "I learned something meaningful and important in this seminar" (cf. Rindermann 2009, p. 398). These items are supplemented by a question on motivation "I found the simulation very motivating" and on the question of whether the simulation strengthened the understanding of the field of study. With a Cronbach's alpha of 0.943, the scale of the selected questions has a very high reliability (Table 6).

Table 6. Items Overall Satisfaction and Learning

Component matrix[a]: Overall satisfaction and learning

	Component
	1
All in all, attending the seminar was worth it for me	**,931**
I learned something meaningful and important in this seminar	**,905**
I found the simulation very motivating	**,888**
I would recommend participation in this course to other students	,886
I learned a lot in the simulation game	**,861**
How satisfied are you with the seminar overall?	**,861**
My interest in the simulation game was at the end of the event…	,844
What grade would you give the event overall?	,839
I learned more than in a normal lecture	,827
My understanding of my field of study has been enhanced by the seminar	**,813**
The intensity of learning was high	,803
The simulation helps me to better understand the content of my field of study	,801
I have been able to develop my skills	,799
The topics covered were meaningful and relevant to me	,789
I was interested in the topic of the event	,687

Extraction method: Principal component analysis.
[a]1 components extracted.

3.8 Final Model

Overall, the empirical analysis confirms the initial model from an exploratory and confirmatory point of view (for detailed information look at the chapters before). However, significant changes result insofar as the two target dimensions (cf. Sect. 3.7) are merged into one dimension and the influencing factors are reduced by one dimension (cf. Sect. 3.3). At the same time, subcategories emerge in individual dimensions, e.g. communication and competence as subcategories of facilitator and comprehensibility and practical relevance as subcategories of the simulation game, that need to be examined more closely on a broader empirical basis (Fig. 3).

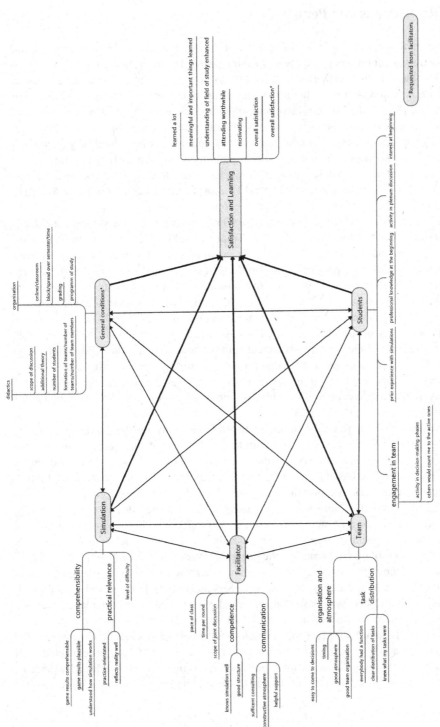

Fig. 3. Final model for evaluating teaching with simulation games. (The questionnaire for facilitators contains some further questions which are not listed in the chart, e.g. for comparison with the student responses.)

4   Restrictions and Perspectives

The central objective of developing a broad-based, low-threshold inventory for the evaluation of simulation game events also imposes some restrictions.

This includes the fact that the learning effects are only evaluated in an undifferentiated manner. A differentiated evaluation of the competence dimensions in which learning has taken place would be desirable and important for assessing in which context and for which learning objectives the use of simulation games is appropriate. Furthermore, valuable insights for the selection of a suitable simulation game could be gained from this. In future surveys, it should therefore be examined in which competence dimensions students see an increase in learning and how these relate to the overall learning success. The results of Trautwein (cf. 2011, p. 171) indicate that students primarily associate learning success with the increase in professional competence.

Furthermore, the data is essentially based on the perception of the students. Although numerous studies (Fondel et al. 2015; cf. Trautwein 2004, 82ff.) refer to the reliability of student evaluations in general, and even in simulation-game-specific research there are references to the reliability of students' self-assessment: "The results indicate significant correlation between the objective measures and the self-assessed measures of knowledge" (Cronan et al. 2012, p. 473). However, this correlation seems to become smaller for more complex learning content (cf. Cronan et al. 2012, p. 473). In view of the high complexity of simulation game events as a learning environment, it is conceivable that the validity of the student assessment is lower here. The aim should therefore be to check the student assessment of simulation games with objective data. Regardless of this, however, it is also explicitly true for simulation game events that, regardless of objective reality, subjective perception is of central importance for the success of simulation game events (cf. Schwägele 2017, p. 61ff.).

Moreover, the empirical results are based exclusively on the survey of students as participants. Future surveys must therefore show whether the questionnaire is also suitable for surveys in a company or school context, for example. In addition, the results presented above are based only on the German version of the questionnaire and future research has to check, whether the results are also valid for the English version.

All the simulation game events evaluated were conducted during online teaching. Therefore one of the next steps will be to check if differences become visible compared to face-to-face teaching. Due to the fact that the theoretical model does not show any specific aspects of online events and the items are taken from survey inventories designed for face-to-face events, there is reason to assume that at least structurally the same factors are relevant for online and face-to-face seminars and that the basic model is confirmed.

With the 182 data sets based on the initial questionnaire, quantitative evaluations would be possible on a univariate, bivariate and multivariate level for a number of questions. These are not planned, as much more robust results can be expected on the basis of the newly developed inventory, with more than 4.000 data sets expected until the end of 2022. In addition the final questionnaire is used for a much broader range of simulation games and it has to be evaluated, whether it really fits for all types of games.

The data from the newly developed inventory will be used to analyse, among others, which factors are decisive for the learning success and the overall evaluation of simulation game events. It will also be examined to what extent there are structural differences in the evaluation of different simulation games. In addition, the data will make it possible to look at a number of individual variables and to analyse, for example, the role of previous experience with simulation games, whether there are gender differences and which aspects should be given particular importance by the facilitators.

Work on further research questions has already started by combining the newly developed inventory with other survey instruments. In an international research project different forms of debriefing are qualitatively analysed in a differentiated way and the data obtained are linked with the game data (success of the teams in the simulation game). In addition a second quantitative questionnaire was used in a sub-sample and offers the possibility to validate the results quantitatively. Furthermore it would be important for future research within the framework of sub-samples to examine the extent to which the students' self-assessment corresponds with objective surveys. With regard to learning success, this would be possible, for example, through pre-post surveys. In addition, the recording of learning success should be more differentiated in different facets. This could be done quantitatively by differentiating the questionnaire or qualitatively through open questions and interviews. It would also be exciting to link the data obtained through the survey with the game data and to address the (de-)motivation effects of the game in a more differentiated way. Through follow-up surveys at later points in time, medium-term learning effects could also be brought into focus and, on the basis of the available data, it could be analysed which factors of the simulation game event itself are responsible for these learning effects. It is also planned to conduct surveys not only in the context of simulation game events at the ZMS, but also at other universities, at schools and in company education. Such surveys would make it possible to check to what extent the results are valid beyond the current survey context. Depending on the results of the evaluations, either a quantitatively sound generalisation or a limitation of the statements would be possible.

5 Conclusion

The questionnaire presented in the article is suitable for evaluating simulation game courses because it specifically collects the influencing factors relevant to simulation games, which is naturally not possible in general teaching evaluation inventories. The present analysis also provides positive findings with regard to the quality criteria of empirical research. The standardised questionnaire and the use of Evasys ensure a high degree of objectivity. The calculation of Cronbach's alpha for the different (sub-)scales indicates a high degree of reliability. The explorative factor analysis shows clear and meaningful components in terms of content, which essentially confirm the theoretically assumed construct. Where this was not the case, the construct was slightly adjusted. Thus, a high degree of construct validity can be assumed. In addition, the factor analysis shows that control variables (interest at the beginning and strategy games) clearly stand out from the actual content of the instrument, which also indicates a high degree of validity.

With this inventory of questions, the Centre for Management Simulation (ZMS) is pursuing the goal of collecting data in a low-threshold manner from a broad spectrum of simulation games. The data should serve to answer a number of previously unanswered questions in simulation game research. This includes, among other things, the fact that the developed questionnaire makes it possible to compare very different simulation games in terms of their acceptance and effect. It is also intended to identify structural factors across all simulation games that are essential for successful simulation game events. Furthermore, the questionnaire is suitable to combine it with research projects on very different questions, in which both qualitative and quantitative research approaches can be pursued. For example, the standard questionnaire could be used to test the representativeness of a smaller sample for a specific question. Likewise, the questionnaire could be further validated through supplementary qualitative and quantitative surveys (for example, also in the form of pre-post surveys).

Until March 2023 the questionnaire has already been used in more than 150 simulation game courses based on more than 30 different simulation games with over 3.000 participants. In addition, it has partly been combined with other quantitative and qualitative research methods. The results so far show, that the ZMS inventory fits as intended for a broad variety of simulation games and that the underlying model can be confirmed on a broad empirical basis for online and face-to-face simulation game courses.

Appendix

Notification/Source Reference

More information towards the development of the ZMS inventory can be found in the ZMS publication series in German language (cf. Trautwein/Alf 2022).

References

Gläßer, E., Gollwitzer, M., Kranz, D., Meiniger, C., et al.: Arbeitskreis "Lehrevaluation" im Fach Psychologie; Zentrum für Psychologische Diagnostik, Begutachtung und Evaluation (2002). TRIL - Trierer Inventar zur Lehrevaluation. Ed. by Leibniz-Zentrum für Psychologische Information und Dokumentation (ZPID). Trier ZPID. https://doi.org/10.23668/psycharchives.355. Accessed 04 2022

Backhaus, K., Erichson, B., Plinke, W., Weiber, R. (eds.): Multivariate Analysemethoden. Springer, Heidelberg (2016). https://doi.org/10.1007/978-3-662-46076-4

Cronan, T.P., Leger, P.-M., Robert, J., Babin, G., Charland, P.: Comparing objective measures and perceptions of cognitive learning in an ERP simulation game: a research note. Simul. Gaming 43(4), 461–480 (2012)

DHBW Stuttgart: Modulhandbuch Studienbereich Wirtschaft. Studiengang Betriebswirtschaftslehre Studienrichtung Handel. https://www.dhbw.de/fileadmin/user/public/SP/STG/Betriebswirtschaftslehre/Handel.pdf. Accessed 03 Feb 2022

Feinstein, A.H., Cannon, H.M.: Constructs of simulation evaluation. Simul. Gaming 33(4), 425–440 (2002) . https://doi.org/10.1177/1046878102238606

Fondel, E., Lischetzke, T., Weis, S., Gollwitzer, M.: Zur Validität von studentischen Lehrveranstaltungsevaluationen. Diagnostica 61(3), 124–135 (2015). https://doi.org/10.1026/0012-1924/a000141

Hossiep, R.: Cronbachs Alpha im Dorsch Lexikon der Psychologie (2021). https://dorsch.hogrefe. com/stichwort/cronbachs-alpha

Hühn, C., Rausch, A.: Collaboration and emotions during simulation-based learning in general management courses. Stud. Educ. Eval. **73**, 1–16 (2022). https://doi.org/10.1016/j.stueduc. 2022.101130

Knödler, E.: Evaluation an Hochschulen. Entwicklung und Validierung eines verhaltensbasierten Messinventars zur studentischen Lehrveranstaltungsevaluation. Springer, Wiesbaden (2019). https://doi.org/10.1007/978-3-658-25553-4

Kriz, W.C., Hense, J.U.: Theory-oriented evaluation for the design of and research in gaming and simulation. Simul. Gaming **37**(2), 268–283 (2006). https://doi.org/10.1177/104687810 6287950

Leigh, E., Likhacheva, E., Tipton, E., de Wijse-van Heeswijk, M., Zürn, B.: Why facilitation? Simul. Gaming **52**(3), 247–254 (2021). https://doi.org/10.1177/10468781211016914

Meßner, M.T., Schedelik, M., Engartner, T. (eds.): Handbuch Planspiele in der sozialwissenschaftlichen Hochschullehre. Wochenschau Verlag, Frankfurt/M (2018)

Rindermann, H.: Lehrevaluation. Einführung und Überblick zu Forschung und Praxis der Lehrveranstaltungsevaluation an Hochschulen mit einem Beitrag zur Evaluation computerbasierten Unterrichts, 2nd, slightly corrected edition. Landau: Verlag Empirische Pädagogik (Psychologie, 42) (2009)

Schwägele, S.: Lerntransfer beim Planspieleinsatz. In: Petrik, A., Rappenglück, S. (eds.) Handbuch Planspiele in der politischen Bildung. Schwalbach (Taunus): Wochenschau Verlag (Politik und Bildung, Band 81), pp. 58–68 (2017)

Trautwein, C.: Unternehmensplanspiele im industriebetrieblichen Hochschulstudium. Analyse von Kompetenzerwerb, Motivation und Zufriedenheit am Beispiel des Unternehmensplanspiels TOPSIM - General Management II, 1st edn. Gabler Verlag, Wiesbaden (2011)

Trautwein, F.: Berufliche Handlungskompetenz als Studienziel. Verlag Wissenschaft & Praxis (Studienreihe der Stiftung Kreditwirtschaft an der Universität Hohenheim, 42), Sternenfels (2004)

Trautwein, F., Alf, T.: Theoriebasierte Entwicklung eines Inventars zur Evaluation von Planspielveranstaltungen. In: Alf, T., et al. (eds.) Planspiele – Erkenntnisse aus Praxis und Forschung: Books on demand (ZMS Schriftenreihe, Band 13), pp. 63–87 (2022)

ZMS Inventory Facilitator (2021). https://zms.dhbw-stuttgart.de/zms/2_Forschung/2.2_Forschu ngsprojekte/ZMS_inventory_facilitator_english.pdf

ZMS Inventory Students (2021). https://zms.dhbw-stuttgart.de/zms/2_Forschung/2.2_Forschungs projekte/ZMS_inventory_students_english.pdf

Exploring the Use of Immersive Virtual Reality Games in a Formal School Environment

Meike Belter[✉], Yuanjie Wu, and Heide Lukosch

HIT Lab NZ, University of Canterbury, Christchurch, New Zealand
meike.belter@pg.canterbury.ac.nz

Abstract. In recent years, immersive Virtual Reality (VR) has gained popularity among young users as a new technology for entertainment gaming. While VR remains majorly used for entertainment purposes, 3D desktop games are already used in schools. This study takes a closer look at the suitability for VR games to be used in a formal educational environment, and its potential to enrich existing game based learning approaches. Based on learning needs of in particular easily distracted and inattentive children, an immersive VR maths game was created and tested on 15 children aged 10–13. This study found VR to be suitable for usage in a school setting, as well as seeming to be an enjoyable addition to learning for this age group. Further research is needed to investigate its concrete potential.

Keywords: Applied Games · Virtual Reality · Education · Game Requirements · Inclusive Games

1 Introduction

In the past two decades, games have been increasingly explored as a new tool in education. Educational games fall under the umbrella of serious games, games designed for a purpose other than pure entertainment [1]. Researchers such as Young et al. [2], found that games are an effective tool for knowledge acquisition and foster a positive student attitude [3]. Kirriemuir and McFarlane [4] indicate that video games may improve communication skills, as well as strategic thinking and planning skills. Moreover, Giannaraki et al. [5] created a multimodal 3D serious game to help young people diagnosed with Attention Deficit Hyperactivity Disorder (ADHD) improve psychosocially (e.g. social skills and collaboration). The game is based on rhythm and music and has shown to be effective in fostering focused attention. The use of game elements and techniques used for game design in an educational context has shown promising findings. In a systematic literature review, Manazano-Leon et al. [6] conclude that this can result in a positive impact on education including increased commitment and motivation. However, the authors also stress the importance of better understanding the challenges and needs of students when applying game elements to education.

Moreover, despite these promising findings, several studies suggest no significant positive effect of desktop video games for learning [7], as well as other methods of instruction in formal education being as effective as video games [8]. For instance

C. Harteveld et al. (Eds.): ISAGA 2022, LNCS 13622, pp. 22–35, 2023.
https://doi.org/10.1007/978-3-031-37171-4_2

Suliyanah et al. [7] find, that in literature, not all educational physics video games or software applications are effective for learning, and often board and physical card games have a higher level of effectiveness. This poses the question how video games may be best implemented in education for maximum learning effectiveness. This can be looked at from different application fields such as pedagogy, educational science, or technology. An interdisciplinary approach to game design seems to be the most promising [9], as educational games are for example, dependent on subject matter specific contents and age and ability appropriate interfaces, thus exceeding the scope of pure software development. Yet, the question in research remains to what extent games may be suitable for school environments.

Lastly, little research exists on exploring other new technologies for serious gaming, such as immersive VR, and their potential to improve and enrich learning effectiveness of gaming in a formal education context. Virtual Reality is a term used for a computer-generated environment that provides its users with the feeling of being physically present, simulating and replicating the real world. Users feel immersed in the three-dimensional (3D) computer-generated world and are not able to see the real world. This is typically achieved by using head-mounted-displays (HDM's) [10, 11].

Immersive VR technology has become increasingly accessible and usable. VR has raised interest in serious game research due to its promising effects on learning. For example, VR seems to motivate users, supports information-retention through immersive visualisation [10, 11]. A study conducted by Araiza-Alba et al. [12], investigated the effect of immersive VR as a problem-solving tool for children. The researchers found that children were more engaged when using VR to problem-solve than when attending traditional lessons. Moreover, Araiza-Alba et al. [12] argue that cognitive load may be reduced due to the nature of VR. Immersive virtual worlds shall also be beneficial to children with special needs, such as children on the Autism spectrum or children with ADHD in schools and on intervention basis [13, 14]. Newbutt et al. [13] tested HMD based VR in a school-based environment on 31 children with autism. It was found that ease-of-use as well as visual and physical comfortability was given and that using VR was perceived as enjoyable and exciting.

Immersive VR has been tested as a learning tool for a variety of subjects and purposes ranging from the use as a clinical intervention tool [14], teaching physics, history and the alphabet [15, 16], to a medium for practising mathematics [17]. As an example for the latter, Akam and Çakır [17] found VR to be effective in engaging children with mathematics while also leading to increased academic performance.

The educational potential as well as customizability and level of immersion, makes VR an interesting field of research. As already outlined in literature today [12–14], this opens up the option to create fully customised learning experiences that are inclusive and individualised to all learner needs. However, many questions remain on how to implement VR in education for optimal learning and user support while finding the right match of learning contents and VR characteristics.

To add to this field of research, this study explores the implementability of VR games for children in formal education, whereby practising maths has been chosen to be the subject matter of the game created. Maths, especially for children with learning difficulties, marks one of the most challenging topics in schooling [18]. Moranyi et al. [18] argue, that innate factors such as cognitive problems, as well as environmental factors, such as insubstantial schooling, can lead to difficulties with maths. This research addresses maths exercises with an immersive VR approach, allowing for cognitive support for children and enrichment of learning tools for educators.

The maths game designed in this research, factors in design requirements for children challenged by attention deficits and hyperactivity, as a large number of children with these traits tend to be cognitively challenged in school. A literature review conducted prior to this study revealed that researchers found approximately 5–10% of all children attending formal education are affected by ADHD [19]. Therefore, building a VR game that considers this group marks an important starting point for working towards the creation of inclusive VR for learning in schools.

This study is explorative and investigates the suitability of a VR game prototype in a school environment, and explores identified game design requirements for immersive VR gaming for children in schools, including children showing traits of hyperactivity and inattention. Here, the usability of the game prototype as well as the user experience (UX) is investigated. This amounts to the following guiding research question for this study: *How could an immersive VR game be used in a formal educational setting?*

The maths game was tested on 15 children aged 10–13 in a school environment, resulting in valuable feedback on its acceptance in an educational setting, and game design elements for immersive VR learning games designed for children. This feedback will be used to further develop and test the prototype.

2 Theory

As an extensive literature review could not reveal guidelines for educational VR game design for children, game elements for the creation of the maths game in this study were constructed in an interdisciplinary manner. Literature on existing (VR) games and their respective elements, mitigation strategies for unique learning needs in schools, and elements from educational science were taken into account. This was accompanied by a situation analysis of formal educational school contexts. In the following, an overview of the defined VR game design requirements is portrayed.

2.1 Designing VR Games for Hyperactivity and Inattention in Schools

Designing inclusive VR games supporting children with special learning needs in schools starts with understanding different learning needs. Some of the most common challenges faced by children in schools relate to hyperactivity and inattention when learning. Both of these traits are key characteristics for ADHD, and frequently lead to poor academic performance [20]. Uncompleted tasks, poor self-regulation, disruptive behaviour in the classroom, trouble with peer relationships, and poor self-esteem are examples of a variety of negative consequences for those affected [20, 21]. Research shows that inattention leads to considerably worse performance in the space of literacy and numeracy skills [22]. While traditional classroom education has come a long way in facilitating different learning needs, due to its nature, it still often fails to accommodate for children struggling with these traits [20, 22]. Considering that approximately 5–10% of all school-aged children are diagnosed with ADHD [19], it is important to think about ways to expand current learning strategies, working towards standardised, inclusive learning tools.

The great increase of technological accessibility over the past decade has opened up new ways of learning, including games for education. Playing computer games has been linked to various educational and skill-strengthening effects such as, improved planning abilities, strategic thinking, decision-making, or acquisition of 21st-century skills [2, 4, 23, 24]. In contrast to difficulties with attention and hyperactivity, games have shown to keep focus and attention of its user and allow for immediate feedback, a factor fostering motivation, often missing in learning [25]. This may lead to reduced off-task behaviour, a major disruptor in learning for children with attention deficits [26]. Moreover, in classroom education it is often required to hold information mentally, an example here is mental-maths [22]. Children with ADHD traits often show impaired working memory and find mentally holding information troublesome, leading to decreased task persistence [22]. Games offer a promising way to customise displayed material, allowing the child to retrieve information as needed to aid mental information retention.

Besides the positive effects desktop games have to offer for learning, children with inattention and hyperactivity difficulties benefit from a non distracting environment [21], which cannot always be achieved by the level of immersion in desktop games. Immersion here refers to the sense of presence, the feeling of being physically in a computer-generated environment [27]. One technology that can provide an increased level of immersion for educational gaming is virtual reality.

In research, the term virtual reality can refer to a variety of things, but this study focuses on virtual reality that requires a HMD. A HMD is worn on the head and functions as eyeglasses with two displays, one in front of each eye. The headset blocks out the real world, leading to a feeling of immersion into the computer-generated world that is displayed [28, 29]. VR can offer a high level of presence, the feeling of being physically present in a place, as well as vividness, and interactivity [28]. These basic characteristics of this technology seem to hold great potential in addressing traits such as hyperactivity, or inattention. A high level of presence may keep attention and focus, whilst interactive environments allow for movement, aiding hyperactivity.

From a technological point of view, VR seems promising for formal education. The game must be designed interdisciplinary, in accordance with the spatial and technological constraints of the school environment. Furthermore, its contents must be designed with the standard curricula in mind, aiming at making it implementable in daily learning activities without adding extra contents [28].

The next Sect. 2.2, provides an overview of the game requirements this maths VR game is based on. The elements are derived from Belter and Lukosch (forthcoming) [30], that are especially well suited for being translated into immersive VR.

2.2 Design Requirements for VR Maths Practice Game

To help children feel comfortable and at ease in the virtual environment, the look and feel should be welcoming, safe and aesthetic, accommodating for all learners [31]. Since VR is a rather new and often unfamiliar technology [10], a training scenario shall precede the game play, helping users to acquaint themselves with the technology and game elements, supporting user acceptance. As VR allows for active movement, which in turn, has been linked to better learning outcomes especially in learners with hyperactivity [32], one design requirement for the game is actively incorporating body movement. To support guiding behaviour and actions, clear verbal cues in task-switching situations are required [33]. Moreover, to stimulate working memory and attention of learners, only little information at a time shall be displayed, comparing distraction and information overload [34, 35]. To further assist children that display self-regulation difficulties, no imposition of time limits should be used, reducing the risk of negative arousal [34], or stress. Lastly, a game design requirement for this study is to create an environment that allows enough time to observe the task as well as visual cues, with no time impositions, and no visual cues that could mislead or confuse the user [36].

For this study, an immersive VR maths practice game was designed keeping the needs of children with hyperactivity and inattention difficulties in mind to work towards an inclusive design. Moreover, a standard consumer HMD was used without extra hardware to accommodate for technological accessibility. The game was designed for a 2.5 × 2.5 m play space area, with the intention to make it implementable in various school areas with spatial constraints.

3 Method

The user test consisted of two different phases: A usability game test, and a post-test user experience evaluation. During the usability test, each child was asked to play the game for 10 min, whereby observations were taken and the screen was recorded. For the experience evaluation, tools were used to gather opinions in child computer interaction. Additionally, the children were each asked 6 semi-structured interview questions which were audio recorded. This mixed-method approach was chosen to receive a variety of self-reported and observed data. The study was approved by the ethics committee of the local university.

3.1 Participants

The participants of the study are 15 school children aged 10–13 in New Zealand. To keep the information collection process for the participating children simple, no extensive demographic data has been collected. The study was carried out in year 7 of the New Zealand school system. Participants had to be enrolled in a school and attending maths classes as default part of their curriculum. This ensured that the participants have gained the maths skills required for the game task. All 15 participants had been recruited from the same local primary school.

As this study aimed at children of 10–13 years of age, caregiver consent was required and collected before the potential participant was able to take part in this study. Each caregiver was provided with an information sheet and consent form. Next to caregiver consent, assent from the children themselves was also a requirement for participation. The child received a simplified version of the information sheet highlighting the most important points including risks. Alongside that, the children received an assent form which they were asked to return before participation was allowed. To put an extra layer of safety in place, on the day of the test, the children were informed again about the study itself and potential risks. Most importantly, they were informed that there were no consequences from participating in the study, and their performance during it. Children were allowed to stop the test at any time without the need of an explanation.

3.2 Material

As experimental material, a VR game in Unity® was created. To provide the option to familiarise the participants with the controls before the actual game play, a series of training sessions was designed. The first scene is the basic controller interaction training session as shown in Fig. 1a.

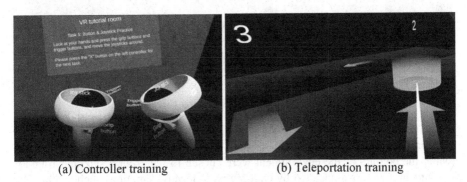

| (a) Controller training | (b) Teleportation training |

Fig. 1. Training room scenarios 1 and 2

The first training session covers technology on-boarding. When a participant puts on the VR headset and holds the two controllers, virtual models of the controllers including buttons can be seen. When the joystick is moved, the virtual joystick moves accordingly. This session was designed to help participants familiarise themselves with the controls and buttons.

The second session is meant to foster locomotion training, introducing options of moving around in the VR environment. A general teleportation method was designed. When the participant pushes the joystick forward, a project line is generated in VR, aimed at the desired location that the participant wants to reach, as shown in Fig. 1b. For turning around in VR, the participant can look and turn around to change the view. Additionally, the joystick can be moved left or right for a so-called snap turn. Snap-turning instead of continuous turning was used to reduce the risk of potential motion sickness.

The third training session is a basic grab-and-throw training in VR, as shown in Fig. 2. Two different grab methods were designed, one is using the indirect way of grabbing (uses an intermediate tool to select or manipulate an object), and the other one uses a direct grab. For the indirect way, there is a red line projected in VR, coming from the right controller. When the red line touches any interactable object, the colour of the line will turn white. This indicates that the participant can grab the object when the grip button is pressed. The direct grab is assigned to the left controller. The participant needs to move close to the interactable object and then press the grip button of the left controller to grab the object. Throwing objects is straightforward. Like throwing an object in the real world, the participant needs to aim in a certain direction and release the grip object by using the power of their arm to throw the object. Two snap zones were placed near the wall. Here, participants can practise throwing virtual number cubes and operator balls into the designated areas.

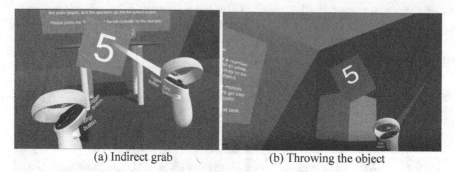

(a) Indirect grab   (b) Throwing the object

Fig. 2. Training room scenarios 3 and 4

After completion of the training sessions, the actual game session starts. For this session, the colours of the environment were chosen to represent a safe and friendly environment. Colours associated by children with negative emotions such as black or dark grey shapes, were avoided, and colours associated with positive emotions, e.g., red, orange, pink, were used wherever applicable [37]. Moreover, a balance was anticipated when using colours to counteract arousal, aiding hyperactivity. When positive, bright and warm colours were used, the tone of the colour was made cooler to promote the restful and non-arousal effect of the colours [38].

The aim of the game is to solve an equation with a predefined result, using number cubes and operator balls within the VR environment, as seen in Fig. 4. The cubes and balls must be thrown, in the right order, into designated snap zones. Figure 3 shows the four cube snap zones for the numbers and the three operator snap zones for the spheres. The participant can pick up the numbers and operators from the ground and throw them into the correct snap zone to calculate the equation and get the correct answer to match the target number displayed right above the snap zone area (Fig. 3). In total, four target numbers must be met, meaning there are four equations in this game to be solved. If the calculation is wrong, hence not all balls or cubes are in the right snap zone, a "wrong" audio sound is heard and the word "wrong" is displayed. Once correct, the word "right" is displayed and accompanied by a sound indicating success. All numbers and operators will drop down and reset to the original positions. The numbers on the cubes will change to the next set and the target number will also change. There is a level bar in the room with four levels. Once the participant finishes one equation, the colour of the level bar changes from red to green, which represents that one level is completed. The level bar can be seen in Fig. 4. Once all four levels are finished, a victory sound is played.

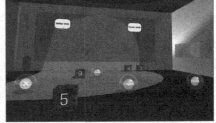

Fig. 3. Game room calculation   **Fig. 4.** Game room environment, level bar.

3.3 Procedure

The study involved two phases; a usability test and a user experience evaluation. A usability test was conducted first with participants playing the game, and being observed while playing. This test functioned as empirical and technical evaluation of the game prototype. Usability testing in this study refers to the general intractability of the game prototype and provides valuable information on how to refine technical and functional game requirements further [39]. Participants were observed on how they interact with the technology, as well as with the game elements. The principal researcher took notes while observing the participants. This phase took 10 min at a maximum to minimise the risk of cyber sickness or any other effects of the immersive VR environment.

After this, the user experience evaluation was conducted. The participants were asked to complete a short questionnaire and 6 semi-structured interview questions on their user experience with the game. The questionnaire utilised elements from the Fun-Toolkit validated by Read and MacFarlane [40], a tool widely used to investigate children's opinions about technology. The interview questions were designed to investigate what the children liked or disliked about the game, as well as questions on the game mechanics. The questionnaire was distributed as hard copy to the children by a second researcher. Upon completion, the second researcher initiated the interview process (Table 1).

Table 1

Activity	Time involvement
Welcome and introduction to the research task/safety briefing	5 min
Usability game test	10 min
User experience evaluation	10–15 min
Debrief	2 min

The study took place in a formal educational setting (school). The researcher set up the equipment needed for the study (HMD, portable computer, desk and chairs for the user interviews) in two separate rooms, which were dedicated to the researcher by a teacher. The principal researcher had all certifications needed to work with children and was accompanied by a second researcher. The whole study received approval from the Ethical Committee of the principal researcher's university.

Data Analysis
To analyse the data collected in this study, a qualitative data analysis tool was used, as well as a statistical tool. As for the observations, all reportings were taken in a manner that ensures the participant's anonymity. The data was entered into ATLAS, and used to identify trends, commonalities and unique opinions and behaviours. The questionnaire was analysed using Microsoft Excel. Moreover, the short interviews were audio recorded and later transcribed, before being processed with ATLAS. All participants were informed about the audio recording beforehand, and their consent was required.

4 Results

The average time for completing the training rooms was 3:12 min, whereby 14 out of 15 (n = 15) participants demonstrated a fast progression through the rooms (>5 min). All participants reported to like the training rooms, while 5 ranked them highest on the scale, as brilliant. Out of 15, 13 participants would train in the room again. All 15 participants liked the game, while 7 found it really good, and 5 brilliant. Moreover, all children reported to at least feel good during gameplay. Further, 14 children would play the game again, and would throw the cubes and balls again. Here, 5 participants reported this to be their favourite part. All 15 participants would use VR glasses again. Other parts enjoyed were learning and figuring out mechanics and controls, teleporting as the choice of locomotion, the freedom to explore the virtual environment, figuring out the maths, finishing a question, and the game's simplicity in regards to look and feel of the environment, as well as receiving guidance from the facilitator. Three children mentioned that they did enjoy the entire experience as a whole. Figure 5 and Fig. 6 show the detailed questions asked and their respective response counts.

Parts not enjoyed were reported by 3 participants and include the handling of controls, doing maths, the throwing mechanism, and brightness of the colour choice. Based on self-report, 12 children were familiar with VR before joining the experiment. It was observed that 13 children moved around rather less in VR, while 13 children also were confident with the technology. In total, 3 children had questions about the technology during the test, and 14 participants handled the technology intuitively. Questions asked about the technology referred to handling of the controls and questions about contents displayed (e.g. target number).

Out of 15 children, 3 purposefully moved outside the defined play area/stationary boundary to explore outside the defined VR space. In all 3 cases this led to distractions for the user. Further, 3 participants completed the first equation in the game, while all 3 individuals appeared engaged and motivated by their success. It was observed that 4 children talked out loud while thinking how to solve the maths equation. On the other hand, 3 out of 15 participants did not talk at all, even when asked a question. This however did not compromise intense focus and concentration, all 15 participants stayed on task. No participant showed hesitation or performance anxiety when completing the task. Lastly, 6 children self-reported that they are having fun and/or enjoy VR. No child

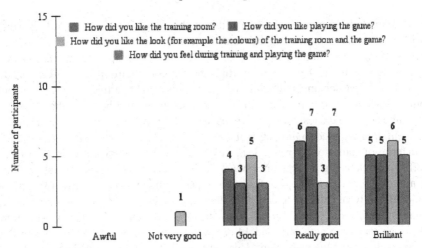

Fig. 5. Smileyometer from Fun-Toolkit, 5 point likert scale (n = 15).

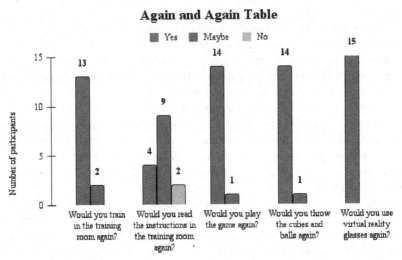

Fig. 6. Again and Again table from Fun-Toolkit, questions on potential repetition of game play elements (n = 15).

reported symptoms of VR motion sickness. However, one child complained of slight dizziness after the completion of the test.

Overall, it was observed that the usage and implementation of a dedicated VR space within the school setting did not show to be of major disruption and inconvenience to other activities within the school. It can be concluded that this VR set up, including the Oculus Quest 2 HMD, a portable computer, and a play space of 2.5 m × 2.5 m seems, from a practicality point of view, to be feasible for school environments.

5 Discussion and Conclusion

It can be concluded that most children in this study enjoyed the usage of VR, as well as learning VR controls and playing the game, indicating that VR may be able to become an accepted learning medium for children. Moreover, the VR setup and gameplay was well implementable into the daily school routine and did not require special space consider- ations, as most participants did not move much. This also underlines its potential appli- cability as a learning tool in educational environments. It must be noted that the school environment where the test took place makes use of an open plan learning environment, where children are used to moving around.

In terms of game design, a simple and clean scene with no time impositions seems to be effective in keeping participants on task. This is in accordance with literature stating that non-distractive environments foster focus and promote staying on task [33, 34]. VR seemed to motivate children to complete the task and lead overall to enjoyment and the feeling of having fun. This is congruent with former research [41, 42]. Most children had prior experience with VR, and 14 did well in the training rooms preparing them for the mechanics of the game play. This may indicate that clear verbal cues may assist control and mechanics learning. No child had major issues with the technology and mostly handled controls intuitively. Hence, barriers in terms of technical knowledge and handling were not identified. This is non congruent with literature used in the preparations of this study, pointing out the unfamiliarity of individuals with VR. This however, may tie into more recent findings in literature stating that in the light of emerging technologies, VR is taking a major role in several areas of education and society as a whole. Therefore, is not unusual to the participants [43]. Especially after two years of a pandemic, children might have become more familiar with all sorts of technology.

In this study, it appears that the throwing of objects (cubes and balls) was enjoyed by the majority of children. This may be explained by findings in literature such as by Rasberry et al. [44], indicating that physical activity was most often positively associ- ated with academic performance. Hence, active movement appears to be enjoyed while practising maths and marks a unique game element of VR compared to non-immersive digital education tools.

In terms of on task behaviour, it was apparent that several children did talk to them- selves the majority of their time in VR, while others did not talk at all and also did not respond to questions asked by the researcher. This demonstrates the variability of cognitive processing and learning in VR. Especially when practising maths, literature states that a reduction in cognitive load can be achieved by presenting isolated and clear tasks rather than tasks that require switching between several mathematical principles [45]. Considering that, the strong level of task engagement, regardless of practising style, might be explained by the simplicity of the maths practice task in this study.

All children seemed to be dedicated to the task without signs of hesitation or per- formance anxiety. Literature suggests that children become more aware of their mathe- matical performance in relation to the performance of their peers, potentially inducing anxiety [46]. The isolating nature of VR might contribute to the confidence to practise in private, without direct peer comparison.

In this study, VR provided an enjoyable experience that could be related to promoting motivation and on task behaviour. The simple nature of the environment and maths task, as well as the attributes of immersive virtual reality may have contributed to various degrees. To what extend these factors are related remains subject to further investigation.

For future studies, customization options for verbal information retention as well as physical movement could be added. One participant for example would have favoured orally communicated instructions. Lastly, the gender balance in this study must be seen as a limitation. While 14 out of 15 children were of the male gender, only 1 participant can be identified as female. This implies the need for further testing this technology on both genders equally.

Acknowledgements. This study receives funding from the Tertiary Education Commission (TEC) New Zealand under the Entrepreneurial Universities Scheme, and the University of Canterbury as part of the Applied Immersive Gaming Initiative. No conflicts of interest result from this funding.

References

1. Bul, K.C., et al.: Behavioral outcome effects of serious gaming as an adjunct to treatment for children with attention-deficit/hyperactivity disorder: a randomized controlled trial. J. Med. Internet Res. **18**(2), e5173 (2016)
2. Young, M.F., et al.: Our princess is in another castle: a review of trends in serious gaming for education. Rev. Educ. Res. **82**(1), 61–89 (2012)
3. Barr, M.: Student attitudes to games-based skills development: learning from video games in higher education. Comput. Hum. Behav. **80**, 283–294 (2018)
4. Kirriemuir, J., McFarlane, A.: Literature review in games and learning (2004)
5. Giannaraki, M., Moumoutzis, N., Papatzanis, Y., Kourkoutas, E., Mania, K.: A 3D rhythm-based serious game for collaboration improvement of children with attention deficit hyperactivity disorder (ADHD). In: 2021 IEEE Global Engineering Education Conference (EDUCON), pp. 1217–1225. IEEE (2021)
6. Manzano-León, A., et al.: Between level up and game over: a systematic literature review of gamification in education. Sustainability **13**(4), 2247 (2021)
7. Deta, U.A., et al.: Literature review on the use of educational physics games in improving learning outcomes. J. Phys. Conf. Ser. **1805**(1), 012038 (2021)
8. Erickson, L.V., Sammons-Lohse, D.: Learning through video games: the impacts of competition and cooperation. E-Learn. Digit. Media **18**(1), 1–17 (2021)
9. Ke, F., Shute, V., Clark, K.M., Erlebacher, G.: Interdisciplinary Design of Game-Based Learning Platforms. Springer, Cham (2019). https://doi.org/10.1007/978-3-030-04339-1
10. Virvou, M., Katsionis, G.: On the usability and likeability of virtual reality games for education: the case of VR-ENGAGE. Comput. Educ. **50**(1), 154–178 (2008)
11. Freina, L., Ott, M.: A literature review on immersive virtual reality in education: state of the art and perspectives. In: The International Scientific Conference eLearning and Software for Education, vol. 1, no. 133, pp. 10–1007 (2015)
12. Araiza-Alba, P., Keane, T., Chen, W.S., Kaufman, J.: Immersive virtual reality as a tool to learn problem-solving skills. Comput. Educ. **164**, 104121 (2021)
13. Newbutt, N., Bradley, R., Conley, I.: Using virtual reality head-mounted displays in schools with autistic children: views, experiences, and future directions. Cyberpsychol. Behav. Soc. Netw. **23**(1), 23–33 (2020)

14. Riquelme, I., Sabater-Gárriz, Á., Montoya, P.: Pain and communication in children with cerebral palsy: influence on parents' perception of family impact and healthcare satisfaction. Children **8**(2), 87 (2021)
15. Kazanidis, I., Palaigeorgiou, G., Chintiadis, P., Tsinakos, A.: A pilot evaluation of a virtual reality educational game for history learning. In: European Conference on e-Learning, pp. 245–253. Academic Conferences International Limited (2018)
16. Ramansyah, W., Aini, N., Fitriansyah, W., Pratama, M.D.: Virtual reality and educational game to learn Madurese history and alphabet for elementary school students. J. Phys. Conf. Ser. **1842**(1), 012012 (2021)
17. Akman, E., Çakır, R.: The effect of educational virtual reality game on primary school students' achievement and engagement in mathematics. Interact. Learn. Environ., 1–18 (2020)
18. Morsanyi, K., van Bers, B.M., McCormack, T., McGourty, J.: The prevalence of specific learning disorder in mathematics and comorbidity with other developmental disorders in primary school-age children. Br. J. Psychol. **109**(4), 917–940 (2018)
19. Faraone, S.V., Sergeant, J., Gillberg, C., Biederman, J.: The worldwide prevalence of ADHD: is it an American condition? World Psychiatry **2**(2), 104 (2003)
20. Barkley, R.A.: Impaired delayed responding. In: Routh, D.K. (eds.) Disruptive Behavior Disorders in Childhood, pp. 11–57. Springer, Boston (1994). https://doi.org/10.1007/978-1-4899-1501-6_2
21. Teichner, G.: Attention-Deficit/Hyperactivity Disorder in Children and Adolescents: A DSM-5 Handbook for Medical and Mental Health Professionals. Momentum Press (2017)
22. Martinussen, R.L., Tannock, R., Chaban, P., McInnes, A., Ferguson, B.: Increasing awareness and understanding of attention deficit hyperactivity disorder (ADHD) in education to promote better academic outcomes for students with ADHD. Except. Educ. Can. **16** (2006)
23. Mayer, R.E., Parong, J., Bainbridge, K.: Young adults learning executive function skills by playing focused video games. Cogn. Dev. **49**, 43–50 (2019)
24. Hewett, K.J., Zeng, G., Pletcher, B.C.: The acquisition of 21st-century skills through video games: minecraft design process models and their web of class roles. Simul. Gaming **51**(3), 336–364 (2020)
25. Teeter, P.A., Semrud-Clikeman, M.: Integrating neurobiological, psychosocial, and behavioral paradigms: a transactional model for the study of ADHD. Arch. Clin. Neuropsychol. **10**(5), 433–461 (1995)
26. Abikoff, H.B., et al.: Observed classroom behavior of children with ADHD: relationship to gender and comorbidity. J. Abnorm. Child Psychol. **30**(4), 349–359 (2002)
27. Tao, G., Garrett, B., Taverner, T., Cordingley, E., Sun, C.: Immersive virtual reality health games: a narrative review of game design. J. Neuroeng. Rehabil. **18**(1), 1–21 (2021)
28. Kwon, C.: Verification of the possibility and effectiveness of experiential learning using HMD-based immersive VR technologies. Virtual Real. **23**(1), 101–118 (2018). https://doi.org/10.1007/s10055-018-0364-1
29. Weidner, F., Hoesch, A., Poeschl, S., Broll, W.: Comparing VR and non-VR driving simulations: an experimental user study. In: 2017 IEEE Virtual Reality (VR), pp. 281–282. IEEE (2017)
30. Belter, M., Lukosch, H.: Exploring the applicability of virtual reality gaming for children with ADHD in formal education. In: International Simulation and Gaming Association Conference 2021. Springer, Cham (2021, forthcoming)
31. Geng, G.: Investigation of teachers' verbal and non-verbal strategies for managing attention deficit hyperactivity disorder (ADHD) students' behaviours within a classroom environment. Aust. J. Teach. Educ. **36**(7), 17–30 (2011)
32. Mulrine, C.F., Prater, M.A., Jenkins, A.: The active classroom: supporting students with attention deficit hyperactivity disorder through exercise. Teach. Except. Child. **40**(5), 16–22 (2008)

33. Kray, J., Kipp, K.H., Karbach, J.: The development of selective inhibitory control: the influence of verbal labeling. Acta Physiol. **130**(1), 48–57 (2009)
34. Chittaro, L., Buttussi, F.: Assessing knowledge retention of an immersive serious game vs. a traditional education method in aviation safety. IEEE Trans. Vis. Comput. Graph. **21**(4), 529–538 (2015)
35. Kalyuga, S., Plass, J.L.: Evaluating and managing cognitive load in games. In: Handbook of Research on Effective Electronic Gaming in Education, pp. 719–737. IGI Global (2009)
36. Jiang, M., Chen, S., Yang, J., Zhao, Q.: Fantastic answers and where to find them: immersive question-directed visual attention. In: Proceedings of the IEEE/CVF Conference on Computer Vision and Pattern Recognition, pp. 2980–2989 (2020)
37. Boyatzis, C.J., Varghese, R.: Children's emotional associations with colors. J. Genet. Psychol. **155**(1), 77–85 (1994)
38. Yildirim, K., Hidayetoglu, M.L., Capanoglu, A.: Effects of interior colors on mood and preference: comparisons of two living rooms. Percept. Mot. Skills **112**(2), 509–524 (2011)
39. Zaidi, S.F.M., Duthie, C., Carr, E., Maksoud, S.H.A.E.: Conceptual framework for the usability evaluation of gamified virtual reality environment for non-gamers. In: Proceedings of the 16th ACM SIGGRAPH International Conference on Virtual-Reality Continuum and its Applications in Industry, pp. 1–4 (2018)
40. Read, J.C., MacFarlane, S.: Using the fun toolkit and other survey methods to gather opinions in child computer interaction. In: Proceedings of the 2006 Conference on Interaction Design and Children, pp. 81–88 (2006)
41. Hui, J., Zhou, Y., Oubibi, M., Di, W., Zhang, L., Zhang, S.: Research on art teaching practice supported by virtual reality (VR) technology in the primary schools. Sustainability **14**(3), 1246 (2022)
42. Holly, M., Pirker, J., Resch, S., Brettschuh, S., Gütl, C.: Designing VR experiences–expectations for teaching and learning in VR. Educ. Technol. Soc. **24**(2), 107–119 (2021)
43. Cardona-Reyes, H., Guzman-Mendoza, J.E., García-Coronado, O.P.: virtual reality environments as a support in elementary school. In: Handbook of Research on Adapting Remote Learning Practices for Early Childhood and Elementary School Classrooms, pp. 463–481. IGI Global (2022)
44. Rasberry, C.N., et al.: The association between school-based physical activity, including physical education, and academic performance: a systematic review of the literature. Prev. Med. **52**, S10–S20 (2011)
45. Friso-Van den Bos, I., Van der Ven, S.H., Kroesbergen, E.H., Van Luit, J.E.: Working memory and mathematics in primary school children: a meta-analysis. Educ. Res. Rev. **10**, 29–44 (2013)
46. Dowker, A., Bennett, K., Smith, L.: Attitudes to mathematics in primary school children. Child Development Research (2012)

Learning Effects and Acceptance in Business Games: A Systematic Literature Review

Susann Zeiner-Fink[1]([✉]) [iD], Angelika C. Bullinger[1] [iD], and Silke Geithner[2] [iD]

[1] Technische Universität Chemnitz, 09235 Chemnitz, Germany
susann.zeiner-fink@mb.tu-chemnitz.de
[2] University of Applied Sciences for Social Work, Education and Nursing, 01307 Dresden, Germany

Abstract. Even though the benefits of learning with business games are well known and accepted among the scientific community, there are only few approaches of making the results of business games measurable by virtue of the difficult evaluation of the multitude of influencing factors of learning effects and success. Moreover, there are only few findings about general conditions influencing learning and high-quality results of business games. In order to gain an overview on the current state of knowledge, the paper provides main results of a literature review about learning effects and success of business games and their influencing components, covering publications from 2010 to 2020.

One of the first and most salient results of the literature review are that the participants' learning effects are strongly connected with the learners' motivation and with their overall satisfaction as well as with the realism of the game. In a similar vein, the acceptance of business games is correlated with the realism of the business game, the group during the game and the acquisition of competencies and learning through the game. Thus, the paper emphasizes which elements are important for evaluating learning effects and acceptance of business games and which components influence them in detail.

Keywords: business games · learning effects · acceptance of business games · further education · systematic literature review

1 Business Games in Further Education

Business games facilitate a close to reality learning environment as they not only simulate dynamic and complex systems but also close to practice problems. The participants are confronted with a specific task or problem in an artificial environment and obtain the possibility to trial different actions. Thereby they acquire knowledge and skills that enable them to act in future real-life situations [1]. Furthermore, business games are characterized by openness, creativity and flexibility giving participants enough space and scope to act [2]. In contrast to genuine problems, wrong decisions in the simulation have no serious effects. Thus, errors provide useful guidance for learning from mistakes by experiencing almost real consequences [2, 3]. Participants receive the opportunity

C. Harteveld et al. (Eds.): ISAGA 2022, LNCS 13622, pp. 36–51, 2023.
https://doi.org/10.1007/978-3-031-37171-4_3

to take part in the game actively and directly by taking over different roles and have an impact on the simulation results. Business games deal with specialized and factual communication and interaction decisions, which are predetermined and regulated by the events as well as the goals of the game in combination with the pre-defined rules and game environments [2].

To sum up, the business game-method supports the participants' ability to reflect as well as to get and to give feedback, to acquire knowledge and to understand the structures and connections in businesses. The method increases the motivation to learn and trains the willingness to compromise. Visual, tactile, auditory and senses which are based on feelings are addressed, whereby long-term professional learning and memorizing can be stimulated [2]. The more sensory channels are addressed, the better the information can be absorbed. The link between motor and visual processes creates a connection to reality allowing a more efficient way of learning. An additional benefit is the integration of emotional aspects and a mostly positive experience of the game situation [3].

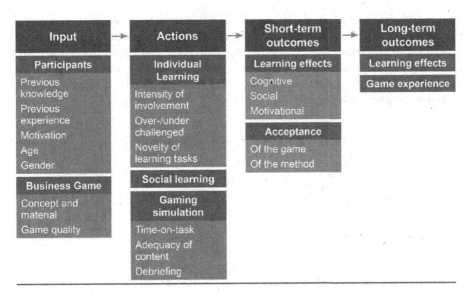

Fig. 1. Logical model of business game evaluation by Kriz & Hense (2006)

Although the benefits of business games are acknowledged and widely spread in research, they are still used very restrainedly in further education [2, 4]. While this is disappointing given the potential benefits, a central reason for this could be that learning effects, game experience or the participants' behavioral changes in the game are difficult to measure. There are only few studies which systematically examine learning through games or influencing factors which support learning and the acceptance of business games [5, 6]. Thus, business games are barely systematically evaluated and are not considered to be scientifically validated [7, 8]. In particular, studies on longer-term and sustainable learning effects are lacking [4, 9]. For this assessment, an evaluation concept must be developed that systematically explores business games. One approach is the logical model of business game evaluation by Kriz und Hense (2006). This model focus on impact analyses that examine the acceptance and achievement of learning effects and are represented as short- and long-term outcomes [56] (see Fig. 1).

Additionally, there is strong evidence in literature that business games are effective learning methods nevertheless, differentiated statements as to which factors influence learning or the success of business games are still lacking [8, 10]. Therefore, a systematic literature review of basic literature and current studies in the field of business games is needed. Hence, after a short overview of learning in games for business education, this paper will answer the *research question* which impact factors influence learning effects and acceptance of business games by using a systematic literature review of current studies from 2010 to 2020. Thus, main results of a systematic literature review will be introduced, and finally, starting points for further research in this field will be explored.

2 Method of the Literature Review

To answer the research question which impact factors need to be considered in simulation game design, a structured literature review according to Wächter (2017) was conducted in addition to statements from previous simulation game and learning research [23f]. Regarding this, four search term groups were applied: business game, evaluation, field of expertise and target group (see Table 1), which were combined step by step and then filtered according to relevance.

Table 1. Core concept of the literature review

Search term 1	Search term 2	Search term 3	Search term 4
business games	evaluation	business	students
simulation	study	production	employees
games	. qualititative	politic	pupils
	quantitative		

EBSCOhost, Web of Science, Google Scholar and additional reviews were chosen as electronical databases. Thus, relevant articles and reference lists of reviews were evaluated. To gain eligibility titles and abstracts were reviewed and articles which obtained the main research criteria according to Kriz and Hense (2006) model were screened and included [24].

The literature review focused on business simulation studies in engineering, business administration, social sciences and humanities in the period from 2010 to 2020. Furthermore, simulation studies were considered in terms of the survey methodology and study group. To be included in the review, the studies needed to be (a) fully available in the scientific database, (b) evaluate a computer assisted or board business game, (c) follow any kind of empirical quantitative or qualitative study design including measurable outcomes, (d) be published in English or German, (e) focus on learning, acquisition of competencies, expert knowledge, satisfaction or success of the game, (f) date from January 2010 to December 2020.

3   Results

In order to report the review process PRISMA statement (see Fig. 2) is used [25].

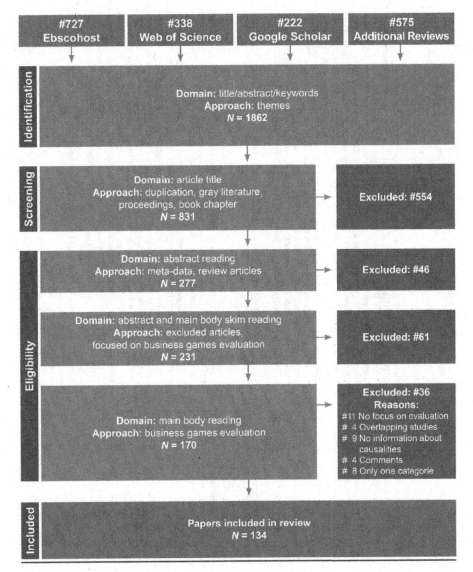

Fig. 2. Overview of the selection process according to PRISMA flow chart

Table 2 summarizes the findings of the four search terms referring the implemented literature review.

Table 2. Studies included in literature review

Variable	N = 134	Keywords	Studies
professional focus			
business administration	57	management, administration team, financial performance, active learning, experimental learning, business games, education, organization, employment, business operations, enterprise, company, corporation, human resources	Dumblekar (2010); Hübscher & Lendner (2010); Mayer & Kriz (2010); De Souza Rodrigues et al. (2011); Peterkova (2011); Trautwein (2011); Arora (2012); Costantino et al. (2012); Leger et al. (2012); Naraharisetty & Vanka (2012); Proserpio & Magni (2012); Riedel & Pawar (2012); Smutny et al. (2013); Barzilai & Blau (2014); Bhardwaj (2014); Chang et al. (2014); Mayer et al. (2014); Katsaliaki et al. (2014); Ranchhod et al. (2014); Vos & Brennan (2014); Boughzala et al. (2015); Poonnawat et al. (2015); Williams (2015); Schwägele (2015); Beltrao & Barcante (2016); Kriz & Auchter (2016); Pavaloiu et al. (2016); Schwade & Schubert (2016); Wang & Wang (2016); Dzeng & Wang (2017); Hwang & Cruthirds (2017); Mustata et al. (2017); Harnada et al. (2018); Hernandez–Lara et al. (2018); Keskin & Brezet (2018); Beranic & Hericko (2019); Brazhkin & Zimmermann (2019); Kaneko et al. (2019); Löffler et al. (2019); Lohmann et al. (2019); Mohsen et al. (2019); Rojo et al. (2019); Weber-Sabil et al. (2019); Bitrián et al. (2020); Thanasi-Boce (2020); Morin, Tamberelli & Buhagiar (2020); Winter, Pryss, Probst & Reichert (2020); Yi, Zhou, Xiao, Ge Qing & Mayer (2020); Shilton, et al. (2020); Peña Esteban, Torralbo, Casas, Concepción & García (2020); Yin (2020); Harta, Margheria, Pacib & Sassone (2020); Teichmann, Ullrich, Knost & Gronau (2020); Yiannakoulias, Gordon & Darlington (2020); Jayakrishnan, Sirigireddy, Vaddepalli, Banahatti, Lodha & Pandit (2020); Pridmore and Godin (2020)
production	6	manufacturing, output, industry, supply, productivity, produced, manufactured, fabrication, end product, process, resource, fabricating	Hauge & Riedel (2012); Pourabdollahian et al. (2012); Bascoul et al. (2013); Uei et al. (2014); Leal et al. (2017); Draghici et al. (2020)
social sciences	15	sociology, psychology, humanities, social research, education	Prinsen & Overton (2011); Dondlinger & Wilson (2012); Bridge & Radford (2014); Brunazzo & Settembri (2014); Elias (2014); Schnurr et al. (2014); Dierßen & Rappenglück (2015); Erb (2015); Meller & Ochs (2016); Weiß & Fischer (2016); Otto (2017); Lohmann (2018); Oberle & Leunig (2018); Davesa & Piros (2019); Leib & Ruppel (2019)
others a. o. Bodnar et al. (2016); Carenys & Moya (2016); Faizan et al. (2019); Hookham & Nesbitt (2019)	59		Biisen et al. (2010); Mahon et al. (2010); Mayer et al. (2010); Remelkas et al. (2010); Chen et al. (2011); Foster (2011); Joiner et al. (2011); Loke et al. (2011); Renda-Tanali & Abdul-Hamid (2011); Beaumont et al. (2012); Cook et al. (2012); Guillen-Nieto & Aleson-Carbonell (2012); Hannig et al. (2012); Loreto et al. (2012); Moreno Cavidad (2012); Buttussi et al. (2013); Chesier et al. (2013); Cronan & Douglas (2013); Lameras et al. (2013); Li et al. (2013); Cheng et al. (2014); Dib & Adamo-Villani (2014); Dzeng et al. (2014); Ferrari et al. (2014); Lee et al. (2014); Mayer et al. (2014b); Misfeldt (2014); Pötter et al. (2014); Reiß (2014); Westera et al. (2014); Bekebrede et al. (2015); Blazic & Blazic (2015); Bramesfeld & Good (2015); Callies et al. (2015); Evans et al. (2015); Lino et al. (2015); Lui et al. (2015); Peixoto et al. (2015); Dankbaar et al. (2016); Gonen & Israeli (2016); Johnsen et al. (2016); Koivisto et al. (2016); Geithner & Menzel (2016); Ribeiro et al. (2016); Castronovo et al. (2017); Henderson et al. (2017); Kaup et al. (2017); Tan et al. (2017); König & Wolf (2018); Su (2018); Taillandier & Adam (2018); Tantan et al. (2018); Verkuyl et al. (2018); Moizer et al. (2019); Pacheco-Velasquez et al. (2019); Salovaara-Hiltunen et al. (2019); Surésh (2019); Alonso-Fernández, Martinez-Ortiz, Freire & Fernández-Manjón (2020)

(continued)

Table 2. (*continued*)

Variable	N = 134	Keywords	Studies
research group			
pupils	5	educate, secondary school, class-room, scolar, learner, graduates, curriculum, educational institution, vocational students, high school graduates	Foster (2011); Cheng et al. (2014); Weiß & Fischer (2016); Kaup et al. (2017); Oberle & Leunig (2018)
students	99	alumni, university, master, bachelor, diploma, academician, academy, studying, seminar, semesters, faculty, academic achievement, degree, students, Phd student	Bilsen et al. (2010); Dumblekar (2010); Mahon et al. (2010); Remeikas et al. (2010); Chen et al. (2011); De Souza Rodrigues et al. (2011); Joiner et al. (2011); Peterkova (2011); Renda-Tanali & Abdul-Hamid (2011); Trautwein (2011); Arora (2012); Cook et al. (2012); Costantino et al. (2012); Guillen-Nieto & Aleson-Carbonell (2012); Hannig et al. (2012); Leger et al. (2012); Moreno Cavidad (2012); Naraharisetty & Vanka (2012); Proserpio & Magni (2012); Riedel & Pawar (2012); Bascoul et al. (2013); Chesler et al. (2013); Cronan & Douglas (2013); Lameras et al. (2013); Li et al. (2013); Smutny et al. (2013); Bhardwaj (2014); Bridge & Radford (2014); Brunazzo & Settembri (2014); Chang et al. (2014b); Dib & Adamo-Villani (2014); Dzeng et al. (2014); Elias (2014); Lee et al. (2014); Mayer et al. (2014); Mayer et al. (2014b); Katsaliaki et al. (2014); Pötter et al. (2014); Ranchhod et al. (2014); Reiß (2014); Schnurr et al. (2014); Westera et al. (2014); Bekebrede et al. (2015); Blazic & Blazic (2015); Boughzala et al. (2015); Erb (2015); Evans et al. (2015); Lui et al. (2015); Peixoto et al. (2015); Poonnawat et al. (2015); Williams (2015); Beltrao & Barcante (2016); Danikbaar et al. (2016); Geithner & Menzel (2016); Gonen & Israeli (2016); Johnsen et al. (2016); Koivisto et al. (2016); Kriz & Auchter (2016); Meller & Ochs (2016); Pavaloiu et al. (2016); Schwade & Schubert (2016); Wang & Wang (2016); Castronovo et al. (2017); Dzeng & Wang (2017); Henderson et al. (2017); Hwang & Cruthirds (2017); Leal et al. (2017); Mustata et al. (2017); Otto (2017); Hamada (2018); Hernández-Lara et al. (2018); Taillandier & Adam (2018); Tantan et al. (2018); Beranic & Hericko (2019); Davesa & Piros (2019); Kaneko et al. (2019); Leib & Ruppel (2019);
			Löffler et al. (2019); Lohmann et al. (2019); Mohsen et al. (2019); Pacheco-Velasquez et al. (2019); Rojo et al. (2019); Suresh (2019); Bitrián et al. (2020); Morin, Tamberelli & Buhagiar (2020); Winter, Pryss, Probst & Reichert (2020); Yi, Zhou, Xiao, Ge Qing & Mayer (2020); Peña Esteban, Torralbo, Casas, Concepción & García (2020); Yin (2020); Harta, Margheria, Pacib & Sassone (2020); Pridmore and Godin (2020)
employees	12	employer, worker, staff members, management, coworkers, business, executives, personal, departments, worksites, shareholders, workforce, administrators, supervisor, transferree, provider, industrial & organizational assessment, workplace	Mayer et al. (2010); Loreto et al. (2012); Pourabdollahian et al. (2012); Buttussi et al. (2013); Lino et al. (2015); Ribeiro et al. (2016); Tan et al. (2017); König & Wolf (2018); Moizer et al. (2019); Salovaara-Hiltunen et al. (2019); Teichmann, Ullrich, Knost & Gronau (2020); Jayakrishnan, Sirigireddy, Vaddepalli, Banahatti, Lodha & Pandit (2020)
mixed	21	Keywords used from category pupils and/or student and/or employees	Hübscher & Lendner (2010); Mayer & Kriz (2010); Beaumont et al. (2012); Hauge & Riedel (2012); Barzilai & Blau (2014); Vos & Brennan (2014); Bekebrede et al. (2015); Bramesfeld & Good (2015); Callies et al. (2015); Dierßen & Rappenglück (2015); Schwägele (2015); Keskin & Brezet (2018); Lohmann (2018); Su (2018); Verkuyl et al. (2018); Weber-Sabil et al. (2019); Draghici et al. (2019); Shifton, et al. (2020); Alonso-Fernández, Martínez-Ortiz, Freire & Fernández-Manjón (2020); Yiannakoulias, Gordon & Darlington (2020)

(*continued*)

Table 2. (*continued*)

Variable	N = 134	Keywords	Studies
research method			
quantitative	124	analytical, quantifiable, quantitative research, quantitative analysis, hypothesis test, valued, statistical analysis, evaluation, variables, modeling, correlations, measurement, descriptive, multivariate, parameters, standardized, evaluating, co-variance, factor analysis, causation, measurement, regression	Biisen et al. (2010); Dumblekar (2010); Hübscher & Lendner (2010); Mahon et al. (2010); Mayer et al. (2010); Mayer & Kriz (2010); Remeikas et al. (2010); Chen et al. (2011); De Souza Rodrigues et al. (2011); Foster (2011); Joiner et al. (2011); Peterkova (2011); Renda-Tanali & Abdul-Hamid (2011); Trautwein (2011); Arora (2012); Beaumont et al. (2012); Cook et al. (2012); Costantino et al. (2012); Guillen-Nieto & Aleson-Carbonell (2012); Hannig et al. (2012); Hauge & Riedel (2012); Leger et al. (2012); Loreto et al. (2012); Moreno Cavidad (2012); Naraharisetty & Vanka (2012); Pourabdollahian et al. (2012); Proserpio & Magni (2012); Riedel & Pawar (2012); Bascoul et al. (2013); Buttussi et al. (2013); Chesler et al. (2013); Cronan & Douglas (2013); Lameras et al. (2013); Li et al. (2013); Smutny et al. (2013); Barzilai & Blau (2014); Bhardwaj (2014); Bridge & Radford (2014); Brunazzo & Settembri (2014); Chang et al. (2014); Cheng et al. (2014); Dib & Adamo-Villani (2014); Dzeng et al. (2014); Elias (2014); Ferrari et al. (2014); Lee et al. (2014); Mayer et al. (2014); Mayer et al. (2014b); Katsaliaki et al. (2014); Pötter et al. (2014); Ranchhod et al. (2014); Reiß (2014); Schnurr et al. (2014); Vos & Brennan (2014); Westera et al. (2014); Bekebrede et al. (2015); Blazic & Blazic (2015); Boughzala et al. (2015); Callies et al. (2015); Dießen & Rappenglück (2015); Erb (2015); Evans et al. (2015); Lino et al. (2015); Lui et al. (2015); Peixoto et al. (2015); Poonnawat et al. (2015); Williams (2015); Beltrao & Barcante (2016); Dankbaar et al. (2016); Gonen & Israeli (2016); Johnsen et al. (2016); Koivisto et al. (2016); Kriz & Auchter (2016); Geithner & Menzel (2016); Meller & Ochs (2016); Pavaloiu et al. (2016); Ribeiro et al. (2016); Schwade & Schubert (2016); Wang & Wang (2016); Weiß & Fischer (2016); Castronovo et al. (2017); Dzeng & Wang (2017); Henderson et al. (2017); Hwang & Cruthirds (2017); Leal et al. (2017); Kaup et al. (2017); Mustafa et al. (2017); Otto (2017); Tan et al. (2017); Hamada et al. (2018); Hernandez-Lara et al. (2018); Keskin & Brezet (2018); König & Wolf (2018); Lohmann (2018); Oberle & Leunig (2018); Su (2018); Taillandier & Adam (2018); Tantan et al. (2018); Verkuyl et al. (2018); Beranic & Hericko (2019); Davesa & Piros (2019); Kaneko et al. (2019); Leib & Ruppel (2019); Löffler et al. (2019); Rojo et al. (2019); Suresh (2019); Weber-Sabil et al. (2019); Moizer et al. (2019); Pacheco-Velasquez et al. (2019); Morin, Tamberelli & Buhagiar (2020); Winter, Pryss, Probst & Reichert (2020); Yi, Zhou, Xiao, Ge Qing & Mayer (2020); Shilton, et al. (2020); Peña Esteban, Torralbo, Casas, Concepción & García (2020); Yin (2020); Harta, Margheria, Pacib & Sassone (2020); Teichmann, Ullrich, Knost & Gronau (2020); Jayakrishnan, Sirigireddy, Vaddepalli, Banahatti, Lodha & Pandit (2020); Pridmore and Godin (2020)
qualitative	61	interview, grounded theory, qualitative research, ethnographic, textual, exploration, exploratory, investigate, participant observation, organizational storytelling, focus groups, case studies, group interview, content analysis	Mahon et al. (2010); Mayer & Kriz (2010); Remeikas et al. (2010); Loke et al. (2011); Primsen & Overton (2011); Dondlinger & Wilson (2012); Guillen-Nieto & Aleson-Carbonell (2012); Hauge & Riedel (2012); Loreto et al. (2012); Moreno Cavidad (2012); Naraharisetty & Vanka (2012); Proserpio & Magni (2012); Riedel & Pawar (2012); Smutny et al. (2013); Barzilai & Blau (2014); Bhardwaj (2014); Bridge & Radford (2014); Brunazzo & Settembri (2014); Dib & Adamo-Villani (2014); Elias (2014); Ferrari et al. (2014); Mayer et al. (2014); Misfeldt (2014); Reiß (2014); Schnurr et al. (2014); Uei et al. (2014); Vos & Brennan (2014); Blazic & Blazic (2015); Bramesfeld & Good (2015); Erb (2015); Peixoto et al. (2015); Poonnawat et al. (2015); Schwägele (2015); Williams (2015); Geithner & Menzel (2016); Johnsen et al. (2016); Meller & Ochs (2016); Ribeiro et al. (2016); Wang & Wang (2016); Weiß & Fischer (2016); Castronovo et al. (2017); Kaup et al. (2017); Hernandez-Lara et al. (2018); Lohmann (2018); Su (2018); Taillandier & Adam (2018); Verkuyl et al. (2018); Brazhkin & Zimmermann (2019); Lohmann et al. (2019); Mohsen et al. (2019); Rojo et al. (2019); Salovaara-Hiltunen et al. (2019); Suresh (2019); Draghici et al. (2020); Thanasi-Boce (2020); Yin (2020); Alonso-Fernández, Martínez-Ortiz, Freire & Fernández-Manjón (2020); Yiannakoulias, Gordon & Darlington (2020)

As a result, 134 simulation studies were scrutinized and identified as relevant to the current review. Figure 3 shows an excerpt of the studies and their classification to the explored categories of learning effects and acceptance of business games.

Study	Business Game	Learning	Expert knowledge	Acquisition of competencies	Satisfaction	Success of the game
⋮						
#125 Pridmore and Godin (2020)	ERPsim simulation game	▪▪		▪▪		
#126 Jayakrishnan, Sirigireddy, Vaddepalli, Banahatti, Lodha & Pandit (2020)	Passworld Game	▪▪		▪▪	▪▪	
#127 Yiannakoulias, Gordon & Darlington (2020)	Decision game			▪▪▪		
#128 Teichmann, Ullrich, Knost & Gronau (2020)	Serious game on Industry 4.0			▪▪		▪▪
#129 Harta, Margheria, Pacib & Sassone (2020)	Risiko game				▪▪	▪▪
#130 Alonso-Fernández, Martinez-Ortiz, Freire & Fernández-Manjón (2020)	First-Aid Game	▪▪				
#131 Yin (2020)	FINS game	▪▪			▪▪	
#132 Peña Esteban, Torralbo, Casas, Concepción & García (2020)	Business Simulation Game			▪▪		
#133 Shilton, et al. (2020)	"Privacy by Design"-Simulation		▪▪▪			▪▪▪
#134 Yi, Zhou, Xiao, Ge Qing & Mayer (2020)	TEAMUP (multiplayer) and DEMOCRACY3 (single player)	▪▪				
Sum		107	42	63	73	9

Research group
▪ employees
▪ students
▪ pupils

Professional focus
▪ business administration
▪ social science

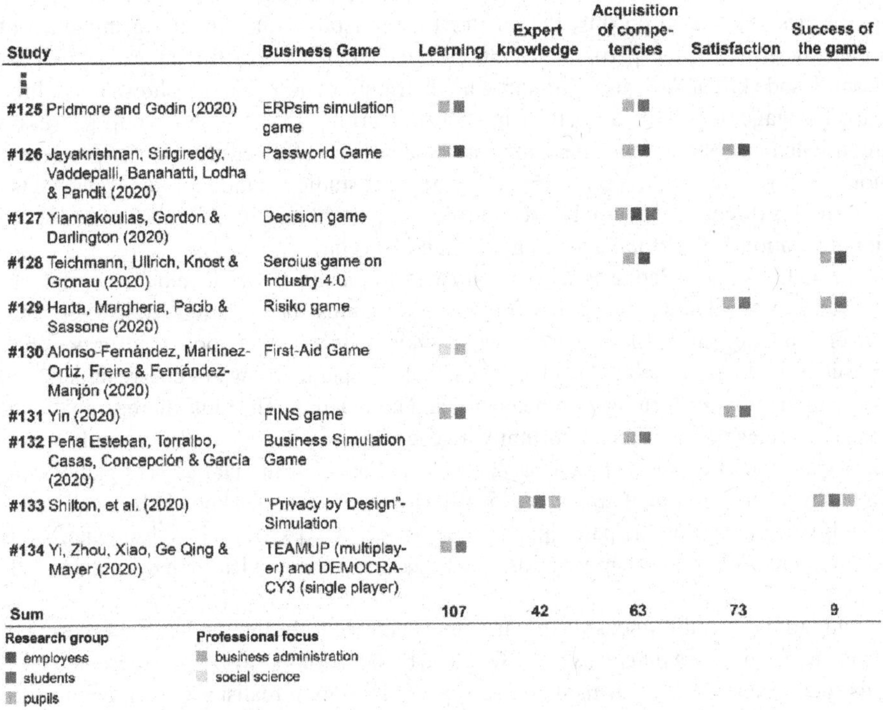

Fig. 3. Extract of the literature review referring variables of learning effects and acceptance of business games

When examining the relevant literature, it is noticeable that different *theoretical approaches* are used to describe and explain learning processes in business games. The most common ones are the situated as well as constructivist learning approaches [5, 11]. A variant of situated learning is the experiential learning according to Kolb (1984) and a variant of constructivist learning is the action-oriented learning which take place in business games [12].

These two approaches supplement each other in relation to potential learning content, whereby the distinctions cannot be considered independently. Common aspects are the activity and dependence on the subjective background and relevance classification of the learner, the difference between expectation and reality which is anticipated by a critical event or irritation, and the processing and reflection of what has happened. However, experiential learning focuses on processing what has been experienced as well as re-experiencing and takes emotional aspects into account. Action-oriented learning focuses on experimentation, physical aspects, and intentional learning [11]. Thus, business games strive for a holistic active sustainable learning that includes content-related and methodological-strategic as well as social-communicative and affective components [2].

107 of the empirical studies confirmed that business games enable *learning* [27, 28ff, 29]. In addition, learners perceive the simulation as authentic thanks to a realistic game setting, as they classify consequences as relevant in the sense of constructivist learning approaches [5]. Based on this, the business game studies show a strong influence of prior experience of the participants [30–32] and of realism of the game [29, 33] on learning and skill acquisition. Similarly, the literature review [22, 34] shows that a high learner engagement have a positive impact on learning [35, 36]. As group processes are initiated and autonomous decisions are made in self-directed learning, the learners' motivation will increase, too [5, 36]. The empirical studies in the literature review also confirm this direct connection between groups of participants [6, 37], autonomy [8, 22] and motivation [38, 39] in business games with learning.

In addition, knowledge is a necessary requirement for the development of competencies. Since knowledge is not transferable, it must be acquired by learners in a self-organized manner. In a narrower sense, knowledge is understood as informational, technical and factual knowledge [15]. Thus, in this paper learning effects are understood as a combination of learning, competencies and knowledge. The multidimensionality of business games provides the opportunity to teach different thematic content and support the acquisition of expertise [40, 44]. 42 of the studies confirm that business games contribute to the *acquisition of expertise* [45, 46]. However, sustained knowledge acquisition is highly dependent on the participants' prior knowledge [43, 47]. Besides, expertise is acquired precisely through motivation, active participation and learner engagement [21, 34].

Due to their multidimensional learning arrangement, business games are designed to promote action *competencies* (n = 37) close to the learners' world of experience [40]. This literature review confirms the influence of simulation realism on skill acquisition [22, 41]. Directly related to the acquisition of competencies in business games is an intrinsic motivation to learn, as it describes the desire to learn and to acquire competencies in the respective educational situation [2, 5]. This relationship is supported by the simulation studies [6, 42]. Moreover, participants groups are discussed as another influencing factor on the acquisition of competencies since they promote social learning [8, 43].

Furthermore, the business game studies indicate that competence acquisition, expertise, and learning correlate strongly with each other due to the similarity in content [21, 47]. Figure 4 provides an overview of the identified influencing variables on learning effects; the number of studies is given in parentheses. Most of the studies (n = 107) focus influencing factors on learning.

Besides, the findings on learning effects are strongly correlated with *acceptance* through the participants' subjectively perceived benefits in a business game [16]. Therefore, this paper discusses satisfaction and simulation success as constructs of business game acceptance.

The construct *satisfaction* is a complex and multi-layered concept and is deemed to be equivalent to the individual attitude, expectation, perception or assessment of the characteristics of an object [17–19]. In relation to the assessment of business games,

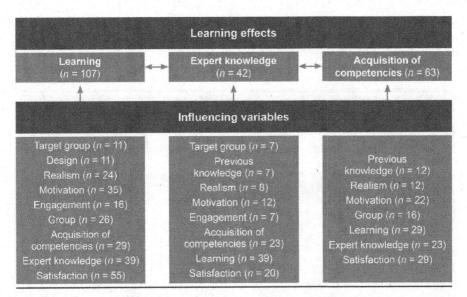

Fig. 4. Influencing variables on learning effects in business games games (number of studies)

satisfaction involves the comparison of perception and assessment of what is experienced with individual expectations [17]. The measurement of satisfaction enables an improvement of the quality of simulation games [5]. Business game studies ($n = 73$) also indicate that participation in a business game is associated with a high level of satisfaction [4, 6]. In addition, professional relevance and thereby relevance to professional reality is crucial for perceived satisfaction [5], which is also evident in the studies examined [4, 50]. Furthermore, a relationship between motivation, skill acquisition, and satisfaction is assumed [5]. In-game feedback is believed to increase motivation and related satisfaction [22]. These correlations are also evident in business game studies [8, 33]. Another influencing factor on satisfaction might be participants' interaction during the simulation game, whereby learning processes only take place to a limited extent in case of dissatisfaction [19], which is also confirmed in the literature review [6, 8].

In addition to satisfaction, the assessment of *success* is indispensable for the acceptance of business games, as a high level of satisfaction is not automatically connected with a successful participation [20]. Therefore, business game success is not necessarily related to learning success [21]. However, perceived success in the game must be attributable to one's actions before business game participation is considered as successful [22]. The literature review ($n = 9$) suggests that business games show a high acceptance if they are assessed as effective and efficient [48, 51]. According to Trautwein (2011), factors influencing the success of simulation games include the learners, the framework, and the group. Different personality characteristics and attributes of the learners can result in different assessments of success [5]. The framework conditions include the subjective perception of the simulation design, whereas realism has the greatest influence on simulation success according to the business game studies [5, 33]. Moreover, the group in which the participants are assigned during the game has a high influence on the success of the simulation through their activity [26, 52], which is also shown by the studies examined [5, 53]. Figure 5 represents the factors influencing the acceptance of business games.

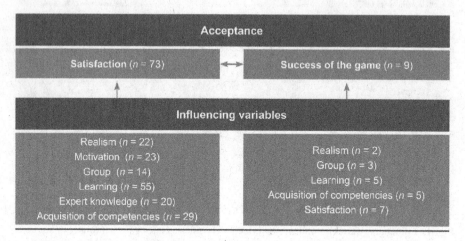

Fig. 5. Influencing variables on acceptance in business games (number of studies)

Overall, the simulation studies suggest that personal influencing factors such as socio-demographic (age, gender) and socio-economic (field of study) variables have only a moderate impact on learning effects and acceptance [5, 54]. However, it is evident that the relevant study group evaluates the learning effects and acceptance in business games differently [49, 55].

4   Discussion and a Future Research Agenda

The literature review indicates that the learning effects of the participants are strongly connected with the target group, the design of the game as well as with engagement during the game. To be more precise, learning is also influenced by realism, learners' motivation, group of participants, expert knowledge, acquisition of competencies and the satisfaction of the game. Expertise is mostly impacted by realism, motivation, acquisition of competencies, learning and satisfaction. Influencing factors of competence acquisition according to the literature review are previous knowledge, realism, motivation, group of the participants, learning, expert knowledge and success of the game. Additionally, the acceptance of business games is correlated with the preconditions of the learners, the group during the game as well as expert knowledge. According to the studies in the literature review, satisfaction is also influenced by realism, motivation, learning and acquisition of competencies. Moreover, the group of the participants, learning, acquisition of competencies and satisfaction with the game influence the success of the business game.

Our literature review also shows that the variables of learning effects and acceptance strongly correlate with each other. In our analysis, we distinguished the factors learning, acquisition of competencies, expertise as well as satisfaction and success. Most of the analyzed papers, however, do not differentiate these categories. Thus, these factors are not perceived individually and distinctly in the analyzed papers. Rather, the terms are partly used synonymously. Therefore, our *first research proposition* is to conceptual clarify and define the analyzed terms. The majority of studies in the literature review examined single variables influencing learning effects or acceptance of business games. In detail 56.7% of the studies examined one to three variables, 31.3% four to five and less than 15% more than five variables. Thus, the studies indicate that an isolated analysis of individual variables has been examined than the interaction between different variables (such as realism, motivation, engagement or group). However, the target variables of learning effects and the acceptance of business games are characterized by different – sometimes interrelated - influencing factors. No study has been found which include several influencing variables by using more complex models like the recommended model of Kriz and Hense (2006). Therefore, our *second research proposition* is to develop complex models that address multiple variables and their interrelationships.

Additionally, there are only a few studies in the literature review that examine business games over a longer period of time. Most studies collect data before, during, and especially immediately after the business game or simulation. Therefore, studies that examine sustainable and long-term learning effects are particularly lacking. However, this is challenging because, on the one hand, the participants must still be reachable six months or a year after the simulation and, on the other hand, because causal effects in the long-term perspective need not be unambiguous. Our *third research proposition* is therefore to invest in studies that systematically investigate sustainable learning effects of simulation participation.

124 studies used quantitative methods, 61 used qualitative methods, and only 48 combined qualitative and quantitative methods. Each research method pursues different goals and addresses different questions. We know that triangulation of methods can yield fruitful and differentiated findings. Our *fourth research proposition* is therefore to invest in studies that combine different research methods (e.g., survey, interview, observation, video analysis).

5   Conclusion

There is profound evidence from the literature that business games are innovative and sustainable learning methods enabling the didactic design of relevant teaching content. Business games enrich the methodical educational offer with a form of learning that allows scope for individual, interactive learning [40]. Besides transferring cognition-based knowledge, simulation games are suitable for the acquisition of competencies and initiating learning processes. Through the combination of authenticity and application reference, social involvement of the participants, as well as the multidimensional learning arrangement, simulation games enable safe problem-oriented trial action [40, 57].

However, since each business game has its own requirements, a separate logical model must be created for each business game and the examined variables need to be integrated [8]. Thus, further evaluation of these learning effects and the acceptance of business games requires the use of an evaluation model that allows statements about learning effects and acceptance.

Moreover, most studies are with students and only a few with employees or pupils due to the accessibility of the participants of business game. In order to promote the use of business games in a corporate context, more studies on the use of business games in enterprises would be useful to evaluate effects on e.g. cooperation in enterprises or increase knowledge of the participants. In addition, there are more studies regarding long-term outcomes and a mixed method evaluation design are needed. In this context, a holistic evaluation of business games appears to be indispensable considering the wide range of possible applications and the assumed high effectiveness.

Acknowledgements. This research was partially supported by the German Federal Ministry of Education and Research (project IMPRESS, 02L17B077). The sponsor had no role in the study design, the collection, analysis and interpretation of data, the writing of the report, or the submission of the paper for publication. We are very grateful to Melisa Tasliarmut and Julia Birke for their assistance with data analysis.

References

1. von Ameln, F., Kramer, J.: Organisationen in Bewegung bringen: Handlungsorientierte Methoden für die Personal-, Team- und Organisationsentwicklung, 2nd edn. Springer, Heidelberg (2016). https://doi.org/10.1007/978-3-662-48197-4
2. Klippert, H.: Planspiele: 10 Spielvorlagen zum sozialen, politischen und methodischen Lernen in Gruppen, 5th edn. Beltz, Weinheim (2008)
3. Riedl, A., Schelten, A.: Grundbegriffe der Pädagogik und Didaktik beruflicher Bildung. Franz Steiner Verlag (2013)
4. Geithner, S., Menzel, D.: Effectiveness of learning through experience and reflection in a project management simulation. Simul. Gaming, 228–56 (2016). https://doi.org/10.1177/1046878115624312
5. Trautwein, C.: Unternehmensplanspiele im industriebetrieblichen Hochschulstudium: Analyse von Kompetenzerwerb, Motivation und Zufriedenheit am Beispiel des Unternehmensplanspiels TOPSIM - General Management II. Springer Fachmedien Wiesbaden GmbH Wiesbaden, Wiesbaden (2011). https://doi.org/10.1007/978-3-8349-6955-2
6. Kriz, W.C., Auchter, E.: 10 Years of evaluation research into gaming simulation for german entrepreneurship and a new study and its long-term effects. Simul. Gaming **47**, 179–205 (2016). https://doi.org/10.1177/1046878116633972
7. Baranowski, M.K., Weir, K.: Political simulations: what we know, what we think we know, and what we still need to know. J. Political Sci. Educ. **11**, 391–403 (2015). https://doi.org/10.1080/15512169.2015.1065748
8. Lohmann, J.R.: Simulations matter: Wirkungsweisen und Mehrwert von Politiksimulationen [Dissertation]: Universität Passau (2019)
9. Lohmann, J.R., Kranenpohl, U.: Kurz- und langfristige Lerneffekte durch Planspiele: Eine Panelbefragung unter studentischen Teilnehmenden. In: Meßner, M.T., Schedelik, M., Engartner, T. (eds.) Handbuch: Planspiele in der sozialwissenschaftlichen Hochschullehre, pp. 85–100. Wochenschau Verlag, Frankfurt (2018)
10. Eberle, T., Kriz, W.C.: Planspiele in der Hochschullehre und Hochschuldidaktik. In: Petrik, A., Rappenglück, S. (eds.) Handbuch Planspiele in der politischen Bildung, pp. 155–168. Wochenschau Verlag, Schwalbach/Ts (2017)
11. Schwägele, S.: Planspiel – Lernen – Lerntransfer: Eine subjektorientierte Analyse von Einflussfaktoren [Dissertation]: Otto-Friedrich-Universität Bamberg (2015)

12. Kolb, D.A.: Experiential Learning: Experience as The Source of Learning and Development. Prentice-Hall, Hoboken (1984)
13. Kriz, W.C.: Qualitätskriterien von Planspielanwendungen. In: Hitzler, S., Zürn, B., Trautwein, F. (eds.) Planspiele - Qualität und Innovation: Neue Ansätze aus Theorie und Praxis, pp. 11–37. Books on Demand, Norderstedt (2011)
14. Ahrens, D., Schulte, S.: Identifikation von Kompetenzbedarfen für den Hafen der Zukunft. In: Bullinger-Hoffmann, A.C. (ed.) Zukunftstechnologien und Kompetenzbedarfe: Kompetenzentwicklung in der Arbeitswelt 4.0, 1st edn., pp. 45–59. Springer, Heidelberg (2019). https://doi.org/10.1007/978-3-662-54952-0_4
15. Erpenbeck, J., Sauter, W.: Wissen, Werte und Kompetenzen in der Mitarbeiterentwicklung: Ohne Gefühl geht in der Bildung gar nichts. Springer, Wiesbaden (2015). https://doi.org/10.1007/978-3-658-09954-1
16. Schüßler, I.: Lernwirkungen neuer Lernformen, Berlin (2004)
17. Bihler, W.: Weiterbildungserfolg in betrieblichen Lehrveranstaltungen. DUV Deutscher Universitäts-Verlag (2006)
18. Fishbein, M., Ajzen, I.: Belief, Attitude, Intention and Behavior: An Introduction to Theory and Research. Addison-Wesley (1975)
19. Jungkunz, D.: Zufriedenheit von Auszubildenden mit ihrer Berufsausbildung. Zeitschrift für Berufs- und Wirtschaftspädagogik 92, 400–15 (1996)
20. Kauffeld, S.: Nachhaltige Weiterbildung: Betriebliche Seminare und Trainings entwickeln, Erfolge messen, Transfer sichern. Springer, Heidelberg (2010). https://doi.org/10.1007/978-3-540-95954-0
21. Williams, D.: The impact of SimVenture on the development of entrepreneurial skills in management students. Ind. High. Educ. 29, 379–395 (2015). https://doi.org/10.5367/ihe.2015.0270
22. Blazic, A.J., Blazic, D.J.: Exploring and upgrading the educational business-game taxonomy. J. Educ. Comput. Res. 52, 303–340 (2015). https://doi.org/10.1177/0735633115572959
23. Wächter, M.: Engineering-Methode zur Gestaltung gebrauchstauglicher tangibler Mensch-Maschine-Schnittstellen für Planer und Entwickler von Produktionsassistenzsystemen [Dissertation]: Technische Universität Chemnitz, 20 December 2017
24. Kriz, W.C., Hense, J.U.: Theory-oriented evaluation for the design of and research in gaming and simulation. Simul. Gaming 37, 268–283 (2006). https://doi.org/10.1177/1046878106287950
25. Page, M.J., McKenzie, J.E., Bossuyt, P.M., Boutron, I., Hoffmann, T.C., Mulrow, C.D., et al.: The PRISMA 2020 statement: an updated guideline for reporting systematic reviews. Syst. Rev. 10, 89 (2021). https://doi.org/10.1186/s13643-021-01626-4
26. Rebmann. K.: Planspiel und Planspieleinsatz: Theoretische und empirische Explorationen zu einer konstruktivistischen Planspieldidaktik. Dr. Kovač, Hamburg (2001)
27. Hernández-Lara, A.B., Serradell-Lopez, E.: Student interactions in online discussion forums: their perception on learning with business simulation games. Behav. Inf. Technol. 37, 419–429 (2018). https://doi.org/10.1080/0144929X.2018.1441326
28. Mayer, I., Kortmann, R., Wenzler, I., Wetters, A., Spaans, J.: Game-based entrepreneurship education: identifying enterprising personality, motivation and intentions amongst engineering students. J. Entrep. Educ. 17, 217–244 (2014)
29. Arora, A.S.: The "organization" as an interdisciplinary learning zone. Learn. Organ. 19, 121–133 (2012). https://doi.org/10.1108/09696471211201489
30. Cheng, M.-T., Su, T.F., Huang, W.-Y., Chen, J.-H.: An educational game for learning human immunology: what do students learn and how do they perceive? Br. J. Edu. Technol. 45, 820–833 (2014). https://doi.org/10.1111/bjet.12098

31. Li, T.M.H., Chau, M., Wong, P.W.C., Lai, E.S.Y., Yip, P.S.F.: Evaluation of a web-based social network electronic game in enhancing mental health literacy for young people. J. Med. Internet Res. **15**, 80 (2013). https://doi.org/10.2196/jmir.2316
32. Thanasi-Boçe, M.: Enhancing students' entrepreneurial capacity through marketing simulation games. Educ. Train. **62**, 999–1013 (2020). https://doi.org/10.1108/ET-06-2019-0109
33. Wang, S.-H., Wang, H.-Y.: Using an epistemic game to facilitate students' problem-solving: the case of hospitality management. Technol. Pedagogy Educ. **26**, 283–302 (2016). https://doi.org/10.1080/1475939X.2016.1234408
34. Suresh, J.: Board room simulation game helps strategic management course. South Asian J. Bus. Manag. Cases **8**, 232–240 (2019). https://doi.org/10.1177/2277977919860274
35. Csikszentmihalyi, M.: Das Flow-Erlebnis: Jenseits von Angst und Langeweile: Im Tun aufgehen. Klett-Cotta, Stuttgart (2010)
36. Hattie, J.: Lernen sichtbar machen. Baltmannsweiler. Schneider-Verl, Hohengehren (2013)
37. Prinsen, G., Overton, J.: Policy, personalities and pedagogy: the use of simulation games to teach and learn about development policy. J. Geogr. High. Educ. **35**, 281–297 (2011). https://doi.org/10.1080/03098265.2010.548508
38. Chang, Y.C., Peng, H.Y., Chao, H.C.: Examining the effects of learning motivation and of course design in an instructional simulation game. Interact. Learn. Environ. **18**, 319–339 (2010). https://doi.org/10.1080/10494820802574270
39. Pacheco-Velazquez, E., Palma-Mendoza, J., Arana-Solares, I., Rivera, T.C.: LOST: a serious game to develop a comprehensive vision of logistics. In: Elbaek, L., Majgaard, G. (eds.) Academic Conferences International Limited, pp. 550–559 (2019)
40. Engartner, T., Siewert, M.B., Meßner, M.T., Borchert, C.: Politische Partizipation "spielend" fördern?: Charakteristika von Planspielen als didaktisch-methodische Arrangements handlungsorientierten Lernens. Zeitschrift für Politikwissenschaft **25**, 189–217 (2015). https://doi.org/10.5771/1430-6387-2015-2-189
41. Vos, L., Brennan, R.: Marketing simulation games: a review of issues in teaching and learning. Mark. Rev. **14**, 67–96 (2014). https://doi.org/10.1362/146934714X13948909473220
42. König, J.A., Wolf, M.: GHOST: an evaluated competence developing game for cybersecurity awareness training. Int. J. Adv. Secur. **11**, 274–287 (2018)
43. Hauge, J.B., Riedel, J.C.K.H.: Evaluation of simulation games for teaching engineering and manufacturing. Procedia Comput. Sci. **15**, 210–220 (2012). https://doi.org/10.1016/j.procs.2012.10.073
44. Capaul, R., Ulrich, M.: Planspiele: Simulationsspiele für Unterricht und Training; mit Kurztheorie: Simulations- und Planspielmethodik, 2nd edn. Tobler, Altstätten (2010)
45. Kaneko, T., Hamada, R., Hiji, M.: Business game promoting supply chain collaboration education at universities. In: Hamada, R., et al. (eds.) Neo-Simulation and Gaming Toward Active Learning. TSS, vol. 18, pp. 137–146. Springer, Singapore (2019). https://doi.org/10.1007/978-981-13-8039-6_13
46. Dib, H., Adamo-Villani, N.: Serious sustainability challenge game to promote teaching and learning of building sustainability. J. Comput. Civ. Eng. (2014). https://doi.org/10.1061/(ASCE)CP.1943-5487.0000357
47. Lohmann, J.R.: Effects of simulation-based learning and one way to analyze them. J. Political Sci. Educ., 1–17 (2019). https://doi.org/10.1080/15512169.2019.1599291
48. Beranič, T., Heričko, M.: Introducing ERP concepts to IT students using an experiential learning approach with an emphasis on reflection. Sustainability **11**, 1–17 (2019). https://doi.org/10.3390/su11184992
49. Davesa, F., Piros, S.: Assessing the effectiveness of EU simulations: do the characteristics of participants impact learning outcomes? Eur. Political Sci. **18**, 535–553 (2019). https://doi.org/10.1057/s41304-018-00199-6

50. Dzeng, R.-J., Lin, K.-Y., Wang, P.-R.: Building a construction procurement negotiation training game model: learning experiences and outcomes. Br. J. Edu. Technol. **45**, 1115–1135 (2014). https://doi.org/10.1111/bjet.12189

51. Hwang, M., Cruthirds, K.: Impact of an ERP simulation game on online learning. Int. J. Manag. Educ. **15**, 60–66 (2017). https://doi.org/10.1016/j.ijme.2017.01.004

52. Duke, R.D., Kriz, W.C.: Back to the future of Gaming. Bertelsmann W. Verlag (2014)

53. Taillandier, F., Adam, C.: Games ready to use: a serious game for teaching natural risk management. Simul. Gaming **49**, 441–470 (2018). https://doi.org/10.1177/1046878118770217

54. Joiner, R., et al.: Digital games, gender and learning in engineering: do females benefit as much as males? J. Sci. Educ. Technol. **20**, 178–185 (2011). https://doi.org/10.1007/s10956-010-9244-5

55. Weber-Sabil, J., Warmelink, H., Martinisi, A., Buijtenweg, T., Hutchinson, K., Mayer, I.S.: Learning efficacy among executives and students of an organizational growth game. In: Hamada, R., et al. (eds.) Neo-Simulation and Gaming Toward Active Learning. TSS, vol. 18, pp. 129–136. Springer, Singapore (2019). https://doi.org/10.1007/978-981-13-8039-6_12

56. Kriz, W.C., Hense, J.U.: Evaluation und Qualitätssicherung von Planspielen. In: Blötz, U. (ed.) Planspiele in der beruflichen Bildung: Auswahl, Konzepte, Lernarrangements, Erfahrungen - aktueller Planspielkatalog 2008, 4th edn, pp. 192–231. Bundesinstitut für Berufsbildung, Bertelsmann Vertrieb, Bonn, Bielefeld (2008)

57. Kriz, W.C.: Planspiele als Trainingsmethode in der Hochschuldidaktik: Zur Funktion der Planspielleitung. In: Meßner, M.T., Schedelik, M., Engartner, T. (eds.) Handbuch Planspiele in der sozialwissenschaftlichen Hochschullehre, pp. 43–56. Wochenschau Verlag, Frankfurt (2018)

About Dinosaurs in Laboratories - Evaluation of the Serious Game Cards for Biosafety

Maria Freese[1,2]([✉]) [iD] and Geertje Bekebrede[1] [iD]

[1] Faculty of Technology, Policy and Management, Delft University of Technology, Jaffalaan 5, 2628 BX Delft, The Netherlands
`maria.freese@ovgu.de`
[2] Faculty of Mechanical Engineering, Otto von Guericke University, Universitaetsplatz 2, 39106 Magdeburg, Germany

Abstract. Cards for Biosafety is a serious game, which was developed as part of a national research project. The aim of this game is to let young biotechnology researchers learn about risks and mitigation measures in different biotechnology environments. To evaluate the game and its learning objective, an online questionnaire was developed and distributed to national and international biosafety experts who had received a print version of the game. In total, 17 participants completed the questionnaire. The results show that Cards for Biosafety supports learning on different cognitive levels of the revised version of Bloom's taxonomy. Especially the influence of fun and humor on the game play and the learning process was emphasized by the respondents. In addition, the creativity of the participants plays a major role in learning. Future research is needed to draw valid conclusions about the effectiveness of learning after playing Cards for Biosafety in comparison to traditional tools.

Keywords: Biosafety · Biotechnology · Cards for Biosafety · Evaluation · Fun · Learning · Serious Games

1 Introduction

Within the T-TRIPP project (Tools for Translation of Risk research into Policies & Practices), which is part of part a National Biotechnology and Safety research programme, different research activities were conducted. One of these research activities focused on the development of a serious game. In order to identify a concrete problem to be addressed by such a serious game, the analyses of the project team were based on the IDEAS approach [1]. The IDEAS approach basically consists of four main steps and defines the participation of the actual target group as a central component. The results of this participatory approach with experts from the field of biotechnology have clearly shown that a) a serious game for education is needed b) to be able to let young biotechnology researchers c) think more deeply about biosafety in an interactive way.

a) The need for a serious game is mainly grounded in the need for an interactive method that makes it possible to discuss topics, such as biosafety and biosecurity and associated risks, with each other in an open and safe environment. The expectation is that

C. Harteveld et al. (Eds.): ISAGA 2022, LNCS 13622, pp. 52–65, 2023.
https://doi.org/10.1007/978-3-031-37171-4_4

the cognitive exchange about these topics in the context of a serious game can contribute significantly to the learning success compared to conventional methods, which have a less strong focus on interaction, engagement, and innovation. The advantage of the latter aspect has already been discussed by Orhan and Sahin [2] for training approaches in biotechnology. Franklin, Peat and Lewis [3] have already addressed the extent to which biology students and teachers find card game discussions useful. The students considered such a method as an added value and the teachers rated the card game discussions as a possibility for active learning.

b) The project analyses have shown that especially junior researchers (Master students, PhD students or Postdocs) should make use of the serious game to give them more active knowledge around biosafety topics.

c) The focus on biosafety has arisen from the content-related discussions with the researchers, who talk about the fact that it is sometimes difficult to explain the rules to researchers, that safety is not always the top priority or that there is a lack of awareness for safety issues. Further results are described in detail in Freese, Tiemersma and Verbraeck [4].

During last year's (online) International Simulation and Gaming Associations conference, we played a prototype of the serious game Cards for Biosafety with workshop attendees in addition to a more content-oriented presentation of the development of this game. Based on the feedback from workshop and conference attendees as well as from subject-matter experts, the game has been further developed to the final version and sent to biosafety experts around the world. The main question for any educational game is if and to what extent the game influences learning and achieves the goal of the game. From a development perspective, the game was designed with 'serious fun' elements. Therefore, the game experience is also examined. The aim of this publication is to discuss the evaluation of this serious game with regard to the achievement of its intended learning objectives and game experiences.

2   Cards for Biosafety

Cards for Biosafety, which was inspired by the entertainment game Cards against Humanity [5], is an analogue card game that can be played with 3 to 8 players. The aim of the game is to let junior researchers think more deeply about safety aspects and thus, create a better understanding of related risks and measures to mitigate these risks in different biotechnology environments. The game is round-based and each round takes about 10 min to play depending on the number of players and the depth and length of the discussions as part of the debriefing. Only the first round takes a bit more time as the players are still busy learning the rules of the game.

2.1   Game Play

The detailed description of the game play can be found in Freese, Tiemersma and Verbraeck [4]. The most important game mechanics that are relevant for a better understanding of this publication are described here. The game is based on different rounds that are independent of each other, making it possible to play as many rounds as possible.

There are three main phases per round: 1) Choosing a scenario, 2) choosing a risk card, and 3) choosing a measure card.

In the first step, the game facilitator selects a scenario (e.g., "fundamental lab research on mutations in the SARS-CoV-2 virus"). This can be done by choosing a scenario consciously or picking it randomly.

In the second step, the facilitator distributes five risk cards (e.g., "non-labelled containers on workbench") to every player. Each of them chooses one of these cards that represents the best, funniest or most realistic risk for the scenario selected in the first phase. The players should not only choose an appropriate risk card, but also think about an argumentation for their choice. Every player pitches their arguments and after the pitches, the players vote for the risk card that symbolizes the most appropriate risk for the scenario. The selected risk card is used as a starting point for the next phase.

In the third step, the facilitator distributes five measure cards (e.g., "make instructions in several languages") to every player. Similar to the previous phase, the players have to choose a measure card that represents the best way to mitigate the previously chosen risk and give a pitch with regard to their choice. This is followed by another voting round, and the players must identify the best measure card.

Cards for Biosafety is seen as a discussion starter. To guarantee this and thus, focus on the serious part of this game, it is important to provide enough space for debriefing moments. During the game play, several debriefing moments exist, meaning that after every phase (risk, measure) or round a debriefing can be initiated. If necessary, the facilitator gives more background information about the selected scenario. The facilitator booklet contains information about the scenarios which can be shared in advance or with participants after a round has finished. To guarantee the achievement of the intended learning goal, a final debriefing can be conducted at the end of the game play to discuss the results from a meta perspective. There are different ways to intensify the debriefing process, because part of the game is of course also the direct exchange process between the players without the facilitator's support. Within the debriefing, different topics are addressed. Besides the players' emotions, concrete experiences related to specific events are analyzed, but above all the connection to everyday life is built up. Here, it is interesting to know why different cards were chosen and how this information (or similar information) on the cards is related to the working world of the players. More concrete debriefing questions can be found in Freese, Tiemersma and Verbraeck [4]. The learning effect increases when the game is played with a diverse group in terms of level of experience [4], which is why we recommend playing this game with both junior (e.g., Master students, PhD students or Postdocs) and senior researchers (e.g., biosafety officers or project leaders). The added value of the debriefing can be supported by the attendance of a senior researcher who can put the element of fun in a serious context making it possible to learn "why a dumb answer could be right".

2.2 Developing an Engaging Prototype

The game was designed with 'serious fun' elements, which means engagement is an important design criterion. To reach the objectives, discussion and creativity is relevant as well. Based on the feedback from gaming and biotechnology experts in numerous iterations, the following aspects were prioritized and implemented in the final Cards for Biosafety prototype.

To encourage and challenge the players as much as possible, the formulations on all cards needs to be neutral. Phrases such as "Due to ..." were removed, as these already provide an argumentation aid. In various playtests, we recognized that pitching for a card should be given greater importance. Therefore, each player gets a short moment to argue their card. To further increase creativity, we have added a number of blank scenario, risk and measure cards with the idea that the players themselves can write down their projects, risks or measures on these cards and thus consider their own projects as part of the game.

Another way to improve discussion and creativity was to work with a competitive element. After the players have presented their pitches, each player will be given the opportunity to vote for the pitch they think is the best (funniest, most realistic, ...). It is not possible to vote for yourself. The player with the most votes wins the phase and round and gets one point. When there is a tie after voting, the players with the same number of votes must defend their cards again. Afterwards, the other players have time to adjust their scoring. A secret voting system is given as option, when the game is played with people with different levels of experience. The players are asked to vote with the corresponding cards upside down and turn over the cards at the same time and thus make the scoring open. In this way, junior researchers are not influenced by the scoring of the more experienced researchers. Our experience from play-testing showed that players considered the competitive element - pitching creative ideas against each other - to be very valuable.

Finally, it was important to check the risk and measure cards with regards to an appropriate balance between fun and seriousness. As already described in Freese, Tiemersma and Verbraeck [4], the cards were validated by experts, but a conscious decision was made to also include funny cards in the game and to work with fun throughout the course of the game play and serious discussions. All this has been incorporated into the final version of Cards for Biosafety (see Fig. 1).

2.3 Learning Objective

As mentioned earlier, we want to let junior researchers think more deeply about biosafety aspects. This learning objective can be classified using the taxonomy of Bloom [6] or the revised taxonomy of Bloom by Anderson and Krathwohl [7]. Generally speaking, these taxonomies assume that there are different levels of cognitive learning goals and that one first needs to acquire knowledge before one can apply it to different situations and thus, create new input. By using Cards for Biosafety, we want players to go through these different phases. After playing Cards for Biosafety, players should have learned something new about specific biotechnology projects, associated risks, and measures to mitigate the risks, and should be able to adapt this to other situations they might or will encounter as well. Based on this, the following research question can be formulated: Does playing Cards for Biosafety support learning on the different cognitive levels of the revised version of Bloom's taxonomy?

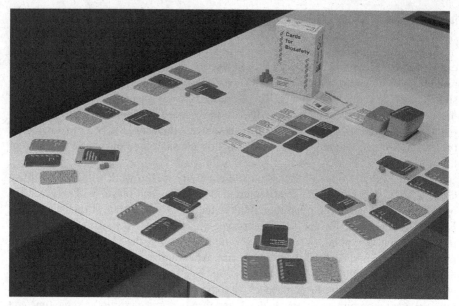

Fig. 1. Impression of the serious game Cards for Biosafety (TU Delft Gamelab, 2021)

3   Experimental Set up

To evaluate the Cards for Biosafety game, we developed and distributed an online questionnaire.

3.1   Online Questionnaire

The online questionnaire consisted of five main parts. First, we asked participants for their consent. Second, we focused on demographical data, such as gender, age, and nationality. Third, we used the Game Experience Questionnaire (GEQ) to measure the game experience of the participants [8]. The GEQ is a well-known and often cited instrument to measure the game experiences based on seven components: competence, immersion, flow, tension/annoyance, challenge, and (positive and negative) affect. Due to the fact that the GEQ was originally developed to measure the players' experience of digital games, we added a 'not applicable' category to the 5-point answer scale of the GEQ in case participants have the impression that an item is less suitable for the evaluation of a card game. The use of the GEQ in order to measure the participants' experience with an analogue game is supported by a study from Johnson, Cuijpers, Pollmann and van de Ven [9]. Fourth, we included several questions regarding the achievement of the intended learning results, the different levels of learning according to the revised Bloom's taxonomy and the participants' chosen strategies in order to try to win the game. Regarding the questions related to the revised Bloom's taxonomy, we chose open-ended questions per level and associated verbs [10] related to that level and let participants self-select what they experienced through the game by selecting the verbs themselves and giving corresponding descriptions. Lastly, the participants could share their general feedback with us.

Within the last quarter of 2021, the Cards for Biosafety game was sent to various people worldwide who expressed interest in receiving the game. After that, in the period from March to April 2022, a standardized email was sent to the contact persons to whom the project team sent the game with a request to forward this link to those who played the game.

Since the game was sent to different organizations, the facilitation was the responsibility of the respective organizers of the gaming session. To allow for comparability between the sessions, the instruction manual provides specific information, such as the recommended number of players. The game developers did not participate in the sessions and do not have specific information about the gameplay itself. The data are based on self-assessments of the participants. This study was approved by the author's university human research ethics committee.

3.2 Participants

In total, 19 people participated. Two participants did not complete the questionnaire and were excluded from further analysis, which means that a total of 17 participants (female = 7, male = 10) will be considered for further analysis. Their age ranged from 21 to 63 years ($M = 34.00$ years, $SD = 14.87$ years). Seven nationalities were represented with a majority of Dutch participants ($N = 11$).

The current position of the participants is diverse. Seven Bachelor students, two Master's students, one PhD student, three Senior researchers and three Biosafety officers completed the questionnaire. In addition, one participant mentioned that he or she works as a Biomedical Laboratory scientist and as a PhD student at the same time.

As Cards for Biosafety got inspired by the entertainment game Cards against Humanity [5], we asked the participants if they knew Cards against Humanity and thus, are familiar with the game play. Ten (58.8%) participants answered "Yes" and seven (41,2%) did not know this game.

In order to understand the setting in which the participants played Cards for Biosafety a bit better, we asked them about the timing and the number of players. One participant (5.9%) mentioned that he or she played the game last week, seven participants (41.2%) answered that they played it last month and nine participants (52.9%) said that they played Cards for Biosafety more than a month ago. This is probably also explained by the fact that the game was distributed at the end of 2021.

With regard to the number of players during such a Cards for Biosafety session, thirteen participants played the game in a session with four, five or six players in total and four participants played the game with either less than three or more than six other players.

4 Results

4.1 Game-Experience Questionnaire

A detailed overview of the descriptive results of the GEQ can be found in Table 1. Considering the description of the results in this section, our attention is mainly focused on the (extreme) mean values of the outer values of the scale (between 1 and 2 as well 4 and 5).

The participants were fairly interested in the story of the game ($M = 4.06$). They found it an aesthetically pleasing game ($M = 4.00$) and felt imaginative ($M = 4.13$). In addition, the participants scored high on positive affect, they felt content ($M = 4.00$), were fully occupied with the game ($M = 4.00$), had fun ($M = 4.41$), were happy ($M = 4.35$), felt good ($M = 4.12$), and enjoyed it ($M = 4.41$). Considering the opposite side of the scale (negative affect), the participants indicated that they were not put in a bad mood ($M = 1.41$), that they just thought a little bit about other things ($M = 1.88$), that the game did not make them tired ($M = 1.41$), and that they were not bored ($M = 1.29$). The scores of the questions whether participants felt annoyed ($M = 1.29$), irritable ($M = 1.24$) or frustrated ($M = 1.24$) ranged from not at all to slightly. Furthermore, they did not feel pressured ($M = 1.88$), while other scores related to the factor challenge where neutral. In contrast to this, they have not forgotten to keep track of the time ($M = 1.87$) and the connection with the outside world ($M = 1.75$).

In order to understand the participants' strategy behind choosing appropriate cards, we asked them about their approach for choosing their risk or measure card. The participants answers can be divided into four categories: 1) Creativity (e.g., "if i didn't have the right cards in my hands I had to be creative to get the right card myself"), 2) experience (e.g., "No strategy at all, rather than just thinking about what I had learned previously"), 3) choice of the funniest cards (e.g., "I chose the funniest or the most accurate ones", and 4) others (e.g., "Pushing the limit a bit what was just acceptable").

4.2 Learning Results

With regard to the statement that Cards for Biosafety gave the participants an opportunity to learn more about biosafety aspects, one participant disagreed (5.9%), one participant chose the neutral category (5.9%), six participants agreed (35.3%) and five participants totally agreed (29.4%) with the statement. In addition, three of them totally agreed (17.6%) and seven participants agreed (41.2%), one was neutral, and two participants disagreed [one of them works as a Biosafety officer]) that the Cards for Biosafety game provided new knowledge on biosafety aspects.

In order to understand what the participants learned, we asked them if they had gained new insights during the Cards for Biosafety game play. Fourteen participants (82.4%) agreed on that. Furthermore, we asked what the insights were:

Table 1. Results of Game Experience Questionnaire.

Factor	Items	Min	Max	M	SD	N
Competence	I felt skillful	2	5	3.76	.97	17
	I felt competent	3	5	3.82	.81	17
	I was good at it	3	5	3.81	.54	16
	I felt successful	2	5	3.62	.81	16
	I was fast at reaching the game's targets	2	5	3.60	.83	15
Sensory and Imaginative Immersion	I was interested in the game's story	3	5	4.06	.83	17
	It was aesthetically pleasing	2	5	4.00	.82	16
	I felt imaginative	2	5	4.13	.72	17
	I felt that I could explore things	2	5	3.82	1.07	17
	I found it impressive	1	5	3.71	1.11	17
	It felt like a rich experience	1	5	3.47	1.07	17
Flow	I was fully occupied with the game	2	5	4.00	.87	17
	I forgot everything around me	1	5	2.59	1.18	17
	I lost track of time	1	4	1.87	.89	16
	I was deeply concentrated in the game	1	5	3.35	1.17	17
	I lost connection with the outside world	1	4	1.75	.86	16
Tension/Annoyance	I felt annoyed	1	4	1.29	.77	17
	I felt irritable	1	5	1.24	.97	17
	I felt frustrated	1	4	1.24	.75	17
Challenge	I thought it was hard	1	5	2.24	1.20	17
	I felt pressured	1	5	1.88	1.32	17
	I felt challenged	1	5	3.53	1.01	17
	I felt time pressure	1	5	2.13	1.41	16
	I had to put a lot of effort into it	1	5	2.65	1.22	17
Negative affect	It gave me a bad mood	1	5	1.41	1.18	17
	I thought about other things	1	4	1.88	.99	17
	I found it tiresome	1	4	1.41	.87	17

(continued)

Table 1. (*continued*)

Factor	Items	Min	Max	M	SD	N
	I felt bored	1	3	1.29	.69	17
Positive affect	I felt content	2	5	4.00	.79	17
	I thought it was fun	3	5	4.41	.71	17
	I felt happy	3	5	4.35	.30	17
	I felt good	3	5	4.12	.60	17
	I enjoyed it	3	5	4.41	.62	17

Note. The participants scored on a 5-point scale ranging from 1 = not at all, 2 = slightly, 3 = moderately, 4 = fairly to 5 = extremely.

– "Provided the participants with insights in each others organizations and the challenges they encounter"
– "Negotiation and persuasion is part of achieving a goal and that is a great addition to practice and get acquainted…"
– "To think about possibilities I never thought of before."
– "Refreshing ideas how to solve problems, that this can also be a way to get a better notion of biosafety issues"
– "As a newbie to biotech topics, all the information I gained was basically new territory for me."
– "Critical Thinking Skills Work within a network of professionals. Discover new things"
– "This game provided a significant insight into how to complete risk assessment whilst also emphasizing how to implement risk assessment in a formal setting. it is a good game."
– "Thinking outside the box"
– "That there is more to biosafety than you'd think!"

These quotes already indicate that the insights are at different levels of cognitive learning objectives which is why the focus in the next section is on the different levels of Bloom's taxonomy.

4.3 Applying Bloom's Revised Taxonomy

The first level 'Remembering (Knowledge)' of Bloom's Revised Taxonomy [7] is mainly about recognizing and recalling information that has been acquired previously [10]. According to quotes formulated by the participants, the Cards for Biosafety game gave them the opportunity to recognize "the challenges of biosafety professionals", that "In everyday life there are always different interests", "That there are multiple forms of biological risk both inside and outside the lab", "Possible solutions", "important aspects of biosafety", and "biosafety aspects in the workplace more easily". These are some of the responses that clearly illustrate the variety of content taught by the play of Cards for Biosafety.

The second level 'Understanding (Comprehension)' basically describes that one is able to understand the meaning based on the used materials [7, 10]. According to the participants, "The game ensures that people listen to each other about certain considerations of different stakeholders and what is behind them. This helps to understand each other". In addition, Cards for Biosafety gave them the chance to understand "how useful is to work together", "The core tenants of risk assessment [...]", "How things can go wrong", "the complexity of biosafety", and "possible dangers outside of the obvious". Furthermore, the game made it possible to explain "what biosafety culture is", "Solutions to these situations", "the concept of biosafety in a very simple way", and "cause and repercussion". It becomes clear that the participants not only perceived information, but were also able to comprehend it.

The third level 'Apply (Application)' means the use of learned input in new situations [7, 10]. With regard to the participants' experiences with Cards for Biosafety, they indicated that the game showed them "the need of a Biosafety officer" and "Where future problems might occur". Furthermore, the participants highlighted that the game gave them the chance to incorporate "safety education in the labs", "Sophisticated ideas", and "biosafety in my daily practices in the lab". These statements of the participants show that a connection and thus a link can be drawn to a new situation.

The fourth level 'Analyze (Analysis)' deals with dividing the 'system' into parts and understanding the relation between the different elements of the system [7, 10]. In a first step, the participants explored "solutions and problems in biosafety", "new mitigation strategies", "The possibilities in biosafety", "an out-of-the-box kind of idea to learn rather strict rules", and "creativity". In addition, they discussed "specific situations [...]", "checks of risk bearing packages", "very different opinions and ideas such as new ideas in dealing with biosafety problems, Key factors and fundamental problems of Biotech, connections and interrelationships between variables", "the need of biosafety in biomedical and research laboratories", "How measures taken to resolve these risks can be beneficial and not beneficial – there is no one-size-fits-all solution", "Extreme situations", "the concept of biosafety in a very simple way", and "strategies for solving the issues". In order to create the basis for discussion, it is necessary to break down information into its components in order to use it appropriately. This also seems to be possible during and after the game play.

The fifth level 'Evaluate (Evaluation)' covers the ability to assess facts and give reasons for certain decisions or opinions [7, 10]. The participants highlighted that the Cards for Biosafety game gave them the chance to argue (= give reasons for) "about biosafety issues", "About possible solutions", and "which danger would be the greatest". In addition, the participants had the chance to evaluate the "Difficult situations" and "[...] knowledge on biosafety". Before one can evaluate information, he or she has to form an opinion to be able to give reasons for it.

The last level 'Create (Synthesis)' means bringing all the information together and creating something new [7, 10]. With regard to this level, the participants said that Cards for Biosafety gave them the chance to learn "about biosafety problems and challenges such as data security", "more about Biosafety", "and revise the various aspects of biological risk management [...]", "Where future problems might be introduced", and "a better way to put biosafety in context". As argumentative decision-making and defending one's own chosen card is also a central mechanic in the game, we also asked the participants whether it was possible for them to defend something. They answered that Cards for Biosafety made it possible to defend "the need of a Biorisk management system.", "The solutions you come up with", "my stands [views]", and "why biosafety exists.

4.4 In-Game Discussions

As the discussions within Cards for Biosafety are expected to make a significant contribution to learning, we asked the participants to what extent they considered the discussions valuable (through an open question). The participants found the discussions:

- "Very interesting"
- "Good"
- "interesting, curious about solutions"
- "multifaceted, exciting, diverse"
- "stimulating, broadening knowledge and career perspectives"
- "Insightful, Helpful, and Useful"
- "Funny"
- "A lot of cards on the table makes it less organized"
- "Fun and interesting"
- "Fun and insightful"
- "hilarious".

5 Discussion and Conclusions

This paper focused on the evaluation of the Cards for Biosafety game which aims to let young biotechnology researchers think more deeply about biosafety. Therefore, an online questionnaire was distributed to different national and international (future) biosafety experts. In total, 17 participants formed the basis of our descriptive analysis. Even though the sample size certainly still has potential to increase, it can be stated at this point that based on the feedback of the sample described in this publication, but also after the use of Cards for Biosafety in several workshops and conferences, it is a well-developed, fun and creative way to learn more about biosafety on different cognitive learning levels.

   With regards to the results of the GEQ, we see that players had the competence to play this game. The players were challenged and the game was not too easy to play. They were generally immersed (except for the rich experience) and were in a flow related to the play intention. They were less in a flow if we look at the environment-related items. The players did not feel annoyed. We see low-scored values in the immersion and flow factors in comparison to other components of the GEQ. Cards for Biosafety was deliberately designed as a simple card game to stimulate discussion. Most likely, a simple cards game is not expected to be associated with a high degree of immersion. This can also be seen in the publication of Johnson, Cuijpers, Pollmann and van de Ven [9], who removed 3-immersion related questions from the GEQ with the argumentation that not all items of the GEQ can be used for analogue games. The question that arises is what one wants to achieve with a high degree of immersion implemented in such a serious game. In our case, we wanted to give the players enough space to explore their own creativity and therefore decided on such a game. This is reflected not only in the GEQ questions in the area of immersion, but also with regard to the flow, which has conceptual overlaps with immersion [11].

The developers of the GEQ recommend using this questionnaire immediately after finishing the game play. Due to different reasons, this was not realized in the setting described in this publication, however, this should be done in future sessions to be able to compare the results of the two different data sets with each other.

If we take a look at the results of the open-ended questions related to the learning objectives, we see that playing Cards for Biosafety supports cognitive learning on different levels. Comparable to Freese, Tiemersma and Verbraeck [4], the feedback of the players highlighted the role of fun and humor and their influence on the game play, which can be seen, among other things, in the responses related to the in-game discussions. During the game, the players may be forced to choose a card that may sound a bit funny, and not too realistic to them. This is an indicator that Cards for Biosafety has successfully made use of the concept of 'serious fun'. Think about the title of this publication which addresses dinosaurs in laboratories. Of course, the chance of meeting dinosaurs in laboratories is quite low, however, exactly this example shows the added value of the debriefing. During the discussions as part of the debriefing, the focus can be on the translation of dinosaurs in the laboratory - used as a metaphor - to visitors who do not have permission to visit a laboratory in a higher safety category. In addition, one of the added values of Cards for Biosafety is its stimulating effect on the creativity of the players. As every player gets random cards, the chance is quite high that they need to come up with creative ideas. The question to what extent creativity (e.g., creative thinking skills) can positively influence cognitive learning has already been discussed by Siburian, Corebima and Saptasari [12]. Learning was in this case primarily supported by the fun and interactive medium of the game. Even though we have received less input regarding the frequency and description of responses in the higher levels of Bloom's taxonomy, we hope that Cards for Biosafety will add value to traditional tools, such as presentations, for both the trainer and the learner. In addition, it must be critically noted that the classification of cognitive learning goals was based purely on the participants' self-assessment. Self-assessments are subjective instruments and what is learned can be both overestimated [e.g., 13] and underestimated [e.g., 14]. Furthermore, the selection of the verbs chosen as well as the interpretation of the corresponding verbs associated with the revised version of Bloom's taxonomy must be critically questioned. With regard to this, Stanny [15] has already described the extent to which the selection of verbs within Bloom's Taxonomy can tell something about learning of students.

6 Future Use and Research

The game has experienced growing interest by national and international biosafety experts. Possible areas of application are wide ranging. In discussions with experts, the use of this game as part of educational and team-building activities and as part of training activities conducted by a Biosafety officer were mentioned. Moreover, they highlighted the use as biosafety awareness tool on the work floor with the aim of designing future learning in such a way that it is more attractive, interesting, and fun. This paper focused mainly on cognitive learning skills. Future research should focus also on the effect Cards for Biosafety might have on the behavior of people.

In addition to the interest in the game, the game concept also received a lot of attention. In discussions with gaming experts, it became clear that Cards for Biosafety is an ideal frame game, which means that the game concept, i.e., the game mechanics, can also be transferred to other areas of application.

Acknowledgements. This article was written as part of the research project T-TRIPP (Tools for the Translation of Risk research into Policies and Practices). The project is funded by the Netherlands Organisation for Scientific Research (NWO) within the programme 'Towards Modernisation of Biotechnology and Safety'. This programme was set up on behalf of the Ministry of Infrastructure and Water Management. The authors are grateful to all project partners for supporting the development process of the Cards for Biosafety game and all participants for taking the time to evaluate the game.

References

1. Freese, M., Lukosch, H.K.: The funnel of game design - proposing a new way to address a problem definition using the IDEAS approach. In: Wardaszko, M., Meijer, S., Lukosch, H., Kanegae, H., Kriz, W.C., Grzybowska-Brzezińska, M. (eds.) ISAGA 2019. LNCS, vol. 11988, pp. 170–180. Springer, Cham (2021). https://doi.org/10.1007/978-3-030-72132-9_16
2. Orhan, T.Y., Sahin, N.: The impact of innovative teaching approaches on biotechnology knowledge and laboratory experiences of science teachers. Educ. Sci. **8**(4), 213 (2018). https://doi.org/10.3390/educsci8040213
3. Franklin, S., Peat, M., Lewis, A.: Non-traditional interventions to stimulate discussion: the use of games and puzzles. J. Biol. Educ. **37**(2), 79–84 (2003). https://doi.org/10.1080/002 19266.2003.9655856
4. Freese, M., Tiemersma, S., Verbraeck, A.: Risk management can actually be fun – using the serious cards for biosafety game to stimulate proper discussions about biosafety. In: Proceedings of the 52nd International Simulation and Gaming Association's Conference, Indore, India, 06 September–10 September 2021
5. Cards against Humanity LLC, 18 April 2022. https://www.cardsagainsthumanity.com
6. Bloom, B.S.: Taxonomy of Educational Objectives, Handbook I: The Cognitive Domain. David McKay Co Inc, New York (1956)
7. Anderson, L.W., Krathwohl, D.R.: A taxonomy for Learning, Teaching, and Assessing: A Revision of Bloom's Taxonomy of Educational Objectives. Longman, New York (2001)
8. IJsselsteijn, W.A., de Kort, Y.A.W., Poels, K.: The game experience questionnaire. Technische Universiteit Eindhoven (2013)
9. Johnson, D.O., Cuijpers, R.H., Pollmann, K., van de Ven, A.A.J.: Exploring the entertainment value of playing games with a humanoid robot. Int. J. Soc. Robot. **8**(2), 247–269 (2015). https://doi.org/10.1007/s12369-015-0331-x
10. Wilson, L.O.: Anderson and Krathwohl Bloom's Taxonomy Revised. Anderson-and-Krathwohl_Revised-Blooms-Taxonomy.pdf, 18 April 2022
11. Procci, K., Bowers, C.: An examination of flow and immersion in games. Proc. Hum. Factors Ergon. Soc. Ann. Meet. **55**(1), 2183–2187 (2011). https://doi.org/10.1177/107118131155 1455
12. Siburian, J., Corebima, A.D., Ibrohim, S.M.: The correlation between critical and creative thinking skills on cognitive learning results. Eurasian J. Educ. Res. **81**, 99–114 (2019)

13. Kajander-Unkuri, S., et al.: Congruence between graduating nursing students' self-assessments and mentors' assessments of students' nurse competence. Collegian **23**(3), 303–312 (2016). https://doi.org/10.1016/j.colegn.2015.06.002

14. Elimelech, E., Ert, E., Ayalon, O.: Bridging the gap between self-assessments and measured household food waste: a hybrid valuation approach. Waste Manag. **95**, 259–270 (2019). https://doi.org/10.1016/j.wasman.2019.06.015

15. Stanny, C.J.: Reevaluating bloom's taxonomy: what measurable verbs can and cannot say about student learning. Educ. Sci. **6**(4), 37 (2016). https://doi.org/10.3390/educsci6040037

Design Consideration of an Educational Video Game Through the Lens of the Metalanguage

Heng Zhang[1,2](✉) [iD] and Vivian Hsueh Hua Chen[1]

[1] Wee Kim Wee School of Communication and Information, Nanyang Technological University, Singapore 639798, Singapore
heng017@e.ntu.edu.sg, chenhh@ntu.edu.sg
[2] Interdisciplinary Graduate Programme, Graduate College, Nanyang Technological University, Singapore 639798, Singapore

Abstract. Educational games have gained popularity. However, the connection between choices of game elements in the design process and the effects educational games can produce is not always clear. It is important to investigate effective educational game design frameworks. The current study, therefore, utilizes the metalanguage for digital gameplay framework to inform the game design decisions and subsequently analyze an educational collaborative video game, *Icebreaker*. It explains how the game is designed to meet educational goals. Implications for future design frameworks are discussed.

Keywords: Metalanguage of Digital Play · Video Games · Ingroup and Outgroup · Collaborative Play · Inclusion

1 Introduction

Playing video games is a prevalent activity among teenagers [2, 3]. Although entertainment is a primary reason for people to play video games, many video games are not designed solely for entertainment purposes. Games also serve serious purposes such as education [4]. Previous studies showed that video games could assist youth in developing pro-social skills and increasing their ability to be inclusive [5–8]. The importance of play in game spaces has been recognized from a pedagogical perspective, as play is fundamental to how humans learn and offers opportunities for practice [9]. Thomas and Brown argue that video games can provide educational experiences for players and describe them as a new "tendency" that requires both adaptability and resourcefulness [10]. Bogost asserts that video games are uniquely "persuasive": "they open a new domain for persuasion through rule-based representations and interactions, different than the spoken word, writing, images and moving pictures" [11]. This project begins with the intention of designing a video game for persuasion and education. In recent years, the world witnessed increased hostility towards people of different identity markers such as race, nationality, political belief, religion…etc. [1]. Promoting inclusion has thus become a pressing social issue. The goal is to utilize video games as an educational and persuasive means to reduce biases and increase inclusion, especially among young people.

C. Harteveld et al. (Eds.): ISAGA 2022, LNCS 13622, pp. 66–79, 2023.
https://doi.org/10.1007/978-3-031-37171-4_5

There has been little research on how games achieve persuasiveness from a linguistic perspective. Video games are distinct from other forms of expression in that they incorporate text, images, sound, moving images, and so on, and players interact with these various elements. Toh and Lim created a framework "metalanguage for digital play" to describe the multimodal semiotic aspect of video game design elements and how it may relate to youth development [12]. This framework serves as a starting point for the current project to design and analyze Icebreaker: an educational game that aims to promote positive attitudes towards different identity outgroups in youth. The metalanguage perspective helps explain how Icebreaker meets its educational goal and the effectiveness of decreasing the level of hostility toward outgroup members.

2 Metalanguage for Digital Play

Toh and Lim proposed metalanguage for digital play (See Fig. 1) in order to help people gain a better understanding of digital games [12]. Metalanguage for digital play is based on the analysis of data from various research fields, including "multimodal discourse analysis, psychological research, new media effects research, critical discourse research, game-based learning research, and game studies" [12]. Based on social semiotics and critical multiliteracies [13, 14], the framework transforms digital game systems into metalanguage functions. It proposes three distinct metafunctions: organization, engagement, and representation.

In metalanguage for digital play, "organization" is conceptualized as a "structure" for digital games and "actions" for youth to interact with the digital game [12]. The term "structure" refers to both the game structure and the narrative structure, and "actions" encompasses both embodiment and subversion [12]. "Engagement" is defined as the perspective or position the player perceives and interprets the digital game; "emotions" the player experience while interacting with the game, and the interactivity of the digital game [12]. It explains how players form social relationships. Perspective encompasses the concepts of "focalization" and "shift," and emotions are aspects that refer to the components of "affect," "judgment," and "appreciation" [12]. Finally, "representation" is defined as what we see in a digital game in terms of "character," "topic," and "context" [12]. Character encompasses "gender," "race," and "ability." "Topic refers to the game type, purpose, and theme, that is, what the game is designed to achieve (e.g., educational purpose)" [12]. Finally, context seeks to expose the digital game developers' ideology [12].

3 The Design and Analysis of Icebreaker

3.1 Description of the Game Icebreaker

Icebreaker is a Unity-based 2D game hosted on a website. The story of the game revolves around a player who is of high social standing and is tasked to collaborate with an antagonistic outgroup in-game non-player character (NPC) Zork, who is of a different race and from a different Village. The game's objective is to save the town they live in from a mysterious natural disaster. The player will eventually go through 7 different game levels and collaborates with the NPC, Zork, to complete various missions to end the natural disaster.

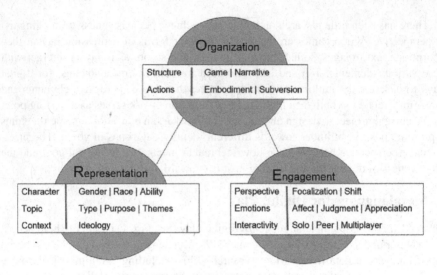

Fig. 1. Metalanguage for digital play

Throughout gameplay, players can choose whether their relationship with Zork is friendly or hostile. In appropriate circumstances, players must decide whether (1) to save Zork from death or harm, or (2) to fulfill their responsibility to save their own citizens. In particular, if the player chooses to save Zork from death or injury, they will lose their only piece of equipment, an enchanted knife that will aid in resolving the crisis that threatens the town's fate. Nevertheless, Lamu and the Frozen Gatekeepers will reunite amicably. Alternately, if players abandon Zork and remain loyal to their tribe, they will be able to save their town from imminent peril. They will lose Zork's assistance and company. The remainder of the performance until the end. Zork returned damaged at the conclusion of the game, and relations between the two tribes deteriorated. The predetermined monologue will inform the player that their choice will affect the outcome of the game, and the player will understand the significance of their choice. This moral dilemma adds complexity to the narrative and has lasting effects on the characters and story's conclusion.

3.2   Organization in Digital Play

3.2.1   Structure-Game

Game structure refers to the rules and mechanics of the game that govern how the various components interact with one another, as well as how video games' multiple components work together to accomplish the objective [12]. The game rules in Icebreaker are based on collaborative gameplay with an NPC outgroup character from a rival tribe who has very different facial features and skin color. The game rules reward collaboration and prosocial choices. Not only can game rules convey discrimination or slander against a specific race, but they can also help improve people's attitudes toward that race [15]. Icebreaker's designer incorporated game mechanics/rules that required players to cooperate with a competitor in order to complete the objective. When players accomplish game objectives, their attitudes toward outgroups can thus be improved.

3.2.2 Structure-Narrative

Narrative structure refers to the various ways a story's plot unfolds depending on the story's design and how youth interact with the game's story [12]. The narrative structure allows players to make their choices in-game and learn about the consequences of how the story progresses. As illustrated in Fig. 2, the player can save or not save the NPC Zork in the early part of the game. Before the task of rescuing Zork, the player will have to go through several different scenarios and game play to understand the background story. Players can combine all pieces of information to create their own narrative in their mental models [16] and create their version of the story [12], allowing them to decide whether or not to save Zork.

Fig. 2. In game Choices in Icebreaker

3.2.3 Action-Embodiment

Embodiment means a digital game's use of multisensory information to encourage players, as well as the "physical and material interactions of youth with the game" [12]. In Icebreaker, players assume the role of a guardian tribe, traversing different environments in search of people and items. Toh and Lim's discussion of embodiment, which focuses on video games' potential to provide youth with authentic learning environments [12], is not exhaustive. Because the game's mechanics permit the player to attempt the mission multiple times, video games are a safe environment for youth to learn and experiment with [16]. When players make a non-prosocial choice or fail a mission in Icebreaker, they are not punished but encouraged to try again. This is in stark contrast to the traditional educational model, in which youth are fearful of answering questions for fear of punishment from teachers or ridicule from classmates if they provide incorrect responses, thereby losing their ability to explore and learn independently.

3.2.4 Action-Subversion

Subversion means the illogical actions to advance in the digital game [12]. Subversion enables players to forget and relearn by compelling them to reconsider their expectations and interpretations in order to adopt new mental models, strategies, and goals [17, 18]. In Icebreaker, the player must choose whether or not to save Zork in order to continue the game. For many players, Zork is a member of a different tribe, the outgroup, and because there is animosity between the player character's tribe and Zork's tribe, they will choose not to rescue Zork. However, regardless of whether the player rescues Zork, the game always continues as saving Zork. At this point, players who did not choose to save Zork must reconsider the game's mode of victory and adopt new strategies and objectives in order to win. Video games can help youth develop their capacity for reflection on their actions [12]. In video games, negative emotions and experiences play a critical role in promoting positive experiences for youth's critical play and learning by robbing the player of control over his or her choice [19]. At the beginning of the game, the player could use an enchanted knife to unfreeze the people in the town.

However, when the player awakens the following morning and discovers that the Enchanted Knife is no longer working to resolve the clan crisis, they may pause the game and consider how the Enchanted Knife can be restored. As a result, they may be more willing to save Zork in the following scenario. Zork had earlier communicated with the player to assist in resolving some of the game's missions. The player may wonder if the enchanted knife can be discovered and restored by rescuing Zork. This process will gradually alter players' attitudes toward outgroups and encourage them to engage in more pro-social behaviors.

3.3 Engagement in Digital Play

3.3.1 Perspective-Focalization

Perspective and focalization are critical concepts in video games. They refer to the vantage point from which the player observes the story [20]. Youth's empathy can be developed through this process, and they combine multimodal elements to create a multimodal set for a specific interpretation of the story [12]. Genette originally defined focalization as describing events that occur within the story world [21]. Toh provides a new definition of focalization based on previous research on video games and empathy, arguing that it has evolved from a passive property of the text to a player's projection of the character's emotional, cognitive, and behavioral states [16]. Genette's focalization is divided into three components: internal, external, and zero [21]. Internal focalization focuses on refers to the character's perspective on what he or she knows and experiences, including their inner thoughts [12]. External focalization focuses on perceptive observations of a character's speech and behavior from the outside rather than the character's inner thoughts [12]. Zero focalization focus transcends a single character's point of view to reveal the inner thoughts and feelings of multiple characters [12].

Internal focalization in Icebreaker refers to the player learning about the character's experiences and emotions through the game's storyline and progression. Throughout the game, the player may be attacked with ice picks, and if they shoot at the game character, they may experience some discomfort or pain. This perception is only felt by the player, not by the game's characters, indicating that it is externally focused. In Icebreaker, players can also observe frozen residents who are immobile, and from these perspectives, players can gain insight into the emotions and thoughts of other NPCs throughout the game. This is referred to as zero focalization.

3.3.2 Perspective-Shift

"Shift" is a term that refers to the concept that in a game with multiple characters, the player can control various characters within the story world and switch perspectives between them to recommend progress [12]. In Icebreaker, the player not only controls his character but also Zork at the game's conclusion. As mentioned previously, the game's final victory requires cooperation between the ingroup and outgroup. As a result, the player may notice that the characteristics of different characters are not identical. Thus, players can better understand how to discover each other's strengths rather than the weaknesses of outgroup members. Players can only create greater value by leveraging one another's strengths and learning from their weaknesses.

3.3.3 Emotions-Affect, Judgment, and Appreciation

Emotion is primarily considered in three dimensions in metalanguage for digital play: "affect," "judgment," and "appreciation." Firstly, affect refers to players' emotions, such as happiness, despair, afraid, disgust, and so on when they interact with video games [12]. Judgment primarily refers to the requirement for players to make moral judgment-based choices throughout the game, with these choices influencing the game's development [12]. Appreciation means an aesthetic assessment of the game's world, including the "settings, music, level design, character design, and so on" [12]. The embodied nature of gameplay enables players to experience the character's emotions throughout the game. Interactivity in games teaches the player how to empathize with others by allowing us to control, reflect on, and recognize the emotions of the player character during play [12].

The player was able to rescue the townspeople at the start of Icebreaker with an enchanted knife and enjoy the positive outcome. However, the player subsequently encounters ice pick attacks, and the enchanted knife stops working, adding to the player's frustration. After experiencing helplessness firsthand, the player is more able to sympathize with Zork's situation and experience an emotional resonance [19, 22]. Moreover, if players have a greater appreciation for the video games, the experience will be more enjoyable [12]. For instance, there are two different models of music in video games: major and minor [23]. The music in the major triads and scales of the Icebreaker contains fine pitches that sound higher. Prior research on Icebreaker demonstrated that the music in the Major model increased players' positive emotions, resulting in increased empathy, pro-social intentions, and favorable attitudes toward outgroup members [24].

In summary, the change in players' moods during the Icebreaker will encourage them to make more ethical decisions in the game, increasing players' empathy and pro-social conduct in real life [25].

3.3.4 Interactivity-Solo, Peer, and Multiplayer

Icebreaker is a single-player game, and single-player games are characterized by a strong emphasis on human-computer interaction [12]. Each player has complete control over their character. As a result, each player can track their own thoughts and progress through the game world without having to compete with others. From an educational standpoint, each youth can track his or her own progress rather than adhering to a unified standard, which can help youth acquire knowledge thoroughly in the real world [16]. There is no cooperation or competition with other players, but the player is required to control NPC Zork at the game's conclusion. Zork and the player-controlled characters each have distinct functions, and the player must combine the two characters' abilities to accomplish the final objective. As a result, players develop their capacity for cooperation and attitude toward outgroup members.

3.4 Representation in Digital Play

3.4.1 Character—Gender, Race, and Ability

Gender is a subject that has been extensively discussed in video games. The gender divide exists not only among the game's characters but also among the technical design and production staff [26]. In the 1980s, male designers primarily created video game technology for male audiences. As a result, the video game industry, which white men in American have long dominated, lacks gender and racial diversity [27]. The flaws reflected in video game content are gradually permeating society [28, 29]. As a result, there is no time to rectify this shortcoming in the video game world. In Icebreaker, players can choose to play as either a man or a woman (See Fig. 3). This undermines society's patriarchal view of gender roles. Not all heroes must be men; in Icebreaker, female guardians of the horde can also be heroic.

Race faces the same issue as Gender. Game designers frequently translate racial representations and identities from real-world contexts into relatively static digital structures in video games [30], resulting in some disparate treatment of race in real life being transferred to video games. If players continue to play these video games regularly, their perception and judgment of race will be influenced subtly. As a result, Icebreaker will eradicate this occurrence. Icebreaker allows players to choose between three races (See Fig. 3). Although not all races are represented in the game, players have the option of experiencing various ethnic identities throughout the game. This defies long-held cultural stereotypes about race in video games.

Customers nowadays have a vast selection of video games. In these games, the player character often has superhuman skills; commercial games idealize the character's talents [12]. As a result, disabled and non-player characters are either forced to play second fiddle or entirely disabled [12]. As an educational game, we must avoid this. We should make each game feel distinct and each character part of the more extensive game process. So, while Zork isn't playable in Icebreaker, his powers should not be ignored. It

Fig. 3. Avatars and instructions in Icebreaker

is necessary to work with Zork, learn from their exchanges, and understand their mutual strengths in order to fulfill the final task. This stops gamers from forming a hegemonic culture and allows them to appreciate others' strengths while polishing their own.

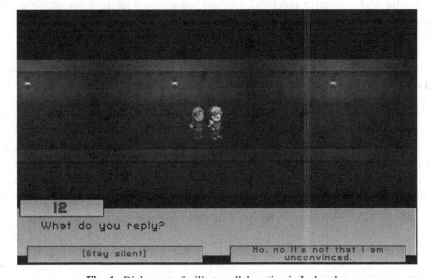

Fig. 4. Dialogue to facilitate collaboration in Icebreaker

3.4.2 Topic—Game Type

Toh and Lim propose distinct categories of games in this category based on previous research on game types [12]. Due to the educational nature of Icebreaker, it falls under the category of Serious Games. The Icebreaker is analyzed using the classification system's four dimensions following Ratan and Ritterfeld's definition of Serious Games (2009). The four dimensions are as follows: "primary educational content," "primary learning principle," "target age group," and "platform" [31]. The primary educational content of Icebreaker should be social change. The game's objective is to foster players' pro-social behavior and to help them develop a more positive attitude toward outgroup members. The primary learning principle is embodied in games where players can explore and acquire knowledge through their practical abilities and ultimately solve cognitive or social problems. After Icebreaker, players must continually improve their skills and find the optimal solution to the game's objectives. Teenagers are the primary target audience for this video game, and the game is presented as a web page.

3.4.3 Topic—Game Purpose, Themes, and Ideology

In the previous paragraph, we indicated that the goal of the game is to change the player's attitude toward the opponent. Players should develop the capacity to recognize and embrace the qualities of their opponents, while simultaneously learning from and progressing together as a team as well (See Fig. 4). At the same time, we encourage prosocial behavior throughout the course of the game. Additionally, video games can help develop the ability to think independently and self-directed learning during the game. Self-directed learning is a critical skill in the twenty-first century, as it has been linked to lifelong learning tendencies, workplace creativity, communication, and teamwork, among other things [12, 32].

Icebreaker explores a variety of topics, including conflict and peace and ingroup and outgroup relations. These two themes are self-explanatory, as the game opens by establishing that the player character and Zork are members of different clans and are on opposing sides. However, the tribal conflict can be addressed only if both sides cooperate and set aside old grudges and animosities.

The game's theme also aims to communicate the game's ideology. Hopefully, players will be more receptive to individuals of many races living in various regions of the world; this reflects the true nature of society in another manner; we should live in peace and mutual respect, not hostility. As a result of humanity's collaborative efforts, the earth will grow more beautiful.

4 Discussion

4.1 Pedagogical Implication

Video games are an effective motivator for students' desire to learn and for the development of numerous students' learning skills, including communication and adaptability [33, 34]. However, developing an educational game that encourages active participation remains difficult [35]. Thus, in the following section, we'll discuss how Icebreaker teaches youth through play.

4.1.1 Perspective Taking

In discussing the metalanguage's engagement function, we believe that youth's ability to use perspective shift in video games can be combined with classroom concepts of focalization [12]. Some studies have shown that video games' perspective shift can improve people's socio-emotional well-being and prosocial behavior and aid the development of their communication skills [36–38]. The game allows players to connect the gaming world and real-world experiences. Players can practice and gain skills, knowledge, and perspectives from the gaming world. Concepts of effective communication, cooperation, and empathy skills they learn in Icebreaker can be transferred to situations where they encounter outgroup members.

4.1.2 Metacognition

Toh and Lim believed they could draw pedagogical principles from the "game," "narrative" structure in the organization function, and "subversive action" in the engagement function of the metalanguage [12]. Players learn how to select, evaluate, and integrate information to create a complete story in their own minds and create meaning through play. Additionally, players were given the freedom to make in-game decisions. They need to assess these tasks and then make decisions based on previously gathered information. A subversive action forces players to constantly think, shattering the framework of their existing cognition and thus acting on a new cognition. Inductively, players will re-build mental models and keep them updated as they interact with the gaming system. They use analogies, mental models, and incomplete representations to figure out how the system works [39]. They connect new concepts with the knowledge they already have.

4.1.3 Challenging Stereotypes

In our representation of the metalanguage, it discusses "topic," gender," "race," and "ability" in "character." Icebreaker highlights those dimensions: The player character and NPC Zork are of different races but have similar abilities. Only when they work together can they solve the problem both tribes face. This kind of gameplay enables open-mindedness. Icebreaker seeks to reduce biases in gameplay.

4.1.4 Embodied Learning

Toh and Lim's engagement function" shows how important it is for youth to be able to actively participate, have agency, and be emotionally involved in learning [12]. Players can interact with virtual environments that use language, action, and gestures in various ways [40, 41]. In Icebreaker, the player is always trying new things: talking to NPCs, going on quests, getting game clues, and keeping players engaged and actively involved in the game. Active learning can help players better understand their learning [42].

4.2 Other Design Considerations

The metalanguage of the digital play framework guided the design and analysis of Icebreaker, but it is not exhaustive. The level of difficulty is a critical characteristic of most games. Many games use Dynamic Difficulty Adjustment (DDA) algorithms to improve the gameplay experience [43]. According to flow theory, a game's complexity must be tailored to the player's expertise in order to offer motivation or keep the player in the flow state [44]. Too much or too little challenge can result in boredom or irritation [43]. So, balancing a game's difficulty is vital. Lowering a game's complexity may reduce the intrinsic value of any interaction in a video game [43]. Players can easily become sidetracked by the game's tasks, missing out on crucial information and failing to grasp the game's worldview [45].

At the beginning of Icebreaker, the player only needs to use the enchanted knife to rescue the tribe's inhabitants, while later in the video game, the player's character is forced to work with Zork. During the initial stages of working with Zork, players were required to complete a relatively simple task in order to become acquainted with the game. After completing the simple task, the final task becomes more difficult. Thus, throughout the game, the difficulty level increases directly to the player's skill level. This not only keeps players immersed in the game's world but also helps them improve their skills and understand that the strength of cooperation far outweighs the strength of individuals.

Because the difficulty of a game is intrinsic to the game development process, attempt to summarize the difficulty within the organization framework; however, as flow theory has demonstrated, a game's difficulty is a critical criterion for engaging players [44]. As a result, difficulty encourages players to engage more actively in the game. From this vantage point, it appears as though the difficulty is also contained within the framework of Engagement.

Icebreaker is a serious game that serves as an educational tool. From a pedagogical standpoint, it is natural for youth to lose interest in games if the difficulty level remains constant. There is no way to improve a youth's ability to continue playing the game once they have mastered the skill. Because the purpose of learning through serious games is to improve a youth's skills, adjusting the difficulty of a game using DDA systems can help motivate youth to continue playing. Youth in the world of video games are not required to follow others; they can learn at their own pace and truly master a skill before moving on to the next level of learning. Youth can perceive their progress, increasing their willingness to engage in play and learn through video games.

Finally, Icebreaker is a self-directed learning experience. Feedback is a necessary component of the game, and including various types of feedback can help players perform better [46, 47]. Self-directed learning via video games is quite different from traditional classroom instruction. If youth receive feedback from teachers in the conventional education style, the feedback can assist youth in completing tasks more effectively. However, game feedback is critical in video games where there is no teacher to provide feedback. As a result, we propose that feedback be classified as "action." In video games, feedback can take on various forms [46], and Icebreaker included text, images, and music as feedback forms. Feedback is provided for each significant action taken by the player in the game, which can assist them in achieving the final goals. According to cognitive load theory, if players fail and do not receive feedback, they may experience cognitive load, reducing their interest in the game [48]. As a result, if video games can provide feedback to the player when they take action, whether successful or unsuccessful, it can assist the player in reducing cognitive load and maintaining a positive state in the game world. Therefore, feedback is an important part of a serious game designed for educational purposes.

5 Conclusion

This is the first study to examine metalanguage for digital play through the video game Icebreaker. According to data analysis, the video game Icebreaker may help youth develop positive attitudes toward various identity outgroups. Then, achieve the educational goal of using video games to educate the youth. Additionally, it has been demonstrated that metalanguage for digital play can be used to explain how video games deliver educational messages. This theoretical framework, however, is not without flaws. It does not cover all aspects of video game content; some are omitted entirely. As a result, the discussion section also makes recommendations for framework components not covered by the framework. This will help educate future video game designers and teachers.

At a time when video games are becoming increasingly popular, it is critical to investigate and comprehend video games from a variety of perspectives. As a result, this study offers some unique perspectives and evidence in favor of serious game design from a linguistic standpoint. However, Toh and Lim believe that metalanguage for the digital play was developed to assist teachers in embedding video games in ways that enhance youth's learning experiences [12]. However, current data analysis indicates that the development of metalanguage for digital play will benefit teachers and game designers, particularly those who specialize in serious games. Metalanguage for digital play can be used as a guide for designing and developing serious games, allowing designers to understand how game elements can be combined to express ideology more effectively and which game mode best stimulates youth's capacity for independent learning. In general, research on metalanguage for digital play is insufficient and should be continuously strengthened. Because video games will evolve into a form of digital education through which youth can develop future-ready abilities, literacy, and so on, they will be well-prepared for the digital age [12].

References

1. Bartoš, V., Bauer, M., Cahlíková, J., Chytilová, J.: Covid-19 crisis and hostility against foreigners. Eur. Econ. Rev. **137**, 103818 (2021)
2. Prot, S., McDonald, K.A., Anderson, C.A., Gentile, D.A.: Video Games Pediatric Clin. North America **59**(3), 647–658 (2012)
3. Gee, J.P.: Situated Language and Learning: A Critique of Traditional Schooling. Routledge (2004)
4. Janarthanan, V.: Serious video games: games for education and health. In: 2012 Ninth International Conference on Information Technology - New Generations, pp. 875–878 (2012)
5. Gentile, D.A., et al.: The effects of prosocial video games on prosocial behaviors: international evidence from correlational, longitudinal, and experimental studies. Pers. Soc. Psychol. Bull. **35**(6), 752–763 (2009)
6. Greitemeyer, T., Osswald, S.: Playing prosocial video games increases the accessibility of prosocial thoughts. J. Soc. Psychol. **151**(2), 121–128 (2011)

7. Li, H., Zhang, Q.: Effects of prosocial video games on prosocial thoughts and prosocial behaviors. Soc. Sci. Comput. Rev. 08944393211069599 (2022)
8. Shoshani, A., Krauskopf, M.: The Fortnite social paradox: the effects of violent-cooperative multi-player video games on children's basic psychological needs and prosocial behavior. Comput. Hum. Behav. **116**, 106641 (2021)
9. Rieber, L.P.: Seriously considering play: designing interactive learning environments based on the blending of microworlds, simulations, and games. Educ. Tech. Res. Dev. **44**(2), 43–58 (1996)
10. Thomas, D., Brown, J.S.: A new culture of learning: cultivating the imagination for a world of constant change. Soulellis Studio (2011)
11. Bogost, I.: Persuasive Games: The Expressive Power of Videogames, p. ix. MIT Press, Cambridge, MA (2007)
12. Toh, W., Lim, F.V.: Using Video Games for Learning: Developing a Metalanguage for Digital Play: Games and Culture (2020)
13. Crafton, L.K., Silvers, P., Brennan, M.: Creating a critical multiliteracies curriculum: Repositioning art in the early childhood classroom. In: Narey, M.J. (ed.) Multimodal Perspectives of Language, Literacy, and Learning in Early Childhood. EYC, vol. 12, pp. 67–86. Springer, Cham (2017). https://doi.org/10.1007/978-3-319-44297-6_4
14. Kress, G., van Leeuwen, T.: Multimodal discourse: the modes and media of contemporary communication. Arnold (2001)
15. Cross, K., Opinion: prejudice as a game mechanic. Gamasutra (2016)
16. Toh, W.: A Multimodal Approach to Video Games and the Player Experience. Routledge (2018)
17. Mitgutsch, K.: Passionate Digital Play-Based Learning. (Re)Learning in computer games like Shadow of the Colossus. Eludamos: J. Comput. Game Cult. **3**(1), 9–22 (2009)
18. Mitgutsch, K., Weise, M.: Subversive Game Design for Recursive Learning, vol. 17 (2011)
19. Bopp, J.A., Mekler, E.D., Opwis, K.: negative emotion, positive experience? emotionally moving moments in digital games. In: Proceedings of the 2016 CHI Conference on Human Factors in Computing Systems, pp. 2996–3006 (2016)
20. Allison, F.: Whose mind is the signal? Focalization in video game narratives. In: Proceedings of DiGRA 2015: Diversity of Play: Games—Cultures—Identities (2015)
21. Genette, G.: Narrative Discourse: An Essay in Method (Lewin, J. E., Trans.). Cornell University Press (1980)
22. Baranowski, T., Buday, R., Thompson, D.I., Baranowski, J.: Playing for real: video games and stories for health-related behavior change. Am. J. Prevent. Med. **34**(1), 74–82, e10 (2008)
23. Husain, G., Thompson, W.F., Schellenberg, E.G.: Effects of musical tempo and mode on arousal, mood, and spatial abilities. Music. Percept. **20**(2), 151–171 (2002)
24. Yi, C.X., Yu, V., Chen, V.H.H.: In the Mood for Doing Good: the influence of positive and negative emotions in game narratives on prosocial tendencies, p. 1365 (2021)
25. Ng, Y.Y., Khong, C.W., Thwaites, H.: A review of affective design towards video games. Procedia. Soc. Behav. Sci. **51**, 687–691 (2012)
26. Julie, P.: Gender Divide and the Computer Game Industry. IGI Global (2013)
27. Fullerton, T., Fron, J., Pearce, C.: Getting girls into the game: towards a. Undefined (2007)
28. Lynch, T., Tompkins, J., Driel, I., Fritz, N.: Sexy, strong, and secondary: a content analysis of female characters in video games across 31 years: female game characters across 31 years. J. Commun. **66** (2016)
29. Williams, D., Martins, N., Consalvo, M., Ivory, J.D.: The virtual census: representations of gender, race and age in video games. New Media Soc. **11**(5), 815–834 (2009)
30. Kim, S.J.: Review of digitizing race: visual cultures of the Internet [Review of Review of Digitizing Race: Visual Cultures of the Internet, by L. Nakamura]. MELUS **33**(4), 211–213 (2008)

31. Ratan, R., Ritterfeld, U.: Classifying serious games. In: Ritterfeld, U., Cody, M., Vorderer, P. (eds.) Serious Games: Mechanisms and Effects, pp. 10–24. Routledge (2009)
32. Eseryel, D., Law, V., Ifenthaler, D., Ge1, X., Miller, R.: An investigation of the interrelationships between motivation, engagement, and complex problem solving in game-based learning. J. Educ. Technol. Soc. **17**(1), 42–53 (2014)
33. Annetta, L.A., Minogue, J., Holmes, S.Y., Cheng, M.-T.: Investigating the impact of video games on high school students' engagement and learning about genetics. Comput. Educ. **53**(1), 74–85 (2009)
34. Squire, K.D.: Sid Meier's civilization III. Simul. Gaming **35**(1), 135–140 (2004)
35. Laine, T.H., Lindberg, R.S.N.: Designing engaging games for education: a systematic literature review on game motivators and design principles. IEEE Trans. Learn. Technol. **13**(4), 804–821 (2020)
36. Dezuanni, M., O'Mara, J., Beavis, C.: 'Redstone is like electricity': children's performative representations in and around Minecraft. E-Learn. Digital Media **12**(2), 147–163 (2015)
37. Hilliard, L.J., et al.: Perspective taking and decision-making in educational game play: a mixed-methods study. Appl. Dev. Sci. **22**(1), 1–13 (2018)
38. Marlatt, R.: Literary analysis using minecraft: an asian american youth crafts her literacy identity. J. Adol. Adult Liter. **62** (2018)
39. Farooq, M.U., Dominick, W.D.: A survey of formal tools and models for developing user interfaces. Int. J. Man Mach. Stud. **29**(5), 479–496 (1988)
40. Hauk, O., Johnsrude, I., Pulvermüller, F.: Somatotopic representation of action words in human motor and premotor cortex. Neuron **41**(2), 301–307 (2004)
41. Pulvermüller, F., Härle, M., Hummel, F.: Walking or talking? behavioral and neurophysiological correlates of action verb processing. Brain Lang. **78**(2), 143–168 (2001)
42. Gee, J.P.: Learning by design: good video games as learning machines. E-Learn. Digital Media **2**(1), 5–16 (2005)
43. Constant, T., Levieux, G.: Dynamic difficulty adjustment impact on players' confidence. In: Proceedings of the 2019 CHI Conference on Human Factors in Computing Systems, pp. 1–12 (2019)
44. Csikszentmihalyi, M., Montijo, M.N., Mouton, A.R.: Flow theory: optimizing elite performance in the creative realm. In: APA Handbook of Giftedness and Talent, pp. 215–229. American Psychological Association (2018)
45. Klimmt, C., Blake, C., Hefner, D., Vorderer, P., Roth, C.: Player performance, satisfaction, and video game enjoyment. In: Natkin, S., Dupire, J. (eds.) ICEC 2009. LNCS, vol. 5709, pp. 1–12. Springer, Heidelberg (2009). https://doi.org/10.1007/978-3-642-04052-8_1
46. Nakamura, T., Miyata, K.: Influence of audiovisual feedback on player behavior and performance in response to video game failure. International Workshop on Advanced Imaging Technology (IWAIT) 2021, vol. 11766, pp. 318–323 (2021)
47. Ruvalcaba, O., Shulze, J., Kim, A., Berzenski, S.R., Otten, M.P.: Women's Experiences in eSports: Gendered Differences in Peer and Spectator Feedback During Competitive Video Game Play: Journal of Sport and Social Issues (2018)
48. Paas, F., Ayres, P.: Cognitive load theory: a broader view on the role of memory in learning and education. Educ. Psychol. Rev. **26**(2), 191–195 (2014). https://doi.org/10.1007/s10648-014-9263-5

Resilience and Sustainability

Quantitative Analysis of Conflict-of-Interest Structures in Consensus-Building Process

Ibu Ueno$^{(\boxtimes)}$ and Shingo Takahashi$^{(\boxtimes)}$

Waseda University, Shinjuku-ku, Tokyo 169-8555, Japan
eve-christmas@ruri.waseda.jp, shingo@waseda.jp

Abstract. Public works projects are required to actively promote public participation from the conceptual stage, but the technology to support consensus-building has not been sufficiently established, and as a result, work related to consensus-building has been avoided. The conflict-of-interest structure is an important element in understanding the characteristics of the consensus-building process. In this paper, we quantitatively and comprehensively analyzed the relationship between the conflict-of-interest structure and the consensus-building process. The conflict-of-interest structure was quantitatively expressed by defining the conflict-of-interest degree using the sum of profits difference squared, and an agent-based simulation was used to conduct a comprehensive analysis. Drama theory was used to model the consensus-building process, and gaming simulation was used to identify parameters of the agents' behavior. The results of quantitative and exhaustive experiments using agent-based simulations, incorporating the behavioral models identified in the gaming simulations, showed that the conflict-of-interest structure is an indicator that characterizes the consensus-building process.

Keywords: consensus-building process · conflict-of-interest structure · drama theory · agent-based simulation

1 Introduction

Consensus-building with residents is one of the central issues in public works planning. According to the Japanese government's "Guidelines for Public Participation Procedures in the Conceptual Phase of Public Works under the Jurisdiction of the Ministry of Land, Infrastructure, Transport and Tourism," public participations are required to be actively promoted from the conceptual phase in implementing public works projects [1]. On the other hand, since the actual consensus-building requires a lot of time and effort and incurs high personnel costs, it is difficult for the private sector to make a profit. As a result, work related to consensus-building is avoided, and materials are not provided at consensus-building [2]. In this situation, the technology to support consensus-building has not been sufficiently established, and the response and efforts in the field are left to the ability and discretion of those in charge, and it is difficult to say that opportunities for fair and appropriate communication are guaranteed [3].

In the consensus-building process in public works projects, there are beneficiaries who receive benefits from the project and bearers (recipients) who suffer disadvantages from the project. Identification of the stakeholders is conducted essentially in conflict assessment, which is extremely important in determining whether consensus-building work should proceed [4]. Yamaguchi [5] showed that the structure of stakeholders, i.e., the relationship between beneficiaries and recipients, influences consensus-building (Table 1). Ninomiya [6] logically characterized the consensus-building process of road improvement projects implemented in Japan as the degree of overlap between beneficiaries and bearers, as shown in Table 2. Since the consensus-building process is affected by the conflict-of-interest structure, it is important to clarify the conflict-of-interest structure in order to capture the characteristics of the consensus-building process. Then the conflict assessment could effectively identify features of agreement and disagreement [4].

Especially in the conflict-of-interest structure of public works, there can be various relationships between public institutions and citizens' power. Arnstein [7] expressed the degree of citizen participation using a "ladder of citizen participation" with eight levels in descending order of degree: Manipulation, Therapy, Informing, Consultation, Placation, Partnership, Delegated power, and Citizen control. It illustrates how powerful public institutions and officials can deny citizens power and how they can increase the level of citizen's independence, control, and power. The conflict-of-interest structure in this paper assumes the partnership stage, in which citizens and authorities share responsibility for planning and decision-making.

Table 1. Effects of conflict-of-interest structure on consensus-building

Stake-holder Structure	There are few recipients, only beneficiaries	Beneficiaries and recipients are somewhat aligned	Beneficiaries and recipients diverge or some of the beneficiaries are recipients
Influence on Consensus-Building	Most of the time, interest alignment is unnecessary	Because of the relative number of beneficiaries and recipients, it is easy to fight for conditions in the participation process	More recipients gathered and less participation by beneficiaries. The main issue is "public interest".

Ninomiya [3] attempted to analyze the theoretical clarification of the problem generation mechanism in the consensus-building process using game theory and drama theory. In the case of a road construction project in Oita Prefecture in Japan, the model analysis based on game theory produced the result that differed from the case study, such as the

Table 2. Classification of road maintenance projects by conflict-of-interest structure

type \ feature	Improved Convenience	Concerns about deterioration of the surrounding environment	Incentives for bearer cooperation	Case
① Beneficiaries and bearers differ Beneficiaries / Bearers	absent	present	absent	• Large-scale public works • Wide-area net-type projects
② Part of the beneficiaries is the bearers Beneficiaries / Bearers	present	present	present	• Medium-Scale Public Utilities • Road-use promotion business
③ Beneficiaries and bearers are aligned Beneficiaries / Bearers	present	absent	present	• Small Business • Lifestyle-oriented business

Beneficiary...Person who benefits from the project
Bearer...Person who is disadvantaged by the project

fact that negotiations could not be settled and ended in cancellation, while the model analysis based on drama theory succeeded to reproduce the characteristics of the case study, in which both sides compromised and reached an agreement. The conflict-of-interest structure was expressed as a profit structure in the game, and the analysis using drama theory was applied to two cases with different conflict-of-interest structures. As a result, it became clear that the consensus-building process was different in terms of the way the gain structure changed until agreement was reached and the number of changes, indicating that the conflict-of-interest structure is a factor that influences the consensus-building process.

While game theory focuses on the strategies of decision makers and their profit structure with respect to outcomes, drama theory describes the process by which decision makers reach agreement through negotiation [8, 9]. Compared to ordinary game theory, drama theory is characterized by its consideration of irrational aspects of decision makers, such as emotions and is appropriate as a model to describe the consensus-building process.

To fully understand the diversity of the consensus-building process and to support consensus-building efforts by the government, it is required to understand in a quantitative way that the consensus-building process has various characteristics depending on differences in the conflict-of-interest structure. Then it is necessary to cover the patterns of diversity in the conflict-of-interest structure as logically as possible.

2 Approach of This Paper

In this paper, drama theory is used as the basic model to describe the consensus-building process. Main consensus-building process expressed in drama theory is shown in Fig. 1 [10].

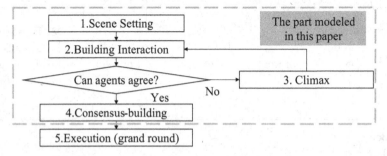

Fig. 1. Consensus-building process in drama theory

The purpose of this paper is to clarify the relationship quantitatively and comprehensively between the conflict-of-interest structure and the consensus-building process. In this paper, the consensus-building process is considered from the two aspects: the profit in agreement and the time it took to reach an agreement. Since the consensus-building process is strongly influenced by the irrational factors of the participants involved in the process, such as their emotions, we use gaming simulation (GS) to identify the parameters for creating a behavioral model of the agent. Next, an agent-based model incorporating the identified parameters is constructed to analyze the relationship quantitatively and comprehensively between the conflict-of-interest structure and the consensus-building process.

The approach of combining GS and ABM is also called GAM [11]. Szczepanska et al. [11] classified GAM into six types based on four characteristics: the order in which GS and ABM are performed, the correspondence between GS and ABM, the relationship with actual phenomena, and the purpose of combination. The approach in this paper corresponds to the third type, in which an agent-based model is created, and then GS is performed. The purpose of the gaming is to verify and validate the simulation and calibrate the parameters. The agent-based simulation is then used to conduct a quantitative analysis of the conflict-of-interest structure.

3 An Agent-Based Model of Consensus-Building Process

In this paper, consensus-building is conducted according to the process shown in Fig. 2. Consensus-building is performed by two agents, who decide on one of nine alternatives. The reason why the game was played with two players was to clarify the relationship between the conflict-of-interest structure and the consensus-building process in the simplest case of conflict of interest, i.e., one-on-one. When the number of participants is increased, such as five, the interactions among the parties that would form subgroups interacted could become highly complex to analyze the relationship between the conflict-of-interest structure and the process of consensus-building. A two-person game performed in this paper has the simplest structure and can reveal the essential relationship between the conflict-of-interest structure and the consensus-building process. Nine alternatives are assigned profits for each agent as shown in Table 3. First, one agent proposes (offers) an alternative with which the other agent seeks agreement. The offered agent decides whether to accept the offer, and if it accepts the offer, an agreement is reached. If it does not accept the offer, the offered agent offers another alternative. This process is repeated till either a consensus is formed or the number of offers reaches 10 or more.

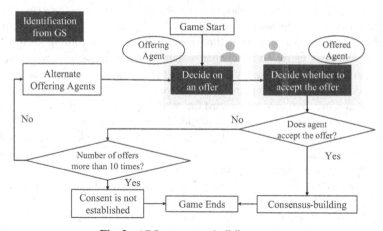

Fig. 2. ABS consensus-building process

Table 3. Profit table (example)

Alternative	1	2	3	4	5	6	7	8	9
Profit of Agent 1	32	14	22	4	30	12	20	2	1
Profit of Agent 2	1	19	11	29	3	21	13	31	32

Then the conflict-of-interest degree is calculated from the profit table. The conflict-of-interest degree indicates the degree of difference in benefits between the agents for each alternative, ranging from 0 to 1, with values closer to 0 indicating a smaller conflict-of-interest and values closer to 1 indicating a larger conflict-of-interest. Let pc_i denote the conflict-of-interest degree in the profit table i. The conflict-of-interest degree is defined as in Eq. (1), where $uc_{i,1,a}$ indicates the profit of agent 1 for alternative a in profit table i, $uc_{i,2,a}$ the profit of alternative a in profit table i for agent 2, and pc_max the maximum value of the sum of squared profit differences across all profit tables.

$$pc_i = \frac{\sum_{a \in A}(uc_{i,1,a} - uc_{i,2,a})^2}{pc\_max} \tag{1}$$

4 Gaming Simulation of Consensus-Building Process (GS)

In this paper, the parameters for performing agent-based simulation (ABS) are identified from subject experiments with GS. Consensus-building is performed according to the process shown in Fig. 2. Each game is performed by two subjects, who decide on one of the nine alternatives. The parameters are identified from the agents' behavior of deciding on the offer, deciding whether to accept the offer and the emotions (friendliness, resignation) used in the decision. In this paper, we define two types of emotions that arise during consensus-building: friendliness and resignation. According to Howard [8, 9], positive emotions cause behavior that is beneficial to the partner, while negative emotions cause behavior that hurts the partner. Although various emotions are mixed in the process of consensus-building, in this paper, we extracted and expressed friendliness as a positive and negative emotion toward the other party, and resignation as a positive and negative emotion toward the passage of time. Friendliness is the degree to which one is willing to approach the other party, and is rated on a 5-point scale, with a score closer to 1 indicating that one is unwilling to approach the other party and a score closer to 5 indicating that one is willing to approach the other party. Resignation is the degree to which one expects the other party to change a move, and is rated on a 5-point scale, with 1 indicating that the other party is unlikely to change a move and 5 indicating that the other party is likely to change a move. The parameters shown in Table 4 are measured using the recording sheet shown in Fig. 3.

In order to have subjects imagine actual consensus-building situation in public works, the setting of GS was designed with reference to a case study [12] of a road construction plan for the Kasumi No. 4 main line of the Yokkaichi Port Harbor Road in Yokkaichi City, Mie Prefecture, where the plan was agreed upon by the actual participants. The road in question is a port road with a bridge connecting the Kasumigaura Wharf at Yokkaichi Port and the Mie-Kawagoe Interchange on the Ise Bay Expressway. Against the backdrop of significant growth in marine container cargo at the Port of Yokkaichi, the project was designed to ensure smooth traffic between the port and the surrounding area. From the case study, five stakeholders are identified: the "port administrator" who manages the proposed new port road, the "employees of the companies in the wharf" who are the employees of the petrochemical companies located in the wharf, the "residents along the national road" who live along the national road, the main road in the region,

Table 4. Parameters to be measured with GS

Parameters to be measured	Meaning	Measurement Timing
Name	Subject's Name	At the start of the game
Conflict-of-interest degree	Calculated based on the profit-difference sum of squares in the profit table 0 to 1 value 0: Interests are completely aligned, 1: Interests are diametrically opposed	At the start of the game
Number of offers	The number of offers made at that point	Per offer
Number of cycles	The number of cycles in which two people make one offer each	Per offer
Degree of friendliness	Degree of willingness to compromise with the other party Rated on a 5-point scale 1: Not wanting to walk up to the other party 5: I want to walk up to the other person	Per offer
Degree of resignation	Degree of expectation that the other party will step up to the plate Rated on a 5-point scale 1: The other party is unlikely to step up to the plate 5: The other party seems to be willing to step up to the plate	Per offer
Offer profit	Profit of the alternatives that were/are offered	Per offer
Offer profit margin	Profit difference of the alternatives that were/are offered	Per offer
Offer preference order	Ranking of each agent's preference for the offered/referred alternative	Per offer

the "residents along the new road" who live near the route where the road is planned to be constructed, and the "environmental protection groups" who work to protect the environment in the region. Roles are randomly assigned to subjects for each game.

In GS, 12 different profit tables were used, and 22 subjects performed the experiment multiple times for each conflict-of-interest degree, as shown in Table 5, for a total of 137 experiments for all subjects. Using that as the number of samples, we estimated the parameters necessary for ABM. With an error of 7.1%, a confidence level of 90%, and a population ratio of 50%, the required sample size is 135, which is sufficient for a significant analysis of GS. To give validity to the experimental results, players were given monetary incentives based on their final score ranking. In addition, a debriefing via questionnaire was conducted after all games and reflections on the games were made.

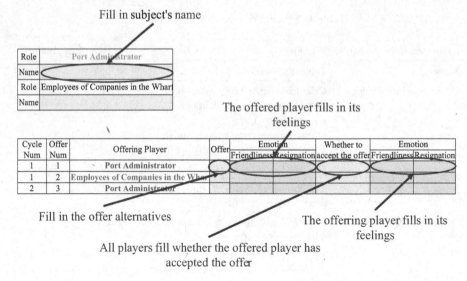

Fig. 3. Recording sheet used in GS

Table 5. Conflict-of-interest degree and number of experiments of GS

Conflict-of-Interest Degree			Game Count
Value	0 ⟷ 1		
0.01			12
0.07			12
0.09			10
0.24			10
0.27			12
0.39			13
0.51			13
0.68			12
0.70			13
0.77			10
0.91			11
0.99			9
Total Amount			137

5 Gaming Simulation (GS) Results

5.1 Cluster Analysis of Behavior Types

To analyze the behavior type of each subject, we conducted a hierarchical cluster analysis based on the average number of offers in all games when the subject agreed (average number of offers) and the average difference in profit between the subject and the opponent when the subject offered (own profit - opponent profit) in all games (average profit difference) for each subject. The analysis resulted in five clusters as shown in Fig. 4, which were characterized as the five behavior types of agents shown in Table 6. The first is the "early settlement" type, which aims for an early agreement because the average number of offers is small. Second, because the average difference in profit is small, we call it the "fairness-oriented" type, which aims for agreement on a proposal with a small difference in profit. Third, the average number of offers is moderate, and the average difference in profit is rather large, hence we call it the "balanced" type, which aims for both an early agreement and one's own profit. The fourth is the "profit-oriented" type, which emphasizes one's own profit because of the large average profit difference. Fifth, because the average number of offers was high, we call it the "long-term negotiation type," in which an agreement is formed over time. This behavior type is incorporated as a behavioral characteristic of the agent.

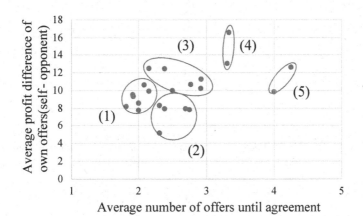

Fig. 4. Results of cluster analysis of behavior types

Table 6. Characteristics of the five behavior types

Behavior Type	Average Number of Offers		Average Profit Difference		Feature
	A little	More	A little	More	
(1) Early Settlement Type	●———————|		|—●——————|		Aim to reach agreement as soon as possible
(2) Fairness-oriented type	|———●———|		●——————————|		Aim to agree on a proposal with a small difference in profits
(3) Balanced type	|———●———|		|————●———|		Aim for both early agreement and one's own profit.
(4) Profit-oriented type	|————————●		|——————————●		Focus on one's own profit.
(5) Long-term negotiation type	|————————●		|——————●——|		Build consensus over time.

5.2 Relationship Between Conflict-of-Interest Structure and Consensus-Building Process

Figure 5 shows the average profit of each player when agreement is reached for the 12 degrees of conflict-of-interest in Table 5, and Fig. 6 shows the average number of offers until agreement is reached. The conflict-of-interest degree defined in this paper represents the characteristics of the profit when agreement is reached and the number of offers until agreement is reached, i.e., the time it takes to reach agreement.

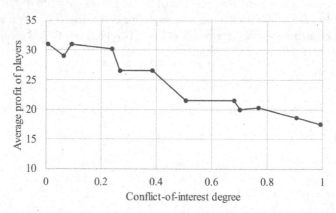

Fig. 5. Conflict-of-interest degree and average profit of each agent when agreeing (GS)

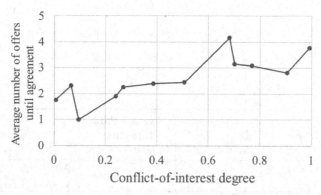

Fig. 6. Conflict-of-interest degree and average number of offers when agreeing (GS)

5.3 Questionnaire Results

The questionnaire asked the questions on emotional determinants, behavioral determinants, agreement satisfaction, and strategies for achieving higher scores.

The most significant factor determining friendliness was the own profit of the other party's offer. Fourteen of the 22 subjects indicated that their own profit earned from the other's offer was the most important factor in determining their friendliness. The most significant factor in determining resignation was time elapsed. Eight of the 22 subjects indicated that elapsed time was the most important factor in their decision to give up. The next most significant factors were: one's own profit from the other's offer, the change in the other's offer, whether the other accepted the offer, the difference between one's own profit from the other's offer and the other's profit from the other's offer, and the other's profit from the other's offer. Most of subjects decided friendliness based on profits, but factors determining resignation were more varied among participants.

The most significant factor in determining the offer to the other party was one's own profit; 16 of the 22 subjects indicated that their own profit was the most important factor in deciding on the offer. The most significant factor in deciding whether to accept the other's offer was one's own profit in the other's offer. Twenty-one of the 22 subjects indicated that their own profit was the most important factor in deciding whether to accept the offer. From these results, we can see, as a whole, subjects tended to place more emphasis on profit in deciding their actions.

Finally, all the subjects were more satisfied with consensus when they got high profits. This result can be naturally interpreted from the objective of the subjects in this game, which was set to increase the profit.

Various types of strategies were found to increase the score, including reaching consensus early, showing strong intent, compromising a little, not giving up, pushing through a proposal with high profits for oneself, and increasing overall profits. The strategy made by each subject is consistent with that derived from the types of behavior classified in 5.1.

6 Agent-Based Simulation (ABS) of Consensus-Building Process

Using ABS, we comprehensively set up conflict-of-interest structures and quantitatively analyze the relationship with the consensus-building process. These features of comprehensiveness and quantifiability cannot be handled by GS which has limitations on such as time and number of participants.

6.1 Agent Behavior Type

From the GS results, the agent's behavior type is determined with the probabilities shown in Fig. 7.

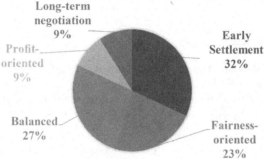

Fig. 7. Agent behavior types and percentages

6.2   Agent Behavior Model

The agent behavior model is identified through a multi-stage stratified analysis from the results of GS. Multi-stage stratified analysis [13] is a method in which an objective variable and explanatory variables are set, and the samples are successively divided into two parts by the explanatory variables so that the difference in the objective variable becomes large. In this paper, the behavioral model was identified by setting the offer alternatives, whether to accept the offer, and emotion (friendliness and resignation) as the objective variables, respectively, splitting the sample data by setting the parameters in Table 4 as explanatory variables, and creating probability distributions within the split groups. As shown in Fig. 8, the agent decides its behavior according to the probability distribution created by the multistage stratified analysis, based on the situation at the time of decision-making, such as the conflict-of-interest degree and the type of behavior.

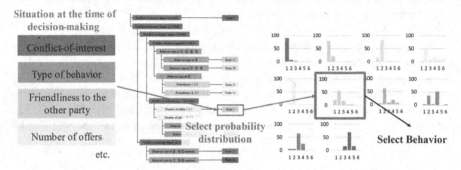

Fig. 8. Agent behavior decision process

6.3   Validation

The agent-based model was validated by examining whether ABS reproduced the distribution of offer alternatives, agreed alternatives, and the average number of offers until agreement obtained from the results to GS. For example, the results for a conflict-of-interest degree of 0.39 are shown in Fig. 9. ABS was run for 1000 trials. We were able to replicate the GS results for other conflict-of-interest cases as well, confirming the validity of the model.

6.4   Experimental Setup in ABS

Figure 10 shows the conflict-of-interest degrees to be experimented with for each of ABS and GS. We see that ABS conducted comprehensive experiments under 62 degrees of conflict-of-interest comparing to GS's 12 ways. In addition, though GS's consensus-building experiment had a total of 137 trials, ABS had a total of 62000 trials with 1000 trials each.

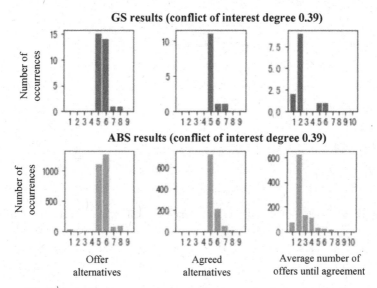

Fig. 9. Comparison of GS and ABS (Conflict-of-interest degree 0.39)

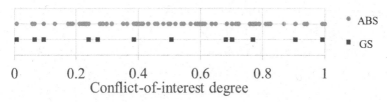

Fig. 10. Conflict-of-interest degrees between ABS and GS

7 Agent-Based Simulation (ABS) Results

The averages of 1000 trials of the conflict-of-interest degree and the profit of the two agents when agreement is reached are shown in Fig. 11, and the averages of 1000 trials of the conflict-of-interest degree and the number of offers until agreement are shown in Fig. 12.

When the conflict-of-interest degree is low, a mutually beneficial agreement is achieved with a small number of offers, while when the conflict-of-interest degree is high, an agreement is achieved with many offers until agreement is reached and with low mutual profits. We can see that the conflict-of-interest degree has a significant impact on the consensus-building process. The conflict-of-interest degree indicates the overall degree of conflict of opinion. When the conflict-of-interest degree is high, there is a conflict of opinion on every proposal, and it is difficult to reach a compromise and it takes time to reach a consensus. As a result, a low-profit, or even undesirable agreement is achieved for both sides.

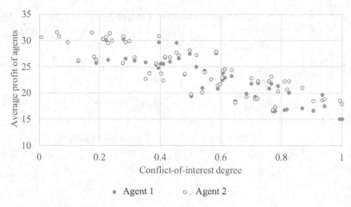

Fig. 11. Conflict-of-interest degree and average of each agent when agreeing (ABS)

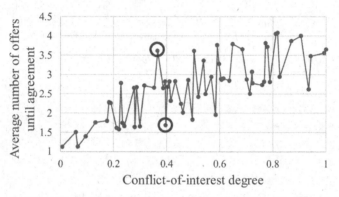

Fig. 12. Conflict-of-interest degree and average number of offers when agreeing (ABS)

While the conflict-of-interest degree captures the overall characteristics of the consensus-building process, there is variation in the number of offers to reach agreement, as in the two cases designated in Fig. 12. The profit tables for these two points are shown in Table 7 and Table 8. It can be seen that even if the conflict-of-interest degree is similar, the number of offers to reach agreement, i.e., the time to reach agreement, varies depending on whether or not there is a mutually beneficial proposal, as shown in alternative 1 in Table 8.

Table 7. Profit tables for conflict-of-interest degrees 0.364

Alternative	1	2	3	4	5	6	7	8	9
Profit of Agent 1	32	14	22	4	30	12	20	2	1
Profit of Agent 2	12	14	2	4	30	32	20	22	32

Table 8. Profit tables for conflict-of-interest degrees 0.395

Alternative	1	2	3	4	5	6	7	8	9
Profit of Agent 1	32	14	22	4	30	12	20	2	1
Profit of Agent 2	31	29	13	11	21	19	3	1	32

8   Summary and Discussion

In this paper, we analyzed the effect of the conflict-of-interest structure on the consensus-building process. First, the conflict-of-interest structure was expressed quantitatively based on the sum of squares of the profit-differences. Next, GS was used to construct a model that quantitatively incorporates emotions, and the parameters of the behavioral model were identified.

Then using the identified behavioral models, ABS was conducted to clarify the relationship between the consensus-building process and variety of conflict-of-interest structures. Using the conflict-of-interest degree defined based on the sum of squares of the differences in profits, we conducted a quantitative analysis of the consensus-building process by capturing the characteristics of the profits when agreement is reached and the number of offers until agreement is reached.

In this paper, we developed a model of GS that can be applied to consensus-building by referring to the framework of drama theory. In drama theory, an agent-based model is not necessarily used, but the equilibrium concept is used primarily in consensus analysis. This shows that GAM can be applied to non-agent-based models of consensus-building, such as in drama theory, and GAM has enough applicability and effectiveness. The method described in this paper also shows an effective way to visualize the conflict-of-interest structure by quantitatively expressing the degree of conflict of interest, and to analyze quantitatively the relationship with other factors.

Future issues include, first, the exploration of an index that expresses the characteristics of the average number of offers until agreement. In this paper, we used the sum of squares of profit differences in our analysis and were able to capture trends in the characteristics of consensus formation, but we observed some variation. This indicates the influence of complex factors on the number of offers to reach a consensus. The search for an index that captures the characteristics of consensus-building in more detail is an issue that needs to be addressed. Another issue is to analyze the combination of more than two stakeholders. This paper clarifies the characteristics of the basic conflict of interest structure between two stakeholders. When three or more stakeholders are involved, the consensus is formed in a conflict-of-interest structure with more complex interactions than in the case of two stakeholders. The findings of this paper on the conflict-of-interest structure between two stakeholders are also fundamental in considering the characteristics of a more complex structure.

References

1. Ministry of Land, Infrastructure, Transport and Tourism, Japan. Guidelines for Public Participation Procedures in the Conceptual Phase of Public Works Projects under the Jurisdiction

of the Ministry of Land, Infrastructure, Transport and Tourism (in Japanese) (2003). https://www.mlit.go.jp/kisha/kisha03/01/010630/0630-2.pdf. Accessed 14 June 2022

2. Seino, S., Uda, T., Hoshigami, Y.: Problems and improvement measures for consensus-building in public works (in Japanese). J. Coastal Zone Stud. **18**(4), 101–107 (2006)

3. Ninomiya, H.: Drama-theoretical analysis of consensus-building process in public infrastructure development (in Japanese). Doboku Gakkai Ronbunshu F **6**(1), 101–116 (2006). https://doi.org/10.2208/jscejf.62.101

4. Susskind, L., Mckearnan, S., Larmer, J.T.: The Consensus-Building Handbook a Comprehensive Guide to Reaching Agreement. SAGE Publications, Inc. (1999)

5. Yamaguchi, S., Miura, R., Suzuki, A., Hayakawa, Y.: A Study on Advancement of Consensus-building Methods in Social Capital Improvement (in Japanese). National Research Institute Annual Report, pp. 90–91 (2005)

6. Ninomiya, H.: A study on factors influencing the consensus-building process in road improvement projects (in Japanese). J. Construct. Manage. **12**, 261–272 (2005). https://doi.org/10.2208/procm.12.261

7. Arnstein, S.R.: A ladder of citizen participation. J. Am. Inst. Plann. **35**(4), 216–224 (1969). https://doi.org/10.1080/01944366908977225

8. Howard, N.: Drama Theory and Its Relation to Game Theory. Part 1 Dramatic Resolution vs. Rational Solution, Group Decision and Negotiation, vol. 3, pp. 187–206 (1994). https://doi.org/10.1007/BF01384354

9. Howard, N.: Drama Theory and Its Relation to Game Theory. Part 2 Formal Model of the Resolution Process, Group Decision and Negotiation, vol. 3, pp. 207–235 (1994). https://doi.org/10.1007/BF01384355

10. Kijima, K.: Invitation to Drama Theory New Developments in Multi-actor Complex Systems Models (in Japanese). Omusha (2001)

11. Szczepanska, T., et al.: GAM on! Six ways to explore social complexity by combining games and agent-based models. Int. J. Soc. Res. Methodol. (2022). https://doi.org/10.1080/13645579.2022.2050119

12. Hayashi, Y.: Road Construction and Stakeholders, A Record of Consensus-building, A Case Study of Yokkaichi Port Harbor Port Road Kasumi No. 4 Main Line (in Japanese). Akashi Shoten (2017)

13. Nagata, Y., Munechika, M.: Introduction to Multivariate Analysis Methods (in Japanese). Science Inc. (2001)

Feedback on a "Territory-Responsive" Participatory Simulation on Coastal Flooding Risk Applied to Two Case Studies in France

Amélie Monfort[1](✉), Nicolas Becu[1], and Marion Amalric[2]

[1] CNRS, UMR LIENSs 7266, 17000 La Rochelle, France
amelie.monfort@gmail.com
[2] University of Tours, UMR CITERES 7324, 37000 Tours, France

Abstract. One of the most important risks that threatens coastal cities is coastal flooding, and the effects of climate change will aggravate this risk. As a response, adaptation strategies need to be developed through the defense of the coastline and planning actions for example. We propose a "territory-responsive" participatory simulation (PS) method called "LittoSIM-GEN" to raise awareness among elected officials and agents of collectivities on different measures of coastal flooding prevention. This PS is carried out during workshops and is based on system modeling and participatory approach to establish links between the reference system and the simulation played. It lies between a descriptive and an abstract model as it does not describe a unique territory but is adapted to some extent to the territory on which it is applied. The analysis of 7 workshops conducted in two French regions questions: 1) the territorial adaptation of the PS through the deployment process, and the development of archetypes and their observability for the participants, 2) how the played experience is used to test strategies and to reconsider how risk management works in reality, and 3) how the attitudes of the participants may depend on the level of territorial adaptation of the PS.

Keywords: participatory simulation · coastal flooding risk · territorial adaptation

1 Introduction

Coastal areas are particularly vulnerable to climate change, both coastal and ocean ecosystems, as well as coastal cities [1]. These are highly populated areas as about 11% of the global population (~900 million people) live in coastal areas below 10 m of elevation above sea level [2]. This number is expected to reach 1 billion by 2050 [3]. Coastal cities are and will be increasingly exposed to the meteorological and ocean impacts of climate change such as sea level rise and extreme storms which can cause and enhance the risks of coastal flooding, extreme water levels, erosion etc. As a result, adaptation strategies need to be developed to reduce the risks, their social, economic, and environmental consequences, and overcome the cascading risks effect on the territories. Among the possible adaptation measures, the defense of the coastline and spatial planning actions participate to reduce the vulnerability of the territory [4]. We generally

© The Author(s), under exclusive license to Springer Nature Switzerland AG 2023
C. Harteveld et al. (Eds.): ISAGA 2022, LNCS 13622, pp. 99–120, 2023.
https://doi.org/10.1007/978-3-031-37171-4_7

distinguish hard infrastructure (e.g. dike, breakwater), nature-based solutions (e.g. beach nourishment, coral reefs, mangroves, marshes), adapted housing (e.g. elevation, refuge area) and managed retreat (i.e. moving people, assets and activities out of the risk area). Hard infrastructure is a widely used measure to protect coastlines from hazards [5], and France is no exception to this trend. Indeed, there is a strong culture of hard protection [6, 7] and studies show how difficult it is for societies to quit this model or to test new ones such as managed retreat [7–11].

Given this observation we propose a "territory-responsive" participatory simulation (PS) method called "LittoSIM-GEN" to raise awareness among elected officials and agents of municipalities and other territorial collectivities, on different measures of coastal flooding prevention in the context of climate change, and on territorial cooperation. PS is a simulation/game which uses system modeling and which intention is explicitly participative (participants share control over the decisions that affect them). It simulates society-environment interactions concerning a complex issue and provides a framework allowing the participants to collectively build ideas, abstractions (concepts, strategies, plans…), which are beneficial to them [12]. As for any other simulation/game, the model can be very specific (descriptive) or generic (abstract). The LittoSIM-GEN model tends towards a descriptive model and is called "territory-responsive" because it is not descriptive of a unique territory but is adapted to some extent to the territory on which it is applied. The model developed corresponds somehow to an archetypal representation of the reference system[1] driven by case study analysis. LittoSIM-GEN aim to support reflection process and to analyze if and how the simulation allows to understand actors' perception of adaptation to coastal flooding risk. How participants manage coastal flooding risk prevention? Do they diversify their practices away from hard defense? Do they experiment managed retreat and how? Do they conceive natured-based solutions as measures to manage the risk or adapt to climate change? Simulation and gaming approach is based on establishing links between the reference system (the 'reality') and the simulation played, and to use the played experience as reflexive elements to reconsider how things work in reality [13]. It is a common practice to support natural resources management and socio-environmental problematics like risk management.

The objective of this article is to propose feedback on the implementation of LittoSIM-GEN in two French territories. In the next sections we briefly introduce the PS by focusing on its territorial intent through the adaptation of its design, and the case studies. Then we present and analyze the results. First, the adaptation of the LittoSIM-GEN model to the territories (3.1). Then, the risk management actions undertake during the simulation (3.2). Finally, the relationship between what happened during the simulation and the participants' reality (3.3). In the discussion, we study how the level of correspondence between the reference system (the 'reality') and the LittoSIM model can influence the simulation experience of the participants.

---

[1] In this paper, to refer to the territory represented by the model, we use the term 'reference system' rather than the term 'reality'.

2 Material and Methods

2.1 LittoSIM-GEN: A "Territory-Responsive" Participatory Simulation

LittoSIM-GEN is a participatory simulation deployed with elected officials and agents of municipalities and other territorial collectivities during half-day collective workshops led by two facilitators who are part of the research team. The process is implemented thanks to a partnership organized in a steering committee between the researchers and some local actors who are in charge of risk and/or coastline management (e.g. inter-municipal cooperation structure, coastal observation network...). Within the steering committee, the local actors examine the need for adaptation of the PS concerning the geographical representation of the territory played, the possible management actions, and the additional objectives of the workshop in relation to local issues. Adaptation requests are discussed and are then validated or not collectively. The actors also help researchers to identify and invite the participants of their territory who then come on a voluntary basis.

The dozen participants are divided into 4 municipal teams whose goal is to manage their territory submitted to a coastal flooding risk with digital tablets. They carry out management actions (construction of a dike, land use change, managed retreat...) according to a budget during about ten game rounds[2], each round corresponding to a period of one year in real time. The game is punctuated by coastal flooding events (about 3 on a game, including one at the beginning) that allow participants to see the consequences of their actions in terms of the extent and height of flooding, and collective times so they can discuss and build an intercommunal management plan. For more information on the design (coastal flooding modeling, representation of land use and coastal defenses, human-computer interactions...) and the deployment (setting up and running a session) of a LittoSIM workshop, see [14, 15].

The PS offers risk stakeholders a simplified representation of their 'reality' and the possibility to freely choose and simulate different flood management scenarios. Its design is described along two axes:

1) First, the *artefact*. The PS is built around 3 elements: an agent-based model [16], a hydrodynamic model of a flooding hazard and a role-playing game. These components form the simulation artefact, i.e. an artificial and "boundary object" [17] that allows actors to interact with their environment in a simplified and comprehensive way. The artefact is a representation of the territory through material elements: geographical and administrative scales, demography, topography, land use, coastal defense...

2) Second, the *deployment*. The artefact is applied on the territories within the framework of a participative process and according to a deployment method: context of

---

[2] It can depend on the workshop, depending on the dynamics of the game. Some workshops have fewer rounds, others have more.

application, local partners, objectives, target audience, selection of participants, scenario… The presence of these elements during the PS "puts this territory back into action by including stakeholders' interactions and its social complexity" [18].

Both axes contribute to the "realism", that is to say the "observability" (i.e. make the reference system visible in the model for the actors) [13], of the simulation and gives it a territorial dimension. LittoSIM-GEN addresses the observability of the artefact through the development of territorial archetypes [19]. A territorial archetype lies between an abstract and a descriptive model and "is the typical example of a situation of inhabited space defined according to physical, socio-economic, historical and governance characteristics" [20]. Therefore, the artefact must be sufficiently observable for the participants from various territories to project their reality onto it.

Several case studies in France have been investigated in the LittoSIM-GEN research project through different archetypes, and this article is based on two of them: Camargue and Normandy.

2.2 Organization and Monitoring of Participatory Simulation Workshops in Normandy and Camargue

Normandy is an administrative Region of 30 000 km^2 in the north of France on the Channel coast (Fig. 1). The landscapes are very varied, especially on both sides of the Seine river. To the north of the river, it is a succession of chalky cliffs and urbanized valleys, it is the Department[3] of Seine-Maritime. These valleys are protected by dikes and pebble ridges and are vulnerable to coastal flooding because their estuary are at a very low level [21]. To the south of the Seine, the territory is located between Deauville and Houlgate in the Department of Calvados and consist of a succession of seaside resorts bordered by seawalls and long sandy beaches.

Camargue is a natural region of southern France on the Mediterranean Sea belonging to the delta of the Rhône, one of the main rivers of Europe (Fig. 1). The deltaic plain forms a triangle of about 1600 km^2 around the two arms of the river (Petit and Grand Rhône) between the cities of Arles to the north, Le Grau-du-Roi to the west and Port-Saint-Louis-du-Rhône to the east. It is a vast natural area particularly rich in biodiversity, consisting of wetlands, agricultural areas, and a few hamlets. The area is protected by 90 km of sandy coastline [22] and hard protection systems in front of highly concentrated urban areas (Saintes-Maries-de-la-Mer, Le Grau-du-Roi…). Camargue is particularly vulnerable to hydraulic hazards, including coastal flooding by overflows and wave overtopping.

We organized 7 workshops (referenced from W1 to W7 in this article) of LittoSIM-GEN between 2019 and 2021 with 2 different "territory-responsive" archetypes (Fig. 2). Three workshops were conducted with a first archetype in Camargue (W1, W2, W3) and 4 with another archetype in Normandy: 1 with the actors of Calvados (W4) and 3 with the actors of Seine-Maritime (W5, W6, W7). Eighty people who were divided in 28 teams, were elected officials (n = 33) and agents of communities and other structures (n = 47) took part (Table 1). They work as mayor, deputy mayor, and/or have areas of expertise focused on the coastline, the environment, urban planning, risk management… Most of

---

[3] A Department is an administrative division of the French territory within a Region.

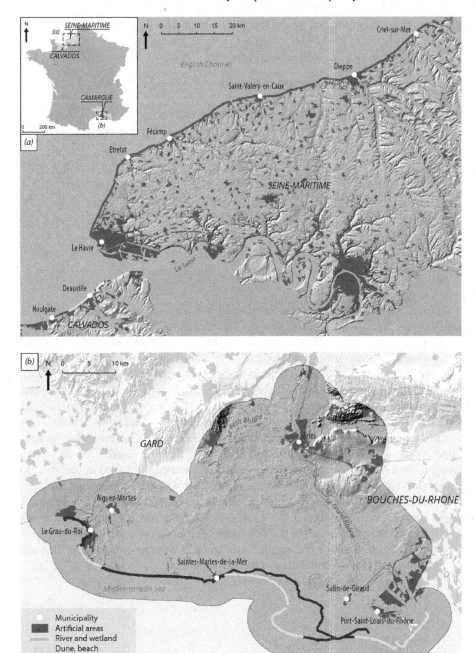

Fig. 1. Study sites of Normandy (a) and Camargue (b), France

them were from the municipal (n = 33) and inter-municipal (i.e., mixed syndicate and inter-municipality, n = 37) levels.

Table 1. Characteristics of the participants of the 7 workshops

| | CAMARGUE | | | NORMANDY | | | |
| | | | | CALVADOS | SEINE-MARITIME | | |
Workshop	W1	W2	W3	W4	W5	W6	W7
Elected officials	1	1	3	7	7	8	6
Agents of collectivities and others	7	10	6	7	9	3	5
Municipal level	1	1	5	12	5	6	3
Inter-municipal level	5	6	4	2	7	5	8

The data used for this article came from various qualitative and quantitative methods. First, we used the logbook that we documented throughout the process to keep track of the implementation of the PS and to analyze the choices that were made regarding the deployment and the artefact of each workshop. Then, during the experiment all the actions of the participants (type of action on land use and coastline), the municipal budget, population trends and the hectares of submerged areas are saved in the model. These raw data are then formatted into graphs and maps thanks to automated R scripts [20] in order to visualize, for example, the evolution of strategies over the rounds and the differences in strategies between the municipalities. The social interactions, in particular the final debriefing phase, were observed, annotated, and partially transcribed. The debriefing phase makes it possible to discuss three points: the strategies followed in the game to prevent the risk of flooding, the collective action that was put in place and the need for coordination between municipalities, and the links between what was simulated and reality. The observation grid and the thematic analysis of the transcripts focuses on identifying the "what and why" of the actions carried out by the participants, reception elements on coastal flooding risk and the management measures, the playful attitude, and the projection into the simulation of the participants.

The results of this study will now be presented.

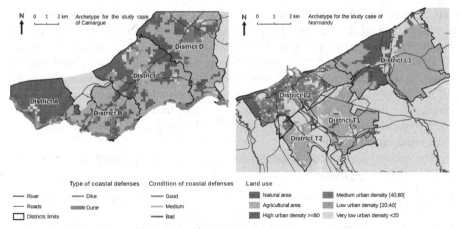

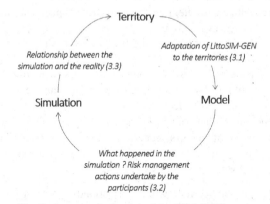

Fig. 2. The two LittoSIM-GEN archetypes for Camargue and Normandy

3 Results

The results below are presented in 3 steps that correspond to the loop "territory-model-simulation" which is often used in participatory modelling [23] (Fig. 3). Such a division allows to analyze successively the simulation model used in the workshops, the simulation experience itself and then the links between the fictional and real worlds.

Fig. 3. Loop analysis of the LittoSIM-GEN results

3.1 Adaptation of the Participatory Simulation to Two Case Studies

The first result of the application of LittoSIM-GEN concerns its adaptation to the territories and the identification of the discrepancies between the reference system (the 'reality') and the model (R/M) for each workshop to determine profiles.

We have chosen to characterize the level of R/M correspondence of the workshops according to different variables drawn from the literature such as [24] for the division into 2 evaluation spheres, [18] for the influence of the design of the artefact, and two previous LittoSIM studies about the spatial and temporal realism of the workshops [15] and the territory-specific elements of LittoSIM that do not belong to the frame-game [19]. We only consider territory-specific variables because they are the ones that are adapted to each case study. Some variables contribute to the observability of the PS but are invariable from one workshop to another: the diversity of the represented spatial scales, the spatial configuration of the simulation room, the time allocated to the flooding event, to the planning of the territory and to the realization and administrative delays of some management actions [15].

The selected 12 variables belong to 2 spheres. First, the sphere of the **deployment** of the participatory process:

1. *articulation of the PS with the missions of the local partners*: how the workshop contributes or not to the partners' missions on their territory;
2. *legitimacy of the organizers on the territory*: is the organization of the LittoSIM workshop by these actors (researchers and local partners) can be perceived as more or less legitimate by the invited and present actors? For example: do the researchers have a particular anchorage on this territory? Do the local partners have the "coastal flooding prevention" administrative competence on the territory? Are there conflicts/tensions on the territory with one or several organizers? Is there a lack of knowledge of the local partners by the participants?;
3. *workshop scenario*: the scenario is the script of the coastal flooding (order and intensity of the hazards launched) and the interventions of the facilitators about collective actions and specific adaptation issues (climate change effects, erosion…). It is the intention of the organizers to integrate these different aspects into the scenario that is taken into account in the evaluation;
4. *group coherence*: do the actors gathered during the workshop work on the same risk territory?;
5. *participation of "strategic actors"*: the management of coastal flooding risk in France is the responsibility of local structures in collaboration with the State. It gives certain actors a greater influence in the decision-making process, therefore some actors have more strategic positions than others. This aspect is considered in the evaluation: as soon as the number of mayors, general manager of services, heads of services and presidents of an inter-municipal cooperation structure represents most of the participants, the workshop is considered "strategic".

Second, the sphere of the **artefact**, which corresponds to the territorial characteristics of the archetype:

6. *district shape*: correspondence between the shape and boundary of the districts played and the municipalities in the territory of the participants;
7. *landforms of the area*: topography and bathymetry;
8. *demographic evolution* of the archetype, based on the trend of the territory of application;
9. *modeling of the coastal physical processes*: how realistic is the flooding event in the game (is it a reference event for the territory or, if not, does the event calibration approximate a known event?) and are there other coastal hazards represented in the model;

10. *local land use issues*: correspondence between the local land use issues of the simulation and the issues of the territory of the participants;
11. *possible management strategies* in the model;
12. *economic system*: cost of the actions, municipal budget and their evolution.

Each variable is qualified with a value from 0 to 3 where 3 is the highest R/M correspondence level. Scores were assigned by expert opinion (the project researchers) based on all the data collected during the implementation process of the workshops in the two territories and their analysis. The explanation of the scores for the 12 variables is detailed in the appendix. We represented the R/M correspondence level of each workshop in radar charts, which is a common way to represent and analyze the territorial dimensions of an object [25]. We have identified 3 workshops profiles (Fig. 4).

The level of correspondence is **accurate** if all the variables of the artefact and most of the deployment variables have important values (2 or 3) and thus contribute to a high observability of the simulation for the participants. A key point in this profile concerns the participation of "strategic actors" during the workshop, which is always very high and helps to anchor the simulation in reality. The W5, W6 and W7 workshops in Normandy are typical of this profile. Indeed, the specific-content of the used archetype, called "coast with cliffs and valleys", for this territory has been significantly adapted and is typical of the Department of the Seine-Maritime. Moreover, many elected officials were present (between 44% and 67% of the total of participants in these 3 workshops), and the workshops directly benefit the local partners of the process who were academics with a scientific project, a coastal observation network and a mixed syndicate whose mission is to develop the Department's coastal strategy.

The level of correspondence is **moderate** if the observability of the PS is both determined by a few artefact variables (that can vary from one workshop to another) and a few deployment variables (mainly the scenario, the legitimacy of the organizers and the presence of "strategic actors" from the same risk territory). In this profile, we observe that the process is not very well articulated with the objectives of the actors of the territory (scores of 0 or 1). These are the profiles of the W2, W3 and W4 workshops in Camargue and Normandy in the Department of Calvados. The difference between the accurate sessions and these can be explained in particular by the fact that the archetype used for Camargue workshops is based on the adaptation of the original archetype of LittoSIM made for another territory [26]. The archetype used for W4 is more typical of the Seine-Maritime than the Calvados. The simulation is therefore *a priori* less observable for the participants of W4.

Finally, the level of correspondence is **superficial** if there is a weak (scores of 0 or 1) participation of the "strategic actors" (elected officials and managers with significant influence in the decision-making process) of a same risk territory and if the observability of the PS is mainly carried out through a few artefact variables such as the representation of possible management actions, the economic system, the local land use issues, or the demographic evolution. This concerns the W1 workshop in Camargue where there was only one elected official and the environmental management actors were over-represented.

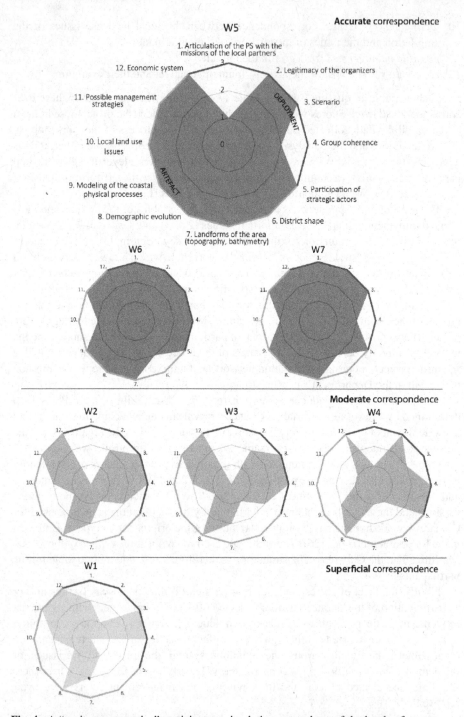

Fig. 4. A "territory-responsive" participatory simulation: a typology of the levels of correspondence between reference system ('reality') and the simulation for each workshop

3.2 Simulate Coastal Flooding Risk Management: Path Dependency to Hard Defense and Multilayer Approach

In this second part of the results, we present how participants used the model to simulate flood risk management options.

In the 7 workshops, different management measures can be and were explored by the participants, from hard shoreline protection to more alternative and flexible solutions (soft defense, managed retreat). Just over a half of the teams (15/28 teams) undertake hard defense actions and all participants implemented alternative measures. This is related to the PS that facilitates the exploration of a diversity of solutions, but also reveals different options of risk management and adaptation policies.

The actions carried out on the dikes show the spontaneous interest of the managers for hard infrastructure. Most of the actions on the dikes are undertake at the beginning of the game during the first 3 to 4 rounds (out of an average of 10 rounds over the 7 workshops) (Fig. 5). They are therefore short-term actions to respond to the emergency after the first flooding at the beginning of the game, as also expressed by the actors during the session:

"The first thing is to repair [...] You have to repair, that's what you always do in these cases. The citizens wouldn't understand if we went to repair where it didn't break." (W2); *"First year you have to do the emergency."* (W2); *"We are talking about dyke failure, apart from initiating a process of repair, of restoration of the dyke, for the moment on this type of event there is no... [he stops]."* (W6); *"The first step is to reinforce the dike."* (W7).

The measures on the dikes are essentially renovation actions, i.e. they maintain and improve the general condition of the dikes. No participants built new dikes (coastal or retro-coastal), and only two teams raised their defenses. This post-disaster reaction and behavior through maintenance leads us to consider the theory of path-dependency of the measure used. Path dependency is the effect of persisting in current practices and resisting to change, even if better solutions exist, because it is difficult to change [27]. Authors have shown that path dependency on dike is notably linked to its physical structure, landscape functions and economic aspects [28, 29].

Despite this strong tendency during the game to rely on dikes to reduce risk, participants also invest in a mix of other measures such as soft defense solutions and planning actions throughout the session.

The defensive actions on natural barriers are widely practiced in the 7 workshops. All teams, except one, rely on natural protections to manage coastal flooding. The actions carried out on the natural barriers (pebble ridge or sand dune) essentially consist of maintenance and reinforcement of the natural accretion of sand dunes through a system of fences. Most of the teams (11/15 who have natural barriers) practice soft defense throughout the game. This shows that the participants are banking on the effectiveness of this strategy from the start. For 6 teams the use of soft defense through coastal sand dunes accelerates after the second flood (change of practice or intensification of the use).

Another management solution implemented focuses on land use planning and is called managed retreat. It involves expropriating and relocating vulnerable urban and agricultural areas to leave more space for the sea in case of flooding (de-polderizing).

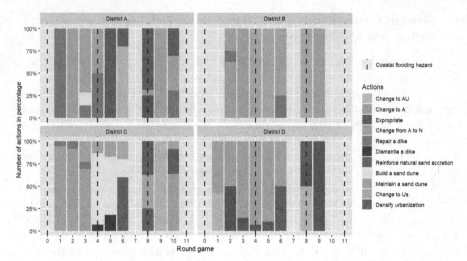

Fig. 5. Illustration of the number of actions per type and round in percentage for the workshop W2 [Actions: Change to AU – *area to be urbanized*; Change to A – *change to an agricultural area*; Change from A to N – *change an agricultural area to a natural area*; Change to US – *adapt an urban area to coastal flooding*]

Almost all participants (25/28 teams) tested this measure and among those who invested in dikes (n = 15) two thirds also implemented strategic withdrawal of urban areas. For some (n = 3) the expropriation was anticipated relatively early in the game, for others (n = 6) the measure was implemented later.

Experimentations of soft solutions and managed retreat show us that participants adopt a variety of management strategies and do not rely solely on hard infrastructure. They favored a multi-layered approach to risk prevention by combining measures on the coastline and land use, either in advance or by adapting as floods occur during the game. But these innovative experiments are not easy to implement in the real world, as shown in the following sub-section by the comments of the participants who refer to their real system.

3.3   From Simulation to Reality: Understanding the Local Issues of the Adaptation to Coastal Flooding Risk

The third part of the results deals with the connection of the simulation to the reality of the territory.

While the PS objectives are mainly focused on testing a variety of management strategies and the importance of building a collective policy, a major concern of the participants in Camargue workshops while discussing adaptation strategies like managed retreat was the consultation of the local population:

"It's easy on the game to say, okay, I'll put my farm in a natural zone and then I'll expropriate it, I'll check the cross. The reality is much more complex." (debriefing, W1); *"I'm working on concertation in Camargue, I find that this tool lacks a*

great deal of humanity because here [in the simulation] we do things, we change agricultural zones into natural zones, in reality it is not at all possible or very difficult." (debriefing, W2)

Indeed, the agricultural stakes in Camargue are particularly high and their vulnerability to coastal flooding risk and climate change's consequences is central. Farmers are therefore key actors in the adaptation of the territory and their absence from the PS highlights their importance in the management of flood risk in the region.

The importance of the social dimension became even more apparent at W3 when participants spent an hour discussing this aspect after the second flood occurred. While group discussions are frequent, and encouraged, in the LittoSIM-GEN PS, especially at this point in the session, the problem was such that participants were stuck. It emerged when the managed retreat of urban areas in the simulation, and therefore of populations, was discussed. To unblock the situation, the facilitator proposed to the actors to integrate concertation measures in the intermunicipal management plan (organization of public meetings and co-construction of adaptation solutions). If the agricultural issues were more highlighted during the other two Camargue workshops, it is interesting to note that this action, described as a "social trauma" (participant, W3), was especially emphasized in the session where actors from the municipality of Saintes-Maries-de-la-Mer were present. Located on the seafront and surrounded by marshes, this actual French district is often designated as particularly vulnerable. However, this majority discourse on consultation quickly expands from the issue of urban retreat to all measures of adaptation to the risk.

In Normandy, at the workshops W5, W6 and W7, simulated experiments of managed retreat, as well, reflected adaptation thoughts widely initiated on the territory regarding the de-polderizing of certain low valleys with little urbanization. For example, in the Seine-Maritime Department, two districts are concerned by the reconnection of their valley to the sea[4] and other similar valleys could see the development of this type of project, such as at the estuary of the Yères river [30]. District L1 of the "coast with cliffs and urbanized valleys" archetype is based on this low valley, which is particularly suitable for testing a de-polderizing strategy. We observed at W5 where elected officials of the estuary of the Yères river were present, that some actors experimented this scenario to demonstrate a certain vision of the territory. In other words, the objective was to convey a message as to how the territory could be developed to manage the coastal flooding risk (see exchange below).

Team L1 explains its management strategy at the workshop: *"(...) and then on top of that we remove the diking system"*. An actual elected official of the municipality that L1 represents reacts, to which some respond: *"It's a game!"*. He replies *"Yeah, that's why I'm not saying anything."* (general laughter) *"It's a simulation!"* *"If you don't have fun in the games, if you don't do it in the games..."* *"You're going to win in tourism!"*

---

[4] Project « Basse Sâane», in the municipalities of Quiberville and Sainte-Marguerite (Seine-Maritime).

This confrontation shows us that there are issues of representation on risk management strategies between actors in Normandy, concerning a de-polderizing adaptation strategy.

Actions carried out in the PS confront their real system and help us to understand the issues and challenges of adapting a territory.

4 Discussion

From the analysis of the simulation actions, the debriefings and the typology of the levels of correspondence, we revealed the different attitudes of the participants to observe the simulation, i.e. project their reality onto the simplified representation proposed to them. The analysis of observability attitudes is useful to question the influence of the levels of R/M correspondence (cf. 3.1) on the simulation experience. The necessary level of realism is a central question for users of simulation models for participative, concertation and pedagogical purposes. Our study led us to identify 3 attitudes that the participants adopted at different moments in the workshops:

1) *Create new simulation rules.* This attitude appeared clearly in W3 (Camargue) when participants created new rules in order to make the simulation more realistic in their eyes. Indeed, two things prevented them from progressing in the game: the absence of the inhabitants in the debate concerning managed retreat, and the pro "managed retreat orientation" of the PS perceived and regretted by some players. This strategy of creating new rules gave the game legitimacy for the participants and allowed them to continue the experiment.

2) *"Play" rather than "simulate reality".* The participants of W2 (Camargue) see the PS essentially as a game, and therefore as a "disconnected" process from their reality. They do a lot of game actions, and their comments show that they are essentially in a playful and critical attitude (*"I only took it as a game."*; *"In reality we would have acted, but we couldn't, we were playing, so we can see that it is an artificial municipality."*). This is particularly evident during the final debriefing, which is supposed to allow the participants to relate the simulation experience to their reality. Instead, they suggested other ways of using LittoSIM (*"I would have liked to do the exercise in the same territory to compare [...]. It is difficult to compare our strategies because we were not all in the same conditions."*), underlined the limitations they feel of the approach and questioned the quality of the method for some:

> *"I'm not sure that between the costs of protection and the costs of the managed retreat measure... are the ratios in the game anywhere near a reality?"*;
> *"You have defined 4 pre-typed communes, different from each other, so with parameters. Does the result correspond to what you have set up? [...] I imagine that you have a probability potential, in a scenario where the parameters are established at the outset, you must be 80% sure that we will behave like this, it seems so logical to me!"*

The objectives of the workshop were therefore not perceived by the participants, which shows a relatively weak echo of the process with respect to local concerns.

3) *Reflexive.* This attitude is more characteristic of the workshops in Normandy (W5, W6 and W7). The dynamics of the game are punctuated by important intra- and inter-teams exchanges and the management actions are weighed. The simulation/reality relationship operates relatively well, and the strategies followed facilitate exchanges on different risk management solutions. For example, in the W6: the double function of defense and tourism of the dike, the consideration of risk in extra-communal planning, the issues of awareness and communication... In some cases, such as W5, the experience leads the participants to wonder if a more advanced adaptation of the PS could be imagined on their territory, which conveys the idea that the workshop allowed them to project themselves in the territorial planning.

This typology of observability driven attitudes highlights differences in the appropriation of the PS depending on the territory. In Camargue, where the R/M correspondence is either moderate or superficial, attitudes are more critical of the artefact. In Normandy, where the R/M correspondence is either accurate or moderate, the interest of the PS to pursue the territory's reflections on risk seems stronger (but does not exclude limits were also mentioned). In all cases, regardless of the attitude, the simulation offered a sufficiently realistic representation to allow the participants to discuss their reality.

5 Conclusion

This paper has studied the question of handling the observability of a simulation/game through the development of territorial archetypes. The results are based on the application in two distinct territories of a participatory simulation (PS) dedicated to coastal flooding risk management. It allowed us to respond to several aspects.

The first one is the question of the territorial adaptation of the PS through archetypes and its observability for the local actors. We have shown that a minimal adaptation was necessary to carry out the process, and we developed a method to characterize the adaptation by evaluating, at the level of the artefact and the deployment of the PS, the degree of correspondence between the reference system ('reality') and the model for each workshop. This allowed us to identify 3 levels of correspondence (accurate, moderate, superficial) for our 7 workshops with the strongest results for those conducted in Normandy. This result contributes to the reflections of previous papers on the advisability, or not, to develop descriptive models to support decision-making process and increase of knowledge about the reference system [15, 18, 31–33]. Our results tend to show that the observability of the gaming/simulation favors a reflexive attitude of the participants towards the questions addressed.

Secondly, we have analyzed the existing bridges between simulation and 'reality' in terms of coastal flooding risk management. Concerning managed retreat that was a particularly tested solution during the workshops, we find that it is a measure that divides the opinions of stakeholders. The simulation is an opportunity to test certain visions and to question the conditions of implementation of this practice (e.g. in consultation with the local population).

Finally, we have shown that realism is revealed on different occasions during the simulation and through different attitudes depending on the level of adaptation of the PS. The workshops in Camargue are more characterized by attitudes of critical posture, either by the fact that people change the rules, or by the fact that people do not take the proposed rules seriously and detach themselves from them by behaving as players rather than actors. This type of attitude can be described as critical observability. It is rather negative and tends to delegitimize the PS and may reduce the interest of LittoSIM-GEN in the short and long term. This tends to be confirmed by the fact that the LittoSIM-GEN action persists after the workshops in Normandy, unlike Camargue. In Normandy, local partners of the process disseminate information about the experiment through articles and seminar, and plan to integrate LittoSIM-GEN into their local policy by conducting further workshops in their territory after the research project to raise awareness on coastal problematics.

As part of the ongoing research, we intend to better assess the need to have a sufficiently "territory-responsive" PS for its legitimacy in the eyes of the actors. The question of the legitimacy of the model used to represent a system of interactions on the one hand, and of its use with a group on the other hand, is a central question for all type of simulation/gaming practices (e.g. [34, 35]).

Appendix

Rationale for scores by variable. *Table likely to evolve over the course of the research.*

Variable	Score 0	Score 1	Score 2	Score 3
1. Articulation of the PS with the missions of the local partners	Marginal articulation with the actions of local actors on the territory. In the speech and in the facts, the partner does not reintegrate the workshop in its own actions	Secondary articulation to the action of peripheral actors of the territory in terms of flooding (academics), who are not in the decision-making process. Moreover, the local decision-makers are mobilized in the last stage of the project (invitation, mobilization of participants)	Partial articulation with the objectives of only some of the major actors in the territory, who are not decision-makers in matters of risk	Close articulation with the actions of local decision makers on the territory

(*continued*)

Variable	Score 0	Score 1	Score 2	Score 3
2. Legitimacy of the organizers (researchers and local partners)	No or weak legitimacy of the organizers	Limited legitimacy because the partners are not the main actors of coastal flooding risk management on the territory and are more identified on other missions (e.g. environmental preservation)	Partial legitimacy because the local partners are well identified in terms of risk management on the territory but the research team is much less so	Strong legitimacy because the partners have a high visibility in the territory on coastal issues and/or have missions directly related to the risk of coastal flooding in the territory
3. Scenario of the workshop	No or weak integration in the workshop scenario of specific and structuring points of interest of the territory	Limited integration in the workshop scenario of specific and structuring points of interest of the territory	Partial integration of some specific and structuring points of interest of the territory. Some aspects have not been mentioned (e.g. erosion dune)	Strong integration of several specific and structuring points of interest of the territory (e.g. climate change effects, erosion, concomitance of climatic hazards)
4. Group coherence	No coherence of the group because the participants come from very different management territories, without relationship	Limited coherence of the group as participants are from very different management territories but with some relationships	Partial consistency of the group because the participants are at different scales of flood management but they are immediately adjacent and belong to the same supra-inter-municipal territory (e.g. the Department)	Strong coherence of the group because all the participants belong to the same management scale, i.e. the scale adapted to decision making regarding the risk of coastal flooding on their territory (e.g. a delta, an intermunicipality, a watershed)

(*continued*)

(*continued*)

Variable	Score 0	Score 1	Score 2	Score 3
5. Participation of strategic actors (mayors, general manager of services, heads of services and presidents of an inter-municipal cooperation structure)	No or low participation between 0% and 17% of total workshop participants	Strong participation, greater than or equal to 50% of total workshop participants	Partial participation between 33% and 50% excluded from the total workshop participants	Strong participation, greater than or equal to 50% of total workshop participants
6. District shape	No or weak correspondence between the shape and boundaries of the municipalities played and the municipalities of the participants' territory	Limited correspondence: the communes played do not correspond to real communes in the participants' territory, but the shapes resemble each other, which allows them to identify themselves	Partial correspondence: the communes played correspond to communes in immediately adjacent management territories that the participants can recognize, so there are few differences	Strong correspondence: the municipalities played correspond to the municipalities of the participants' management territories, so they can recognize them
7. Landforms of the area (topography, bathymetry)	No or weak correspondence: the proposed representation does not correspond at all to the local specificities of the participants' territory	Limited correspondence: the proposed representation omits a non-negligible part of the local specificities of the relief of the participants' territory	Partial correspondence: the representation tends to be close to the 'reality' of the participants' territory without representing all its landforms specificities	Strong correspondence between the relief represented in the game and the reality of the participants
8. Demographic evolution	Not at all representative of the demographic dynamics of the participants' territory	Poorly representative of the demographic dynamics of the participants' territory	Partially representative of the demographic dynamics of the participants' territory	Strongly representative of the demographic dynamics of the participants' territory

(*continued*)

(*continued*)

Variable	Score 0	Score 1	Score 2	Score 3
9. Modeling of the coastal physical processes	Null integration: the flooding event is not calibrated on the reference storm of the territory and the model does not consider other hazards than the coastal flooding	Limited integration: the flooding event is not calibrated on the reference storm of the territory but the model takes into account another hazard	Partial integration: the flooding event is calibrated on the reference storm of the territory and the model takes into account another hazard	Strong integration: the flooding event is calibrated on the reference storm of the territory and the model takes into account several hazards other than coastal flooding
10. Local land use issues	Zero correspondence between the land use issues of the simulation and the real territory of the participants	Limited correspondence: the issues of the participants' territory are present in the simulation but some local specificities are not taken into account and other issues are represented even though they are not present on the real territory	Good representation of the different types of issues but some local specificities of the real land use are not well highlighted in the simulation	Strong correspondence between the land use issues of the simulation and the participants' real territory
11. Possible management strategies	Zero correspondence between the possible management actions in the simulation and the reality	Limited correspondence: the possible management actions in the game correspond to reality, but some actions are missing and/or do not exist on the real territory	Partial correspondence: several possible management actions on the participants' real territory are not taken into account in the simulation	Strong correspondence between the possible management actions in the simulation and the reality

(*continued*)

(*continued*)

Variable	Score 0	Score 1	Score 2	Score 3
12. Economic system (cost of the actions, municipal budget and their evolution)	No match: the economic aspects of the simulation were not at all linked to elements of the real system and the evolution of the budgets of the communes over the course of the game appeared very unbalanced	Limited match: only some economic aspects of the simulation were linked to elements of the real system and the budgets of the communes evolved in an unbalanced way	Partial match: only some economic aspects of the simulation were linked to elements of the real system and the budgets of the communes evolved in a balanced way	Strong match: the economic aspects of the simulation are linked to elements of the real system and the budgets of the communes have evolved in a balanced way

References

1. IPCC: Cross-Chapter Paper 2: Cities and Settlements by the Sea. IPCC WGII Sixth Assessment Report, p. 42 (2021)
2. Haasnoot, M., Winter, G., Brown, S., Dawson, R.J., Ward, P.J., Eilander, D.: Long-term sea-level rise necessitates a commitment to adaptation: a first order assessment. Clim. Risk Manag. **34**, 100355 (2021). https://doi.org/10.1016/J.CRM.2021.100355
3. Oppenheimer, M., Glavovic, B.: Chapter 4: sea level rise and implications for low lying islands, coasts and communities. IPCC SR Ocean and Cryosphere. In: Pörtner, H.-O., et al. (eds.) IPCC Special Report on the Ocean and Cryosphere in a Changing Climate. Press, vol. Chapter 4, no. Final Draft, pp. 1–14 (2019). https://report.ipcc.ch/srocc/pdf/SROCC_FinalDraft_Chapter4_SM.pdf. Accessed 23 March 2022
4. Meur-Ferec, C., et al.: Une méthode de suivi de la vulnérabilité systémique à l'érosion et la submersion marines. Développement durable Territ. **11**(1), 24 (2020). https://doi.org/10.4000/developpementdurable.16731
5. Mamo, L.T., Dwyer, P.G., Coleman, M.A., Dengate, C., Kelaher, B.P.: Beyond coastal protection: a robust approach to enhance environmental and social outcomes of coastal adaptation. Ocean Coast. Manag. **217**, 106007 (2022). https://doi.org/10.1016/J.OCECOAMAN.2021.106007
6. Bawedin, V.: L'acceptation de l'élément marin dans la gestion du trait de côte : une nouvelle gouvernance face au risque de submersion? Ann. Georgr. **692**, 422–444 (2013). http://www.cairn.info/revue-annales-de-geographie-2013-4-page-422.htm
7. André, C., Boulet, D., Rey-Valette, H., Rulleau, B.: Protection by hard defence structures or relocation of assets exposed to coastal risks: contributions and drawbacks of cost-benefit analysis for long-term adaptation choices to climate change. Ocean Coast. Manag. **134**, 173–182 (2016). https://doi.org/10.1016/j.ocecoaman.2016.10.003
8. Meur-Ferec, C., Lageat, Y., Hénaff, A.: La gestion des risques côtiers en France métropolitaine: évolution des doctrines, inertie des pratiques? Géorisques **4/Le litt**, 57–67 (2013). https://hal.archives-ouvertes.fr/hal-00430767/document

9. Mineo-Kleiner, L., Meur-Férec, C.: Relocaliser les enjeux exposés aux risques côtiers en France : points de vue des acteurs institutionnels. [VertigO] La Rev. électronique en Sci. l'environnement **16**(2) (2016). https://doi.org/10.4000/vertigo.17656

10. Guéguen, A., Renard, M.: La faisabilité d'une relocalisation des biens et activités face aux risques littoraux à Lacanau. Sci. Eaux Territ. **23**(2), 26 (2017). https://doi.org/10.3917/set.023.0026

11. CGEDD, IGA, and IGF. Recomposition spatiale des territoires littoraux, Rapp. Mission pour le Gouv. sur le Financ. la recomposition Spat. des Territ. littoraux dans le Context. du recul du Trait côte, p. 234 (2019)

12. Becu, N., Crookall, D.: Companion modelling and participatory simulation: a glimpse. The European Geosciences Union Conference (2020)

13. Klabbers, J.H.G.: The magic circle: principles of gaming and simulation. Magic Circ. Princ. Gaming Simul. (2009). https://doi.org/10.1163/9789087903107

14. Becu, N., et al.: Participatory simulation to foster social learning on coastal flooding prevention. Environ. Model. Softw. **98**, 1–11 (2017). https://doi.org/10.1016/J.ENVSOFT.2017.09.003

15. Amalric, M., et al.: Sensibiliser au risque de submersion marine par le jeu ou faut-il qu'un jeu soit spatialement réaliste pour être efficace? Sci. du jeu **8** (2017). https://doi.org/10.4000/sdj.859

16. Voinov, A., Bousquet, F.: Modelling with stakeholders. Environ. Model. Softw. **25**(11), 1268–1281 (2010). https://doi.org/10.1016/j.envsoft.2010.03.007

17. Star, S.L., Griesemer, J.R.: Institutional ecology, 'translations' and boundary objects: amateurs and professionals in Berkeley's museum of vertebrate zoology, 1907–39. Soc. Stud. Sci. **19**(3), 387–420 (1989)

18. Becu, N.: Les courants d'influence et la pratique de la simulation participative : contours, design et contributions aux changements sociétaux et organisationnels dans les territoires, La Rochelle Université (2020). https://hal.archives-ouvertes.fr/tel-02515352. Accessed 27 Jan 2021

19. Becu, N., et al.: Applying a descriptive participatory simulation to specific case studies: adaptation of LittoSIM coastal flooding management simulation. iEMSs, p. 10 (2020)

20. Laatabi, A., et al.: LittoSIM-GEN: a generic platform of coastal flooding management for participatory simulation. Environ. Model. Softw. 105319 (2022). https://doi.org/10.1016/J.ENVSOFT.2022.105319

21. Caspar, R., Costa, S., Jakob, E.: Fronts froids et submersions de tempête dans le nord-ouest de la France: Le cas des inondations par la mer entre l'estuaire de la Seine et la baie de Somme. La Météorologie, no. 57, pp. 37–47 (2007). http://documents.irevues.inist.fr/handle/2042/18188. Accessed 13 Mar 2020

22. Sabatier, F., Suanez, S.: Evolution of the Rhône delta coast since the end of the 19th century. Cinématique du littoral du delta du Rhône depuis la fin du XIXe siècle. Géomorphologie Reli. Process. Environ. **9**(4), 283–300 (2003). https://doi.org/10.3406/morfo.2003.1191

23. Le Page, C., et al.: Models for sharing representations. In: Étienne, M. (ed.) Companion Modelling, pp. 69–101. Springer, Dordrecht (2014). https://doi.org/10.1007/978-94-017-8557-0_4

24. Hassenforder, E., Pittock, J., Barreteau, O., Daniell, K.A., Ferrand, N.: The MEPPP framework: a framework for monitoring and evaluating participatory planning processes. Environ. Manage. **57**(1), 79–96 (2015). https://doi.org/10.1007/s00267-015-0599-5

25. Amalric, M.: Habiter l'environnement pour une géographie sociale environnementale: nature, paysage, risque. Volume 1 : positionnement & projet de recherche, Université de Bretagne Occidentale (2019). https://hal.archives-ouvertes.fr/tel-02371925. Accessed 3 Mar 2020

26. Becu, N., et al.: Participatory simulation of coastal flooding: building social learning on prevention measures with decision-makers (2016). https://scholarsarchive.byu.edu/iemssconf erence/2016/Stream-D/73, http://www.iemss.org/society/index.php/iemss-2016-proceedings

27. Barnett, J., et al.: From barriers to limits to climate change adaptation: path dependency and the speed of change. Ecol. Soc. Publ. **20**(3) (2015). https://doi.org/10.5751/ES-07698-200305

28. Gerrits, L., Marks, P.: Complex bounded rationality in dyke construction. Path-dependency, lock-in in the emergence of the geometry of the Zeeland delta. Land Use Policy **25**(3), 330–337 (2008). https://doi.org/10.1016/j.landusepol.2007.09.001

29. van Buuren, A., Ellen, G.J., Warner, J.F.: Path-dependency and policy learning in the dutch delta: toward more resilient flood risk management in the Netherlands? Ecol. Soc. **21**(4),(2016). https://doi.org/10.5751/ES-08765-210443

30. Lafond, L.-R.: Le réaménagement du littoral Haut-Normand à Criel-sur-Mer (Seine-Maritime). Rapp. Assoc. "RIVAGES," p. 11 (1990)

31. Le Page, C.: Simulation multi-agent interactive: engager des populations locales dans la modélisation des socio-écosystèmes pour stimuler l'apprentissage social, p. 126 (2017)

32. Medema, W., Furber, A., Adamowski, J., Zhou, Q., Mayer, I.: Exploring the potential impact of serious games on social learning and stakeholder collaborations for transboundary watershed management of the St. Lawrence River Basin. Water **8**(5), 175 (2016). https://doi.org/10.3390/w8050175

33. Delay, E., Becu, N.: Overcoming the final frontier of climate change in viticulture: exploring interactions between society and environment using Agent Based Modelling and Companion Modelling approaches. In: Sustainable Grape and Wine Production in the Context of Climate Change, no. December, pp. 204–212 (2017)

34. Barnaud, C., Van Paassen, A.: Equity, power games, and legitimacy: dilemmas of participatory natural resource management. Ecol. Soc. **18**(2) (2013). https://doi.org/10.5751/ES-05459-180221

35. Daré, W., et al.: Difficultés de la participation en recherche-action : retour d'expériences de modélisation d'accompagnement en appui à l'aménagement du territoire au Sénégal et à la Réunion. [VertigO] La Rev. électronique en Sci. l'environnement **8**(2) (2008). https://doi.org/10.4000/vertigo.5012

Simulation Games
on Sustainability – A Comparative Study

Tobias Alf[✉] and Friedrich Trautwein

Centre for Management Simulation, Baden-Wuerttemberg Cooperative State University,
Stuttgart, Germany
`tobias.alf@dhbw-stuttgart.de`

Abstract. Sustainability is an essential factor for the future of mankind. This applies to all areas of society, but especially to the economy, which is responsible for a significant part of resource consumption. Therefore, the education of business students as future executives is of essential importance for the successful change towards sustainability.

Against this background, the following article compares simulation games on sustainability and business simulations. The results are based on a quantitative empirical survey with a total of 1101 participants, of whom 125 took part in a total of 6 simulation game seminars on sustainability. On the one hand, the acceptance of simulation games on the topic of sustainability among business students at the DHBW Stuttgart is investigated. On the other hand, essential components that are responsible for the success of simulation game events are recorded and similarities and differences between business management simulation games and simulation games on sustainability are analysed. The results show a high acceptance, satisfaction and learning success of business students with the sustainability simulation games used at the ZMS. In addition, despite many similarities, some practically significant structural differences can be observed, especially in the field of teamwork and engagement during plenum discussion.

Keywords: Sustainability · Simulation Game · Common-Action-Problem

1 Introduction

At the DHBW Stuttgart business school simulation games are widely used in teaching. Therefore in 2008 a specialized lab, the Centre for Management Simulation (ZMS) was founded to support with infrastructure and to train lecturers in the facilitation of simulation games (DHBW Stuttgart). Since then, with responsibility for the European Conference on Simulation and Gaming as well as the German Simulation and Gaming Award, the ZMS has developed to the leading teaching and research centre for simulation games in Germany.

Typically, business simulation games are integrated into lecturing on bachelors level to provide students with a comprehensive understanding of business using "total enterprise simulations" (Mayer, Dale, Fraccastoro, & Moss 2011, p. 65) or to address specific business topics like for example the bullwhip effect, that can be displayed by the beer game (Zensimu SAS 2022, p. 682). Due to climate change and a newly awakened awareness of finite resources on our planet the idea of sustainability has become a major topic not only in many areas of society but also in business education. Therefore, in the last years simulation games addressing sustainability have become part of the portfolio of simulation games at the ZMS.

Besides introducing simulation games on sustainability, it was important for the ZMS as a research centre to evaluate the simulation game-based lectures. Based on this research the article addresses the question how well simulation games on sustainability are accepted by business students and whether there are structural differences in the gameplay process compared to management orientated simulation games.

2 Sustainability and Simulation Games on Sustainability

In a first step the idea of sustainability was developed in the 17th and 18th century in European forestry as a "response to dwindling forest resources" (Purvis, Mao, & Robinson 2019, p. 682). In a global sense the idea of sustainability was introduced by Meadows et al. questioning the assumption of growth as an ongoing basis for the worldwide economy in "Limits to Growth" demanding the need for a global sustainable system (Meadows, Meadows, Jorgen, & Behrens 1972). The authors criticize the idea of unlimited economic growth in a world of limited resources. Beginning there the "concept snowballs" (Purvis et al. 2019, p. 682). In 1987 the idea of sustainable growth was introduced by the UN emphasizing that development is needed to fight poverty in third world countries and developing countries (UN 1987). The concept of sustainable development combines economic growth with the idea of social and environmental sustainability (Purvis et al. 2019, p. 684). The nowadays mostly used and widely accepted definition (Brandt 2021, p. 5; Fisher & Bonn 2011, p. 564) of sustainable development comes from the so called Brundtland Report: Sustainability is "development that meets the needs of the present without compromising the ability of future generations to meet their own needs" (UN 1987) and has become a widely accepted definition (Brandt 2021, p. 5; Fisher & Bonn 2011, p. 564).

Also very common is the graphical representation of sustainability as pillars or similar to a venn-diagramm. In both cases sustainability is represented by a balanced composition of society, environment/ecology, and economy. This also fits to the idea of "Our Common Future" (Brundtland Report), where the balance between economy (growth), environment and society is often mentioned even though not made explicit with a graphic: "What is needed now is a new era of economic growth - growth that is forceful and at the same time socially and environmentally sustainable." (UN 1987) (Fig. 1).

At least with the United Nations release of the 2030 Agenda for Sustainable Development describing 17 Sustainable Development Goals and 169 targets specifying the goals (UN 2015) the matter of education has been discussed in the context of sustainability. The fourth goal is explicit on education. Next to a broader view on education (e.g., literacy and numeracy, equal education for girls and boys) it explicates as a target: "that all learners acquire the knowledge and skills needed to promote sustainable

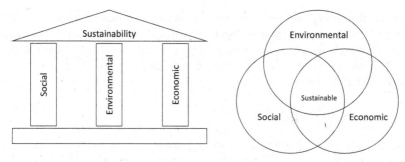

Fig. 1. Representations of Sustainability (Squires; thwink.org 2020)

development (…) through education for sustainable development…" (UN 2015, p. 17). Education is therefore not only a goal but also a main resource to reach the overall goal of sustainable development. In this context education is also described as a catalyst for sustainability (Brandt 2021, p. 6). The role of university teaching for education for sustainable development is emphasized by Sonetti et al. because it may lead to "behavioral change in future citizens and decision makers" (Sonetti, Brown, & Naboni 2019, p. 17).

The two simulation games used at the ZMS referring to the topic of sustainability are The Fishing Game and Fountains. Compared to many business simulation games the two games are rather short and can be played in about three hours.

The Fishing Game (Molleindustria 2013) is a free license round based game that addresses the problem of overusing common resources (problem of the common). Four teams are playing against each other harvesting and selling fish from the same lake. At the beginning of the game every team can use a rod that catches one fish. Continuing the game teams can also invest in boats to catch more fish and eventually make more money with selling more fish. After each round of fishing the lake is regenerated by one for three remaining fish. After a couple of rounds players become aware of overfishing. This problem can only be solved by all four teams cooperating. If only one or two teams start a sustainable strategy the lake can still be overfished by the other teams that might even profit from the reserved strategy of teams looking for sustainability. The three pillars of sustainability are represented in the game: Players want to sell fish and make money (economy/growth). Players have to nourish the population by providing enough fish (society) and they have to take care for a balanced number of fish in the pond (ecology).

In Fountains (Männamaa 2015; Männamaa & Leijen 2015) teams operate in a desert and represent different tribes. Each tribe cares about its horses, for which they seek watering places at the country's wells. For this task, the tribes have several rounds to negotiate, coordinate or fight with each other. The winner of the game is the tribe that has found the best arrangement for its horses, thus scoring the most points in the end. The game is designed rather abstract and can be applied to various topics (Bundeszentrale für politische Bildung 2021). One main insight students can win from the game is that useless attacks and competition leads to a waste of resources that can be used more effective by cooperating with other tribes (Männamaa & Leijen 2015, p. 103). In the last years both games were used at the ZMS to enable business students with awareness for sustainability.

Against this background this research addresses two main questions regarding simulation games on sustainability using The Fishing Game and Fountains as examples:

RQ1: How well are games on sustainability accepted by students at the ZMS?

RQ2: What structural differences can be seen in gameplay process compared to business simulation games?

3 Method and Design

Basis for this study is a questionnaire for the evaluation of simulation game-based teaching that was developed at the Centre for Management Simulation. This inventory for the evaluation of simulation game-based teaching combines inventories for lectures in general with the specific circumstances of simulation games. It is oriented on the influencing factors described by Rindermann (Student, lecturer, framework conditions) (2009, p. 66) and adds the simulation game and the teamwork as relevant factors for simulation game-based teaching. All aspects together contribute to learning and satisfaction in simulation-based lectures (Trautwein & Alf 2022).

The ZMS questionnaire consists of 27 Likert scaled items (and other non-Likert-scaled items, that are not used for this research). These items can be combined to 7 scales. Two scales are addressing aspects of the simulation game: How well the game is understood by students (Comprehension) and how well the simulation represents the real world (Practical Orientation). For both scales data used in this research show acceptable values for Cronbach's alpha of .795 and .860 (Table 1). A scale of five items measures the Facilitation and the Communication between students and lecturer (Facilitation, Instructor and Communication). It shows an alpha value of .873. Again, two scales refer to aspects of Teamwork. Atmosphere combines items that tell how "easy" or "well" the team-collaboration is (alpha .799). Task orientation gives insight into the distribution of tasks within the team with a Cronbach's alpha of .810. The Engagement scale shows how intensive students are engaged in the gameplay and learning process. It shows an alpha of .686 for all three items and an alpha of .794 calculating only with the items S2 and S3. S1 that asks for the engagement in the plenum discussion reduces the alpha value of the scale. This is very comprehensible since the possibility of active participation in the plenum is reduced by the fact that more students are participating. It could give the scale a broader view on student engagement but is not interpreted since the alpha value drops under 0.7. So, the student engagement in this research is calculated only by S2 and S3 whereas S1 is still be used as a single item. In the logic of the model the scale for Learning and Satisfaction can be described as the dependent variable because it stands for the goal of simulation game-based teaching. It is represented by three items referring to learning and three items referring more to general satisfaction with an alpha value of .930.

Using the described instrument business simulation games and simulation games on sustainability can be compared with each other. With the single item Interest at beginning (I) and the scale for Learning and Satisfaction (LS) RQ1 can be addressed. Using the other scales RQ2 can be addressed. Differences in gameplay process between business simulations and simulations on sustainability might be seen.

The data used in this research was gathered with the described ZMS inventory between February 2021 and December 2021 in simulation-based seminars at the ZMS in

Table 1. Overview: Items and Scales

	Item	Scale	alpha
I	My interest at the beginning of the simulation game was…		
SG1	The results of the simulation are very comprehensible	Simulation Game Comprehension	.795
SG2	The results of the simulation are plausible		
SG3	I understood how the simulation works		
SG4	The simulation has a close practical orientation	Simulation Game Practical Orientation	.860
SG5	The simulation game is a good representation of reality		
F1	The instructor is very familiar with the simulation	Facilitation, Instructor and Commumication	.873
F2	The seminar was well structured		
F3	There was sufficient opportunity to consult with the instructor		
F4	Consultation with the instructor took place in a constructive atmosphere		
F5	Support of the instructor was professionally helpful		
T1	We found it easy to come to decisions as a group	Teamwork Atmosphere	.799
T2	The timing in the group worked well		
T3	The atmosphere in the group was good		
T4	I would say that our team was well organized		
T5	Everybody in the group had a function	Teamwork Task orientation	.810
T6	There was a clear distribution of tasks in the group		
T7	I knew what my tasks were		
S1	I actively participated in the evaluation phases (joint discussion of the game results in the plenum)		
S2	I actively participated in the decision-making phases (work in small groups)	Student Engagement	.794

(continued)

Stuttgart, Germany. All seminars were taught at the DHBW Stuttgart Business Faculty and are part of the mandatory curriculum for business students on bachelor's level. As

Table 1. (*continued*)

	Item	Scale	alpha
S3	When others look at my role, they would count me as one of the more active participants		
LS1	I learned a lot in the simulation game	Learning and Satisfaction	.930
LS2	I learned something meaningful and important in this seminar		
LS3	My understanding of my field of study has been enhanced by the seminar		
LS4	All in all, attending the seminar was worth it for me		
LS5	I found the simulation game very motivating		
LS6	How satisfied are you with the seminar overall?		

it is common at the ZMS all seminars were held as block courses. The data used in this research was gathered in 58 seminars using nine different simulation games, of which two are Fountains and the Fishing-Game. One seminar out of 58 seminars used Fountains (n = 27) and in five seminars The Fishing Game (n = 98) was used (together n = 125). In the other 52 seminars (n = 976) seven different business simulation games were used, that are regularly applied at the ZMS (DHBW Stuttgart): BTI Factory, BTI Global Strategy, BTI Store Manager, coludo-Industry, Riva SysTeamsChange, TOPSIM Easy Management and TOPSIM General Management. These simulation games address various management topics like accounting, change-management and organization, logistics, financing, international business and more.

Even though the evaluation data used in this research is not normally distributed (but mainly right skewed) t-tests are calculated for test statistics, due to the fact that the number of samples is clearly over n = 30 and robust results can be expected (Bortz & Schuster 2010, p. 122; Kubinger, Rasch, & Moder 2009; Rasch, Teuscher & Guiard 2007). The sample size of groups compared in this research is very unequal. The business simulation group consists of n = 976 and the sustainability simulation group consists of n = 125. Due to such unequal samples the statistical power might be questioned. Therefore, using G*Power version 3.1.9.7. an A priori power analysis for "Difference between two independent means (two groups)" was calculated to find appropriate sample sizes (Universität Düsseldorf 2022). G*Power can be used to calculate required sample sizes for acceptable statistical power for various tests (Mayr, Erdfelder, Buchner, & Faul 2007, p. 52). Assuming an effect size of at least d = 0.35, accepting an alpha error probability of 0.05, a 1-beta error probability of 0.95 and estimating that one group is 8 times as big as the other G*Power suggests having at least n = 120 and n = 956 in the compared groups. Since sample sizes used in this research fit the required sample sizes t-tests can be calculated and trustworthy results can be expected if the effect size d is at least 0.35. In case of unequal variances in the groups the Welch's Test (Johnson 2017, p. 93) is reported, as automatically calculated by SPSS 27.

4 Results and Findings

4.1 RQ1: How Well Are Games on Sustainability Accepted by Students at the ZMS?

The single item "interest at beginning" and the scale "Satisfaction and Learning" can be used to answer RQ1. Regarding the interest at the beginning of a simulation-based seminar we see a slightly higher interest for simulations on sustainability. This should not be overinterpreted for various reasons. The difference is not significant (Table 2), and the effect size (d = .175) is very low. Other reasons might also play a role for the slight difference. Compared to business-simulations the simulations on sustainability are rather short. Maybe students are in the beginning more motivated to participate in shorter simulations than in longer simulations lasting two or three days. Looking at the Satisfaction and Learning scale almost no difference can be seen between the two groups. Simulations on sustainability as well as business simulations games are rated with a mean of 4.5 rather good on a scale from one to six (1 = strongly disagree, 6 = strongly agree for all items). Comparing the interest at the beginning and the overall Satisfaction and Learning an improvement of 0.7 for business simulations and an improvement of 0.5 for sustainability simulations can be seen. For both groups the general assessment regarding Learning and Satisfaction is better than the expectation at the beginning of the seminar. To answer RQ1 we can say that games on sustainability (as well as business simulations) are well accepted by students at the DHBW Stuttgart, especially looking at Learning and Satisfaction. We do not see significant differences in the student's appraisal of business simulation games and simulations on sustainability.

4.2 RQ2: What Structural Differences Can Be Seen in Gameplay Process Compared to Business Simulation Games?

The ZMS inventory grants insight into various aspects of gameplay processes (e.g., teamwork, communication between students and facilitator, comprehension of the game). Comparing simulation games on sustainability and business simulation games structural differences might be seen.

Looking at the scales for the simulation we find a highly significant result for the comprehensibility and a non-significant result for the practical orientation of the simulations. The comprehensibility of business games and games on sustainability is rated with a mean difference of .266 (Table 2) while the practical orientation is rated with a difference of only .014. With a small effect (d = .334) we find that games on sustainability are understood better by students at the ZMS. Most probably this result is not a structural difference between business simulations and sustainability simulations but due to the fact that sustainability simulation games represented in this research are rather short games compared to business games, of which some last very long and are accordingly

Table 2. Mean Differences and t-tests for Business and Sustainability Simulation Games

Group Statistics		N	Mean	Std. Deviation	t	Mean Difference	Sig. (2-tailed)	cohen's d
						t-test for Equality of Means		
Interest at Beginning	Sustainability	124	4,05	1,361	1,837	0,25	0,067	.175
	Business	974	3,80	1,407				
Simulation - Comprehensability	Sustainability	125	5,26	0,703	3,516	0,27	0,000	.334
	Business	976	5,00	0,808				
Simulation - Practical Relevance	Sustainability	125	4,45	1,029	0,141	0,01	0,888	.013
	Business	976	4,44	1,048				
Facilitator - Competence and Communication	Sustainability	125	5,43	0,713	1,186	0,09	0,236	.113
	Business	975	5,33	0,815				
Team - Task Orientation	Sustainability	125	4,22	1,210	−2,890	-0,33	0,004	.275
	Business	969	4,55	1,213				
Team - Atmosphere	Sustainability	125	4,82	0,894	−4,875*	−0,41	0,000	.338
	Business	971	5,22	0,735				
Student Engagement Team	Sustainability	125	4,99	1,079	−0,669	−0,07	0,504	.064
	Business	970	5,06	1,019				
Student Engagement Plenary	Sustainability	125	4,61	1,301	6,383*	0,81	0,000	.532
	Business	969	3,80	1,542				
Satisfaction and Learning	Sustainability	125	4,52	1,018	−0,738	−0,07	0,461	.070
	Business	968	4,59	1,063				

* Welch-Test for unequality of variances

more complex. This result should be interpreted with slight caution, because Cohen's d is a little bit under .35 for which value trustful results can be expected due to statistical power analysis. The items for practical relevance of the simulation measure whether the simulation has a practical relevance and does represent reality well. Business and management topics like cost accounting or product development can be assumed as more concrete and practical than the more abstract topic of sustainability. From this point of view the two considered simulations on sustainability seem to address their topics well and being able to make it relevant for business students.

For the Facilitation-scale (Table 2) very high values of 5.43 (sustainability) and 5.33 (business) are found. With 0.1 no significant mean difference between the two groups can be seen. The slight difference is most probably due to coincidence. To find no differences regarding questions on facilitation is not surprising. The items building the facilitation scale refer to communication, consulting during the gameplay and how well the facilitator knows the game. Structural differences between games on sustainability and business regarding facilitation would be surprising. First, many lecturers use both types of games and facilitate both in the same quality. Second, a significant difference would mean that one type of game was structurally facilitated by better facilitators than others, which is very unlikely. The results for both types of games (5.3 and 5.4 on a scale from one to six) show a good quality of facilitation for various simulation games at the ZMS.

For both team scales (task orientation and atmosphere) highly significant results are found. Task orientation in business games is by 0.333 points higher than in simulations on sustainability with a small effect of $d = .275$. As mentioned before many business simulation games used at the ZMS last longer than the simulations on sustainability. Some require complex calculation and the division of teams in specialized areas during the game (e.g. TOPSIM – Business Simulations | Learn by Doing 2021), whereas in both games on sustainability teams always work together on their decisions. So, the difference in task orientation becomes very plausible. It might not be a structural difference between games on sustainability and on business simulations but rather a difference between simulation games with or without a specialization on subtopics by team members. Interestingly the atmosphere in business simulations is by 0.407 points better than in games on sustainability, showing a higher but still small effect of $d = .338$. In all business simulations considered in this research teams work together to achieve successful game-results. The better their commonly taken decisions are the better results they achieve. Both considered games on sustainability work with gameplay mechanics that represent "collective action problems" (Fennewald & Kievit-Kylar 2013, p. 435). This means that reasonable in-team decisions do not automatically lead to success, but teams are very dependent to decisions of other teams. One team cannot be successful, but inter-team collaboration (collective action) is required to deal with a problem that affects everyone. Usually, teams become aware of that mechanism during gameplay and start to negotiate within their teams and with other teams, which can be a frustrating process. So, it becomes plausible to see a lower value for team atmosphere in simulation games on sustainability. This difference might be seen as a typical and structural difference for simulations on sustainability, since simulation games addressing sustainability often work with similar game mechanisms (Eisensack & Petschel-Held 2022; Fennewald & Kievit-Kylar 2013; Männamaa & Leijen 2015). Both results on team scales seem to be plausible but should be interpreted with slight caution since Cohen´s d is lower than .35, which is the value for full statistical power for the number of samples included in this study.

Looking at the student engagement we can analyze two different measures: The Student Engagement scale that measures mainly the engagement during teamwork and a single item that refers to engagement during discussions in plenary. First of all, we can state that the engagement in plenary is lower than engagement during teamwork (Table 2). This is very plausible since plenary discussions are usually led by the facilitator and involves more participants than work in small groups, so the possibility of active participation is reduced. On the Student Engagement scale (measuring engagement during teamwork) no significant differences between business games and games on sustainability are found. For both types of games the engagement is high with means of 4.99 and 5.06. Comparing business games and games on sustainability with regard to engagement in plenary discussion the greatest difference found in this study can be reported. In games on sustainability students are with a mean difference of 0.807 and a medium effect size ($d = .532$) highly significant more engaged during plenary discussion than in business games. We might see here a similar effect as already described above when the Team Atmosphere scale was analyzed. Since games on sustainability use collective action problems as game mechanics inter-team collaboration is necessary to play the game successfully. This requires greater participation in plenary from students. In typical round based business simulation games students reflect the results of their own team in plenary and collect ideas to improve in the next rounds. In games on sustainability the plenary is not only a place for reflection, but a necessary forum for inter-team collaboration to resolve the collective action problem. Once students have discovered the common action problem, the plenary becomes the most important forum for gameplay and requires activity and communication between the teams. It can be noted that a higher activity during plenary discussion might be a typical effect of simulations on sustainability because they very often represent sustainability as a goal that can only be achieved by inter-team collaboration.

5   Summary and Discussion

This research discusses the acceptance of simulation games on sustainability among business students as well as structural differences between business simulation games and games on sustainability. As an empirical database we used 58 simulation-game based seminars that were evaluated with the ZMS inventory. In six seminars simulation games on sustainability were used and in 52 seminars business simulation games were played. With RQ1 we addressed the question how well games on sustainability are accepted by business students at the ZMS. No significant differences were found for satisfaction between the two types of games. All games are accepted well, especially in comparison with student's interest at the beginning. With RQ2 we researched structural differences between business games and games on sustainability comparing means on various scales and items included in the ZMS inventory. Structural differences were especially found for the two team scales and student engagement in plenary. Whereas the difference in Team Task Orientation can be attributed to a higher demand of differentiation in teamwork for (longer) business simulation games the significant differences for Team Atmosphere and Student Engagement in plenary discussion may be rooted in the same ground: simulations on sustainability very often work with common action problems. Therefore, the game success lies not only in a team's hand but in common actions between teams that lead to overall success. This may disturb team atmosphere and lead to a deliberate level of frustration because one team's success can easily be violated by other teams. The same mechanic requires a higher participation and engagement of students in the plenary discussion. The plenary becomes the forum for inter-team discussion to solve the common action problem. Whereas the plenum in business simulations is often seen as a place for debriefing (actual as a place to interrupt the gameplay for reflection) the plenum becomes an essential forum for the gameplay in sustainability simulations. This can be noted as a critical difference between business simulations and simulations on sustainability.

Results found in this study were sometimes highly significant but looking at the mean differences and on the effect sizes (Cohen's d) rather small or medium. To find only small differences was expectable because the objects of differentiation have a lot in common. Simulation games were compared with simulation games differentiating only in the topics the games address. In addition, the evaluation tool used to measure the differences was not theoretically designed to find differences between these two types of simulation games, but as a general inventory for simulation games. The small differences found are still remarkable, because they describe typical characteristics for business simulation games and for sustainability simulations: competition on the one hand and the need for collaboration on the other hand.

The ZMS inventory is a relatively young instrument introduced at the ZMS in Stuttgart, Germany. Apart from analysis regarding its reliability and validity this is the first published data gathered with the inventory. The results of this research can also be considered as an indicator for an acceptable content validity of the instrument. As described, it is able to visible meaningful differences between two types of simulation games.

6   Limitations

All data used in this research was gathered among business students at the DHBW in Stuttgart. Further research should evaluate whether these results on simulation games on sustainability can be confirmed with other target groups. It might be criticized that some effect sizes reported and discussed in this study are under d = .35 which was the limit for solid statistical power as described in the chapter Method and Design. Up to now not more than the reported seminars on sustainability simulations were evaluated with the ZMS inventory. Future evaluations are planned, and greater number of data sets will allow trustful results for even smaller effect sizes than d = .35. With further data it will also be possible to compare different simulation games for sustainability with each other on a quantitative basis.

As described before both simulation games use game mechanics that make it necessary for students to start inter-team collaboration. Future research might evaluate games on sustainability using different game mechanics to see whether the results found in this study are confirmed or contrasted. In addition it would be possible to take only business management games which roughly take the same time, to eliminate the length of the simulation game as a disruptive factor. With a mean of 4,52 for Learning and Satisfaction on a 6 point Likert scale the students clearly see positive learning effects. Due to the fact that sustainability is not a core topic for business students that is a very positive result. Due to the fact that the inventory is used on a large scale and has to be very short, there are no specific questions referring to sustainability games in detail. Further research should therefore extend the standard questionnaire with quantitative as well as qualitative instruments measuring specific aspects of sustainability games. This would allow a closer look on what business and other students learn from sustainability games and whether they have the potential to change future behaviour for the sake of nature and people.

References

Bortz, J., Schuster, C.: Statistik für Human- und Sozialwissenschaftler. Springer, Berlin. Heidelberg (2010). https://doi.org/10.1007/978-3-642-12770-0

Brandt, J.-O.: A Matter of Connection: Competence Development in Teacher Education for Sustainable Development (Dissertation). Leuphana University Lüneburg, Lüneburg (2021). https://pub-data.leuphana.de/frontdoor/index/index/docId/1145

Bundeszentrale für politische Bildung: Fountains. Bundeszentrale Für Politische Bildung (2021). https://www.bpb.de/lernen/angebote/planspiele/datenbank-planspiele/502804/fountains/

DHBW Stuttgart. The Centre for Management Simulation (ZMS). https://zms.dhbw-stuttgart.de/en/the-zms/

DHBW Stuttgart. Our Simulation Games. https://zms.dhbw-stuttgart.de/en/the-zms/our-simulation-games/

Eisensack, K., Petschel-Held, G.: KEEP COOL – Gambling with the Climate (2022). https://www.climate-game.net/en/

Fennewald, T.J., Kievit-Kylar, B.: Integrating climate change mechanics into a common pool resource game. Simul. Gaming 44(2–3), 427–451 (2013). https://doi.org/10.1177/1046878112467618

Fisher, J., Bonn, I.: Business sustainability and undergraduate management education: an Australian study. High. Educ. 62(5), 563–571 (2011). https://doi.org/10.1007/s10734-010-9405-8

Johnson, D.L.: Statistical Tools for the Comprehensive Practice of Industrial Hygiene and Environmental Health Sciences, 1st edn. Wiley, Hoboken, NJ (2017)

Kubinger, K.D., Rasch, D., Moder, K.: Zur Legende der Voraussetzungen des t -Tests für unabhängige Stichproben. Psychol. Rundsch. 60(1), 26–27 (2009). https://doi.org/10.1026/0033-3042.60.1.26

Männamaa, I.: FOUNTAINS. Simul. Gaming 46(1), 113–126 (2015). https://doi.org/10.1177/1046878115591248

Männamaa, I., Leijen, Ä.: The simulated acculturation model in the FOUNTAINS-Game. Simul. Gaming 46(1), 98–112 (2015). https://doi.org/10.1177/1046878115591393

Mayer, B.W., Dale, K.M., Fraccastoro, K.A., Moss, G.: Improving transfer of learning: relationship to methods of using business simulation. Simul. Gaming 42(1), 64–84 (2011). https://doi.org/10.1177/1046878110376795

Mayr, S., Erdfelder, E., Buchner, A., Faul, F.: A short tutorial of GPower. Tutor. Quant. Meth. Psychol. 3(2), 51–59 (2007). https://www.psychologie.hhu.de/fileadmin/redaktion/Fakultaeten/Mathematisch-Naturwissenschaftliche_Fakultaet/Psychologie/AAP/gpower/GPower ShortTutorial.pdf

Meadows, D.H., Meadows, D.L., Jorgen, R., Behrens, W.W.: The Limits to Growth: A Reporte for the Club of Rome's Project on the Predicament of Mankind. Universe Books, New York (1972)

Molleindustria. The Fishing Game – Molleindustria (2013). https://www.molleindustria.org/blog/fishing-game/

Purvis, B., Mao, Y., Robinson, D.: Three pillars of sustainability: in search of conceptual origins. Sustain. Sci. 14(3), 681–695 (2019). https://doi.org/10.1007/s11625-018-0627-5

Rasch, D., Teuscher, F., Guiard, V.: How robust are tests for two independent samples? J. Statist. Plan. Infer. 137(8), 2706–2720 (2007). https://doi.org/10.1016/j.jspi.2006.04.011

Rindermann, H.: Lehrevaluation: Einführung und Überblick zu Forschung und Praxis der Lehrveranstaltungsevaluation an Hochschulen mit einem Beitrag zur Evaluation computerbasierten Unterrichts (2., leicht korrigierte Auflage). Psychologie: vol. 42. Landau: Verlag Empirische Pädagogik (2009)

Sonetti, G., Brown, M., Naboni, E.: About the triggering of UN sustainable development goals and regenerative sustainability in higher education. Sustainability 11(1) (2019). https://doi.org/10.3390/su11010254

Squires, G.: Sustainable Urban Development – Connecting Urban and Environmental Economics – Professor Graham Squires. https://www.grahamsquires.com/economics-and-sustainable-urban-development/

Thwink.org: The Three Pillars of Sustainability (2020). https://www.thwink.org/sustain/glossary/ThreePillarsOfSustainability.htm

TOPSIM – Business Simulations | Learn by Doing. Business Simulations & Experiential Learning | TOPSIM (2021). https://www.topsim.com/en/education-solutions#portfolio

Trautwein, F., Alf, T.: Theoriebasierte Entwicklung eines Inventars zur Evaluation von Planspielveranstaltungen. In: Tobias, A., et al. (eds.) Planspiele – Erkenntnisse aus Praxis und Forschung. Books on Demand, Norderstedt (in press)

UN: Report of the world commission on environment and development: our common future (1987)

UN: Transforming our world: the 2030 Agenda for Sustainable Development. New York (2015)

Universität Düsseldorf: G*Power: Statistical Power Analyses for Mac and Windows (2022). https://www.psychologie.hhu.de/arbeitsgruppen/allgemeine-psychologie-und-arbeitspsychologie/gpower

Zensimu SAS: The Beer Game App - Supply-chain Serious Games for Continuous Improvement (2022). https://beergameapp.com/

Stop Work: Serious Games as Intervention Method to Enhance Safety Behavior

Maria Freese[1,2,4(✉)] [iD] and Karen van Vliet[3]

[1] Faculty of Technology, Policy and Management, Delft University of Technology, Jaffalaan 5, 2628 BX Delft, The Netherlands
[2] Raccoon Serious Games, Schieweg 15D unit Z25, 2627 AN Delft, The Netherlands
[3] Quattor P, Binckhorstlaan 36 unit C3.69, 2516 BE Den Haag, The Netherlands
[4] Faculty of Mechanical Engineering, Otto von Guericke University, Universitaetsplatz 2, 39106 Magdeburg, Germany
maria.freese@ovgu.de

Abstract. Organizations will go through great lengths to prevent accidents from occurring. This is shown in the implementation of safety management systems in which all procedures are captured describing how work can be done safely. Stopping the work is seen as one of the last barriers in risk management. Our theoretical analyses and conducted interviews have shown that no interactive, innovative and analogue tools exist that effectively enable the use of the Stop Work Policy in a safe space. Serious games and the associated provision of a safe environment make it possible to let personnel speak up about perceived unsafe situations, as there are no consequences to fear. The present paper describes and discusses the development of the two serious games Dare to Repair and Danger Dialogue that aim to support the implementation of the Stop Work Policy effectively and thus enhancing the dialogue on working safely.

Keywords: Human Errors · Intervention · Learning · Safety · Serious Games · Stop Work Policy

1 Introduction

According to the National Institute for Public Health and the Environment [1], 230.000 of the 7 million employees in the Netherlands have an accident every year. This means 600 injured people per day who can no longer work - temporarily or for life. Organizations, such as companies within high-risk industries in the maritime sector, will go through great lengths to prevent accidents from occurring. This is shown, amongst others, in the implementation of safety management systems in which all procedures are captured describing how work can be done safely. Furthermore, organizations will most often have implemented a risk management system - whether or not as part of the safety management system - which guides the organization in identifying, assessing, and mitigating the risks related to the operations. However, not all hazards can always be foreseen and therefore organizations working in high-risk environments have implemented a so-called 'Stop Work Policy' for which all personnel have the mandate to stop the work in case of an unsafe situation.

C. Harteveld et al. (Eds.): ISAGA 2022, LNCS 13622, pp. 134–148, 2023.
https://doi.org/10.1007/978-3-031-37171-4_9

Stopping the work is seen as one of the last barriers in risk management. Workers are trusted to judge the situation and be able to identify whether a situation is deemed safe or unsafe, and to act accordingly. Hazardous situations should be resolved prior to continuing the job. To recognize the stopping of work as a last defense, it can therefore be considered an important factor in safe working environments. The right to stop work in case of hazardous situations by employees is often part of the law (for example; Article 29 in the Dutch Working Conditions Act). However, implementing a Stop Work Policy as such is not required by law, but is today more or less common knowledge within high-risk organizations [2].

Supporting the implementation of the Stop Work Policy effectively and thus enhancing the dialogue on working safely, is one of the goals of the Safety Deal project. To practice the application of a Stop Work Policy in a safe environment, two innovative and interactive serious games, Dare to Repair and Danger Dialogue, have been developed that motivate personnel in high-risk environments to speak out and to communicate risks. The present paper focuses on the design and development phase of both games as intervention methods to strengthen safety behavior.

2 Safety-Related Concepts

In the following, concepts in the field of safety that are relevant to the understanding of this publication are further elaborated.

2.1 Safety Knowledge and Skills

Knowledge on what is safe and what is unsafe is rather important as this is necessary to make a judgement and stop the work. Effective safety training improves knowledge and helps to make accidents more predictable [3]. Lack of training is a contributing factor to high incident rates [4]. Employees new to the job or organization should obtain sufficient training to learn about the risks associated with the work, as otherwise they would not be able to stop the work as they do not recognize the risks [5].

Not only knowledge and training of individuals is important, however, also the perceived knowledge of others is of importance to increase safety. The 'Perceived Colleagues Safety Knowledge / Behavior' (PCSK/B) is positively related to safety compliance and safety participation [6]. If employees perceive that their colleagues have knowledge and skills, and do act accordingly, they will do so as well.

Safety performance is influenced by safety culture [4], meaning that safety culture is an important aspect in the prediction of accidents [7]. This is also shown in relation with the PCSK/B. With a lower safety climate, the effects of PCSK/B were found weaker - meaning that with a higher safety climate, employees will follow and copy their colleagues' behavior regarding safety [6]. In addition, the safety culture within an organization is of importance, as this reflects the willingness to reflect on the situation.

2.2 Safety Culture

There is no consensus on the definition of safety culture. Safety culture and safety climate are often used interchangeably. See Guldenmund [8] for an elaborate review on the distinction made and definitions used. Safety culture often involves the attitudes [9–11]), beliefs as well as perceptions [9, 12–14], and values [9, 15] that employees share in relation to safety. It is the frame of reference through which interaction, symbols and behavior are interpreted [16], and is dynamic and constantly and continuously adjusted and (re)created [17]. Once new in the group, one will be taught all norms and values [18] by socialization, meaning that individuals learn from others or the group [19]. According to Pidgeon [10], a good safety culture is characterized by three attributes: (1) Norms and rules for handling hazards, (2) attitudes towards safety, and (3) reflexivity on safety practice.

Culture is the frame of reference for people to rely on to act. They do so as they have limited capacity to process information, and base thereupon what information they can ignore, or should, creating certain blind spots [16]. Furthermore, the frames of reference, through which information is interpreted, influence whether hazards are seen, judged, or overlooked, but also how they are evaluated [20]. Training adds to knowledge about safety [21], and to discuss safety issues [4]. The Stop Work Policy being the last safety barrier for incidents to happen, is therefore only to be found effective as this is part of the norms of the safety culture.

2.3 Stop Work Policy

Due to its nature, it is difficult to implement a Stop Work Policy effectively. Weber et al. [2] conducted research towards the hampering factors in implementing a Stop Work Policy. They found that the decision to stop the work is influenced by procedural, social, technical and non-technical / personal aspects. Furthermore, it is stated that though the Stop Work Policy is a behavioral approach, it is limited for that matter as it leaves out the context the person is in. Havinga et al. [22] have further pursued the research of Weber et al. [2] and draw different conclusions as it was seen in their research that the decision to stop the work was made all the time, and workers found stopping the work a suitable way for them to completing their work, instead of linking this to safety reasons. Therefore, they conclude that it should be more useful for organizations to focus on alternative methods to complete a job instead of focusing on training to support workers in stopping the job for safety reasons. It should be noted that the conclusions refer to research conducted by one organization.

Although having a Stop Work Policy is common in high-risk industries, it is not easy to implement it well and to ensure that all employees are indeed making use of this policy and stop the work when deemed necessary. Some state that Stop Work Policy programs empower the employees to be more pro-active, and that workers are expected to speak up in an unsafe situation [23]. Workers are to be encouraged to speak up without fear of retribution [24]. Weber et al. [2] refer to Johnson [25] who stated that Stop Work policies are mostly built upon unrealistic assumptions such as that people will always stop work when an unsafe situation occurs, that all warning signs are clearly visible, that safety can always be the first priority and stopping colleagues is always possible.

Though not supported by the findings of Havinga et al. [22], van Vliet [5] did find various factors that were hampering the use of the Stop Work Policy within different organizations. These findings, together with the findings of Weber et al. (2018), show that Stop Work Policies cannot be taken 'for granted', and require much more attention in implementation that is currently done.

3   Intervention Tools

According to Wilkins [26, p. 1017], "[...] *it is apparent that non-compliance with safety procedures and inadequately delivered training are among the key factors resulting in such a high rate of injury and fatality in this sector* [construction industry]." In addition, Tezel et al. [27] summarized success factors for safety training and concluded that, among other factors, the absence of training can affect safety practices in organizations and thus, represents a critical factor.

3.1   State of the Art

According to Burke et al. [28], there are different traditional tools for safety training which can be distinguished from each other based on their level of engagement, such as toolbox talks (low level of engagement) or hands-on training (high level of engagement).

Dyreborg et al. [29] have conducted a review towards the effectiveness of various behavior change safety interventions and have found that the effectiveness is still rather unclear. Mullan et al. [30] have found similar results, as for the studies reviewed, the methodologies lacked a scientific foundation - meaning that control groups were missing, or the conditions of test groups were not equal - resulting in it being difficult to draw the conclusion that the interventions had a positive effect.

In the Netherlands, research has been conducted by van Kampen et al. [31] on the safety interventions safety professionals most often use to train workers in their organization, and which interventions were considered most useful. Their results show that mainly very traditional tools are used, such as general risk inventory and assessments, reporting and investigating (near) misses, and emergency preparedness exercises.

Gao et al. [32] have performed a literature review and conclude that traditional tools about the safety domain ignore the real on-site physical environments, fail to take care of workers who have low English proficiency and low literacy, fail in attracting trainees' attention and are less engaging, are limited in developing workers' spatial awareness ability, and have an unsatisfied knowledge retention.

To conclude, traditional intervention tools are not sufficient enough to provide effective and efficient training in order to initiate a change in behavior. Thus, a different type of intervention is needed to enhance safety knowledge and skills of operational personnel in high-risk environments. This is supported by Zuidema et al. [33] who concluded that the development of and implementation of behavioral training is a must-have.

3.2   Use of Serious Games as Intervention Methods in Safety Domains

Having people change their behavior on this rather complex phenomenon and to get the Stop Work Policy implemented effectively, a traditional tool would not be deemed effective. It is important that people have the appropriate knowledge to react in the best possible way to the demands of a potentially dangerous situation, but it is also about the reaction itself, i.e., the behavior of the people. In addition, other contextual factors [2], but also socio-economic aspects [34, 35], play a role that make the phenomenon of a Stop Work Policy a complex system.

Serious games are a suitable method for presenting these complex phenomena in a more simplified version and thus, making it possible for people to experience them and (interactively) participate in a safe environment [36]. Regarding the safety domain and according to Gao et al. [32], serious games are seen as a suitable and promising tool for training. With regard to safety in general, a number of serious games exist [see 37–38 for an overview of examples]. In the area of construction safety, Kazar and Comu [38] conducted a study with students and tested different safety trainings. Their results show that the participants who received safety training based on a serious game significantly improved their knowledge of occupational safety compared to participants who received traditional training. This was not influenced by the participants' game experience. Furthermore, their results (p. 04021091–1) "[…] *show that serious game-based training provides effective training that ensures the maintenance of safety knowledge acquired over time.*" Also, Martínez et al. [37] see serious games as an adequate alternative to traditional training formats, as during a serious gaming session the participants can make experiences that they most likely could not make in real life due to safety-critical, financial aspects and time.

Weber et al. [2] found that training is a factor that supports stopping work and recommend offering training to train less experiences employees in particular. Training is not described further at this point. To the best of the authors' knowledge and based on the discussed literature, (longer-term) interventions that address the Stop Work Policy and make it possible to physically interact with the subject and colleagues without fearing any consequences are not present. Based on the theoretical background information discussed in this publication, it became visible that an innovative and interactive tool is needed with the aim to address and discuss the use of the Stop Work Policy in a safe space and according to Martínez et al. [37, p. 107], "*serious games provide an opportunity to emphasize safe behaviors in the workplace.*"

In order to develop such an intervention method that makes it possible to let personnel experience the Stop Work Policy in an interactive and safe space, interviews have been conducted with experts to (a) gain more insight in the factors that hamper and motivate stopping the work, and (b) to gain an understanding of the context the game should fit in.

4   Development and Design of an Intervention Method

To get a more thorough understanding of why the Stop Work Policy is such a difficult policy to be implemented effectively, and therefore to know what a proper intervention should do, interviews were held with various managerial and operational personnel in different organizations operating in high-risk environments. In total, 48 people from 7 different companies were interviewed: a steel manufacturer, a logistic services provider, a crew and shipping management company, a yachts builder, a shipyard, a construction company, and an offshore construction company. All companies were based in the Netherlands, except for the crew management company that has offices worldwide and employs international crews with their international clients. Almost all other companies work with multiple nationalities and cultures amongst their operational personnel.

The interviews took place both online and offline – this varied due to location and COVID19 restrictions, and were ranging from 30 min to 1 h. The goal for the interviews with the managerial personnel was to understand how their perspective was on the Stop Work Policy, what their role was in implementing, and whether they saw the same hampering and motivating factors as operational personnel. Amongst the questions asked were 'to what extend do people use the Stop Work Policy according to you?', 'what hampers operational personnel to use the Stop Work Policy?', and 'how do you motivate your employees to use the Stop Work Policy?'. The goal for the interviews with the operational personnel was to understand whether they knew what the Stop Work Policy was, whether them or colleagues have ever stopped the work, and whether they or others have encountered situations in which the work should have been stopped for safety reasons but was not done. A more fundamental analysis can be found in van Vliet [5].

4.1   Target Group and Working Environment

The people designing and implementing the Stop Work Policy in organizations are most often not those that will use them. The difference is in the type of role and the physical work environment. Staff in the 'Quality, Health, Environment and Safety' (QHES) department will design the Stop Work Policy, but those in the line of fire most will be in the need of using it in a hazardous situation. The intervention developed is therefore targeted at operational personnel; those who are in the line of fire, and can be physically injured in case of an accident happening. As high-risk organizations can be very different from each other, the context also varies from company to company, however, workers often work in teams managed by a supervisor in hazardous environments characterized by noise, different materials, machines, and tools. The game should take this into account.

4.2   Conclusions for Intervention Design Based on Interviews

The interviews provided 13 different factors that hamper the effective implementation of a Stop Work Policy. An overview of the most important factors can be found in Table 1.

4.3   Designing the Intervention Method

Duration of the Intervention Method.

The intervention to be developed should consist of several units, as it has already been concluded by Mullan et al. [30] that a single intervention is less successful compared to a longer lasting intervention measure. To support this, the intervention method to be developed consists of one central unit, the main game, followed by so-called refresher moments, the building blocks.

Table 1. Description of relevant factors that hamper stop work.

Factor	Description	To what extent does this factor hamper stop work
Knowledge and risk perception	Stopping work in an unsafe situation, sufficient knowledge about the hazards are necessary to be able to judge the situation Perceiving the situation as safer than it actually is	Not having the right knowledge in order to judge the situation will lead to not stopping the situation Perceiving the situation as safer than it actually is, one will not stop the work
Complacency	Complacency is a type of risk perception in which one has a lack of awareness and a feeling of uncritical satisfaction	Especially when people have experienced a situation many times, their risk perception might change to the task of being of lower risk. This interpretation results in the frequency of stopping the work to decline
Hierarchy (Power distance; Social hierarchy)	Power distance refers to the relationship between higher-ranking and lower ranking individuals [40]. Social hierarchy refers to the relationship between individuals based not on a formal hierarchy but on the unofficial hierarchy, related to e.g. popularity, experience, or length of employment	People new in an organization have shown to have difficulties speaking up to people who are employed for the organization much longer. They might have newer, more complete or updated knowledge than those already working in the organization, the newly employed personnel find it hard to speak as they still need to find their place in the group and do not want to thorn on the legitimacy of others
Time pressure	Time pressure is the perception of people of having too much to do in too little time	Time pressure results in risk perception to change. Where situations might be stopped if there is sufficient time to conduct the activity; they will pursue in case of time pressure

(*continued*)

Table 1. (*continued*)

Factor	Description	To what extent does this factor hamper stop work
Being afraid to use Stop Work / how one has been treated before when using Stop Work	Not willing to stop work in case of an unsafe situation as one is afraid for the reaction of others, either because of a negative reaction that one got in the past, or one is just being afraid for the reactions of others without having a negative experience earlier	Having experienced a negative reaction when stopping the work, one will be less likely to do so again. Also, the feeling of potentially getting a negative reaction might result in people not speaking up

The Most Important Game Mechanic.

The task of the players in the game is focused on finding the right balance between three main elements. First, the players need to ensure that they can do the job safely. Second, they must be able to use Stop Work accordingly. Third, it is the task of the players to solve in-game challenges.

Use of Metaphor.

To take into account, as much as possible, the needs of different companies and to develop the game as generically as possible, it was decided to work with metaphors. A metaphor can help to reduce the complexity of a specific subject and can be beneficial for the relation between game and player(s) [39]. The use of metaphors often has the aim to reduce the complexity (abstract) of the implemented model of reality, which should make it possible to enter the gaming world more quickly.

Analogue Versus Digital.

As we aim to design an interactive and innovative game, we want to develop a physical game which makes this possible. In addition to this, we strongly believe that the idea of speaking up to someone is way easier to realize in a face-to-face situation than in a digital setting. Last but not least, we want to give the players the space to touch and thus, play with the game materials ('look and feel') in order for the game to be appealing for the players.

Number of Players.

Since an exact number of players per session cannot be determined in advance, it is decided to keep both games open for up to 3 to 6 players and make them adjustable according to the number of players.

Theoretical Frame.

According to Mullan et al. [30], it is important to have a theoretical basis for designing an effective intervention that aims to change behavior. The intervention presented in this paper is based on Kirkpatrick's model, which, however, is not the subject of further consideration as part of this publication.

Duration of Game Play.

To make the game still playable for personnel in high-risk environments, it was decided to target a maximum playing time (excluding briefing and debriefing) of 60 min for Dare to Repair and 30 min for Danger Dialogue.

Not all the factors listed in Table 1 have been explicitly implemented in the serious games. Some of them were implicitly incorporated (see Table 2). Based on the requirements described above, the following intervention method has been developed.

Table 2. Factors that hamper stop work and their implementation in the serious games.

Factor	Implemented in	Implicit / explicit	Description
Knowledge and risk perception	Dare to Repair	Explicit	Finding the right balance between risky and safe decisions
	Danger Dialogue	Explicit	Explaining the correct answer from one's perception
Complacency	Danger Dialogue	Implicit	Hearing out other's perceptions, challenging yours
Hierarchy (Power distance; Social hierarchy)	Dare to Repair / Danger Dialogue	Implicit	The game does not work with different in-game roles, but can certainly be played with different people from different hierarchy levels
Time pressure	Dare to Repair	Explicit	The implementation of time pressure plays an important role. The tasks to be solved have to be completed within 45 min
	Danger Dialogue	Explicit	Per round, players have approximately 7 min time to work on their tasks
Being afraid to use Stop Work / how one has been treated before when using Stop Work	Dare to Repair	Implicit → Explicit	In the course of playing Dare to Repair, the implicitly implemented benefits of stopping work are made explicit by taking too many risks

5 Description of Intervention Method

The intervention method presented in this publication consists of two parts: Dare to Repair and Danger Dialogue. Whereas the learning objective of Dare to Repair is mainly to make people more aware of the importance of safety in the workplace and in particular the Stop Work Authority, the idea of Danger Dialogue is to make safety-specific topics discussable.

5.1 Dare to Repair

Goal of the Game.

Dare to Repair is a cooperative board game for 3 to 6 players. The goal of this game is to learn how to use the Stop Work Policy and thus, speak up accordingly. The game was developed by Raccoon Serious Games and Quattor P and is available both in English and Dutch.

Goal in the Game.

The goal in the game is to repair a number of machines in a factory within a given time limit. This can only be achieved by the players playing and discussing together. While repairing these machines, all players face different challenges. The challenges are characterized by the fact that the players need to make decisions related to the trade-off between safety and risks for each machine. Through the conscious decisions made by the players, they experience the advantages of the Stop Work Policy based on the results of their decisions, which may result in a machine being repaired, not being repaired due to an accident, or having the work stopped early. Risk taking, time pressure and budgeting are three central key performance indicators that were implemented in the game, whereas the general idea is to have as few accidents as possible while focusing on costs and time. Each of the decisions made by the players is associated with the key performance indicators. In Fig. 1, the serious Dare to Repair game is depicted.

Fig. 1. Dare to Repair (left side) and Danger Dialogue (right side) game set-up (Quattor P & Raccoon Serious Games, 2022).

Role of the Facilitator.

The game is facilitated by a facilitator. His / her task is to make sure the game runs smoothly, meaning that he / she is responsible for setting up the game, explaining it (briefing), observing the game play carefully, and conducting the debriefing. It is extremely important throughout the course of the game that the facilitator does not actively intervene in the game, but only answers questions that have to do with understanding the game.

Debriefing.

In order to let participants exchange their thoughts, reflect on the game play and make connections with their real working environments, a structured debriefing guideline has been developed. This is based on the 4 E's [41]. The 4 E's, a short description of each of them, and an exemplary debriefing question is shown in Table 3.

Table 3. Overview of some exemplary debriefing questions.

E	Explanation	Example
Emotion	How did you feel?	What are the first three words that come to your mind when you think of 'Dare to Repair'? Why?
Events	What happened?	Are you satisfied with the outcome of the game? Why (not)? What would you do differently?
Everyday life (translation game to reality)	What did you learn?	What elements or experiences from the game do you encounter in day-to-day life at work?
Experiences	How would you translate it to real life?	Has this game brought you any insights?
Every day application (future)	How can this game support you in future day to day life?	Did you learn or experience anything today that might help you to do things differently?

5.2 Danger Dialogue

Goal of the Game.

Danger Dialogue[1] is a card game playable with 3 to 6 players. The goal of the game is to let players discuss the risks that may affect different situations in their workplace.

Goal in the Game.

The game itself consists of several question and risk cards that are played in three different rounds. Each round consists of the following phases: (1) Randomly select a question card that describes a specific scenario, (2) select and explain a risk card that fits the question card, and (3) vote for the risk card that best fits the described scenario. At the end of the game, a fourth round is followed. In this phase, the players look at the chosen combinations of three question cards and risk cards and discuss them on a meta

[1] The illustrations are made by de Visuele Verbinders.

level with the goal to identify the most important one for the corresponding organization and to derive measures. A photo of the game is depicted in Fig. 1. This game can be played several times as new combinations can be drawn at each session, giving new input for discussions.

Role of the Facilitator.

There is no facilitator needed for this game, as this short game is meant to be self-learnable. A player is designated to be a facilitator, but only to make sure each card has sufficient reasoning behind it.

Debriefing.

There is room for discussion during the game. The results of the discussions during playing Danger Dialogue are documented in a book, which can be further used in follow-up sessions.

6 Discussion

The present paper focused on the development of an interactive and innovative intervention method to enhance safety behavior of personnel in high-risk environments. Therefore, a conscious decision was made to make use of serious gaming. Serious games and the associated provision of a safe environment make it possible to let personnel speak up about perceived unsafe situations, as there are no consequences to fear. Interviews with the target group of the intervention method were conducted to consider appropriate requirements of the interventions based not only on theoretical considerations from literature, but also potential end-users (user-centered design approach). The results of the interviews can be read in detail in van Vliet [5]. In summary, several factors resulted that should be considered in the development of the intervention method. In addition, other requirements with the design of the intervention method were defined. The results of all these analyses resulted in the development of Dare to Repair and Danger Dialogue. Dare to Repair - defined as the main game - follows the idea of a one-time intervention which should be used to give personnel the opportunity to speak up about perceived unsafe situations. In addition to Dare to Repair, the aim of Danger Dialogue - defined as a building block - is to function as a regular refresher making it possible to make personnel in high-risk environments more aware of the importance of safety (measures) in their workplace.

The theoretical analyses and conducted interviews have - to the best of the authors' knowledge - shown that no interactive, innovative and analogue tools exist that effectively enable the use of the Stop Work Policy in a safe space. During the playtests and in exchange with the players, it became visible that experiencing a serious game for personnel in these environments can also mean leaving one's own comfort zone. Associated with this, the acceptance of the target group towards serious games plays a major role. For many, this approach of using a game for serious purposes was completely new. On the other hand, it became apparent that some people also saw it as an opportunity to finally be able to talk about safety-related problems in a safe environment.

Furthermore, the interventions developed within the Safety Deal project aim to be used in diverse high-risk environments. As described earlier, the safety culture can also play a role in the experience of such an intervention and its subsequent implementation.

Future research should address this issue and explore the extent to which culture influences the active experience of these interventions. It is particularly interesting to see to what extent the discussion of risk-related topics is experienced in different cultural settings.

7 Outlook

Due to the fact that the Safety Deal Project mainly deals with Dutch organizations, future research activities should look at what forms of training tools are used in other countries. The authors of this publication are strongly convinced that these are similar tools, however, this should be elaborated scientifically.

To answer the research question of whether and to what extent the intervention (playing the serious games Dare to Repair and Danger Dialogue) have an effect on the safety behavior of personnel in high-risk environments, workshops are currently being organized at different organizations in the heavy industry sector (with high-risk environments). Groups of 3 to 5 employees are tested per workshop. In order to measure the effectiveness of the intervention, various conditions were defined: (1) One group that plays 1x Dare to Repair and 4x Danger Dialogue, (2) one group that plays 1x Dare to Repair and 2x Danger Dialogue, and (3) one control group that plays neither Dare to Repair nor Danger Dialogue. Fortunately, the sessions are not only planned in Europe, but also in Asia, which makes it possible to analyze cultural differences as well. In addition, the influence of the attitude towards serious games and a possible influence on the learning success remains a subject for future research.

Acknowledgements. This article was written as part of the research project Safety Deal (Enhancing the dialogue on working safely through serious gaming), which has received funding from RVO (Netherlands Enterprise Agency). The authors are grateful to all involved colleagues from Raccoon Serious Games and Quattor P for the development of these great tools and all related work, to all project partners for giving valuable feedback on the two serious games, and to all participants for taking the time to test the games.

References

1. National Institute for Public Health and the Environment (RIVM): Occupational accidents. https://www.rivm.nl/en/occupational-safety/occupational-accidents#:~:text=In%20the% 20Netherlands%2C%20approximately%207,work%20due%20to%20their%20accident. Accessed 18 Apr 2022
2. Weber, D.E., MacGregor, S.C., Provan, D.J., Rae, A.: We can stop work, but then nothing gets done. Factors that support and hinder a workforce to discontinue work for safety. Safety Sci. **108**, 149–160 (2018). https://doi.org/10.1016/j.ssci.2018.04.032
3. Vinodkumara, M.N., Bhasib, M.: Safety management practices and safety behaviour: assessing the mediating role of safety knowledge and motivation. Accid. Anal. Prev. **42**, 2082–2093 (2010)
4. Guo, H., Li, H., Chan, G., Skitmore, M.: Using game technologies to improve the safety of construction plant operations. Accid. Anal. Prev. **48**, 204–213 (2012)

5. Van Vliet, K.J.A.: It might be the small things that keep people from speaking up, but the consequences can be big. An analysis of Stop Work Authorities and their hampering and supporting factors [White paper]. Quattor P..https://www.quattorp.com/2022/01/05/whitep aper-it-might-be-the-small-things-that-keep-people-from-speaking-up-but-the-consequen ces-can-be-big-an-analysis-of-stop-work-authorities-and-their-hampering-and-supporting-factors/. Accessed 1 8Apr 2022

6. Jiang, L., Yu, G., Li, Y., Li, F.: Perceived colleagues' safety knowledge/behavior and safety performance: safety climate as a moderator in a multilevel study. Accid. Anal. Prev. **42**, 1468–1476 (2010)

7. Aburumman, M., Newnam, S., Fildes, B.: Evaluating the effectiveness of workplace interventions in improving safety culture: a systematic review. Safety Sci. **115**, 376–392 (2019). https://doi.org/10.1016/j.ssci.2019.02.027

8. Guldenmund, F.W.: The nature of safety culture: a review of theory and research. Safety Sci. **34**(1–3), 215–257 (2000). https://doi.org/10.1016/S0925-7535(00)00014-X

9. Cox, S., Cox, T.: The structure of employee attitudes to safety: an European example. Work Stress **5**(2), 93–106 (1991). https://doi.org/10.1080/02678379108257007

10. Pidgeon, N.F.: Safety culture and risk management in organziations. J. Cross-Cult. Psychol. **22**(1), 129–140 (1991)

11. Coyle, I.R., Sleeman, S.D., Adams, N.: Safety climate. J. Safety Res. **26**(4), 247–254 (1995). https://doi.org/10.1016/0022-4375(95)00020-Q

12. Brown, R. L., Holmes, H.: The use of a factor-analytic procedure for assessing the validity of an employee safety climate model. Accid. Anal. Prev. **18**(6), 455–470 (1986). https://doi.org/10.1016/0001-4575(86)90019-9

13. Ostrom, L., Wilhelmsen, C., Kaplan, B.: Assessing safety culture. Nucl. Saf. **34**(2), 163–172 (1993)

14. Cooper, M.D., Philips, R.A.: Validation of a safety climate measure. Presented at the British Psychological Society, Annual Occupational Psychology Conference, Birmingham, United Kingdom, 3–5 January 1994

15. Lee, T.R.: Perceptions, attitudes and behaviour: the vital elements of a safety culture. Health Saf. 1–15 (1996)

16. Antonsen, S.: The relationship between culture and safety on offshore supply vessels. Saf. Sci. **47**(8), 1118–1128 (2009). https://doi.org/10.1016/j.ssci.2008.12.006

17. Schein, E.H.: Organizational Culture and Leadership, (3rd edition). Jossey-Bass, San Francisco (2004)

18. Schein, E.H.: Organizational Culture and Leadership, (2nd Edition). Jossey-Bass, San Francisco (1992)

19. Nordlöf, H., Wiitavaara, B., Winblad, U., Wijk, K., Westerling, R.: Safety culture and reasons for risk-taking at a large steel-manufacturing company: investigating the worker perspective. Saf. Sci. **73**, 126–135 (2015). https://doi.org/10.1016/j.ssci.2014.11.020

20. Turner, B.A., Pidgeon, N.F.: Man-Made Disasters, (2nd edition). Butterworth Heinemann, Oxford (1997)

21. Topf, M.D.: General next? Occup. Hazards **62**, 49–50 (2000)

22. Havinga, J., Bancroft, K., Rae, A.: Deciding to stop work or deciding how work is done? Saf. Sci. **141**, 105334 (2021). https://doi.org/10.1016/j.ssci.2021.105334

23. Maurer, R.: SHRM. https://www.shrm.org/resourcesandtools/hr-topics/risk-management/pages/stopping-unsafe-work.aspx. Accessed 18 Apr 2022

24. Gaddis, S.: OHS Online. https://ohsonline.com/Articles/2019/12/02/Stop-Work-Authority-A-Principled-Based-Approach.aspx. Accessed 18 Apr 2022

25. Johnson, D.: Beyond BP: can you handle a hazmat incident? Indus. Saf. Hyg. News, 40–43 (2010)

26. Wilkins, J.: Construction workers' perceptions of health and safety training programmes. Constr. Manag. Econ. **29**, 1017–1026 (2011). https://doi.org/10.1080/01446193.2011.633538
27. Tezel, A., Dobrucali, E., Demirkesen, S., Kiral, I.A.: Critical success factors for safety training in the construction industry. Buildings **11**, 139 (2021). https://doi.org/10.3390/buildings110 40139
28. Burke, M.J., Sarpy, S.A., Smith-Crowe, K., Chan-Serafin, S., Salvador, R.O., Islam, G.: Relative effectiveness of worker safety and health training methods. Am. J. Publ. Health **96**(2), 315–324 (2006). https://doi.org/10.2105/AJPH.2004.059840
29. Dyreborg, J., et al.: PROTOCOL: safety Interventions for the Prevention of Accidents at Work. Campbell Syst. Rev. **11**(1), 1–70 (2015). https://doi.org/10.1002/CL2.146
30. Mullan, B., Smith, L., Sainsbury, K., Allom, V., Paterson, H., Lopez, A.L.: Active behaviour change safety interventions in the construction industry: a systematic review. Saf. Sci. **79**, 139–148 (2015). https://doi.org/10.1016/j.ssci.2015.06.004
31. Van Kampen, J., Lammers, M., Steijn, W., Guldenmund, F., Groeneweg, J.: The effectiveness of 48 safety interventions according to safety professionals. Chem. Eng. Trans. **77**, 307–312 (2019). https://doi.org/10.3303/CET1977052
32. Gao, Y., González, V.A., Yiu, T.W.: Serious games vs. traditional tools in construction safety training: a review. In: Lean and Computing in Construction Congress (LC3), vol. I - Proceedings of the Joint Conference on Computing in Construction (JC3), Heraklion, Greece, pp. 653–660, 4–7 July 2017
33. Zuidema, V., Bruijnen, C., Vriend, I., van de Laar, K.: Effecten van interventies om gedrag gericht op veiliger werken te beïnvloeden: Ervaringen uit de praktijk. http://docplayer.nl/56296909-Effecten-van-interventies-om-gedrag-gericht-op-veiliger-werken-te-beinvloeden-ervaringen-uit-de-praktijk.html. Accessed 18 Apr 2022
34. Christian, M.S., Bradley, J.C., Wallace, J.C., Burke, M.J.: Workplace safety: a meta-analysis of the roles of person and situation factors. J. Appl. Psychol. **94**(5), 1103–1127 (2009). https://doi.org/10.1037/a0016172
35. Urlings, I., Nijhuis, F.: Determinants of safe behaviour of construction workers. Mag. Soc. Health Care, **66**, 134–138 (1988)
36. Lukosch, H.K., Bekebrede, G., Kurapati, S., Lukosch, S.G.: A scientific foundation of simulation games for the analysis and design of complex systems. Simul. Gaming **49**(3), 279–314 (2018). https://doi.org/10.1177/1046878118768858
37. Martínez-Durá, R.J., Arevalillo-Herráez, M., García-Fernández, I., Gamón-Giménez, M.A., Rodríguez-Cerro, A.: Serious games for health and safety training. In: Ma, M., Oikonomou, A., Jain, L.C. (eds.) Serious Games and Edutainment Applications, pp. 107–124. Springer, London (2011). https://doi.org/10.1007/978-1-4471-2161-9_7
38. Kazar, G., Comu, S.: Effectiveness of serious games for safety training: a mixed method study. J. Construct. Eng. Manag. **147**(8), 04021091 (2021). https://doi.org/10.1061/(ASC E)CO.1943-7862.0002119
39. Allegra, M., et al.: The role of metaphor in serious games design: the bubblemumble case study. In: de Rosa, F., Marfisi Schottman, I., Baalsrud Hauge, J., Bellotti, F., Dondio, P., Romero, M. (eds.) GALA 2021. LNCS, vol. 13134, pp. 198–207. Springer, Cham (2021). https://doi.org/10.1007/978-3-030-92182-8_19
40. Hofstede, G.: 2003. Sage Publications, Culture's Consequences (2003)
41. Bartschat, D., Schwägele, S.: SAGSAGA-Netzwerktreffen zum Thema Debriefing [SAGSAGA network meeting on the subject of debriefing]. PLANSPIEL+ - DER BLOG. https://zms.dhbw-stuttgart.de/de/planspielplus/blog/details/2014/12/01/sagsaga-net zwerktreffen-zum-thema-debriefing/36/. Accessed 18 Apr 2022

Gaming Simulation Design to Learn Best Mixes of Power Sources

Ryoju Hamada[1](✉), Noritaka Yusa[2], and Tomomi Kaneko[3]

[1] National Institute of Technology, Asahikawa College, Asahikawa, Hokkaido, Japan
hamada@edu.asahikawa-nct.ac.jp
[2] Tohoku University, Sendai, Miyagi, Japan
noritaka.yusa.d5@tohoku.ac.jp
[3] National Institute of Technology, Tomakomai College, Tomakomai, Hokkaido, Japan
t_kaneko@tomakomai.kosen-ac.jp

Abstract. To confront the global warming crisis, reducing greenhouse gas emission amounts is an important issue for electrical power providers. However, understanding the business model and characteristics of power sources simultaneously is quite difficult. The authors designed a new Gaming Simulation called the "Power Mix Game (PMG)" to provide opportunities for understanding electrical power generation business operations. The game was evaluated at two schools in 2021: 50 students participated. According to a comparison of responses given to questionnaires before and after playing, PMG has been demonstrated as an effective learning tool. Using PMG for learning can lead to better consensus for issues that have divided people and the power supply industry.

Keywords: Best mix of power sources · Consensus building · Global warming · Greenhouse gas

1 Introduction

Global climate change can no longer be regarded as someone else's misfortune. The world environment is our shared difficulty: practical solutions must be found to prevent ruination of the Earth environment. Cultivating proper understanding of such issues requires increased consciousness of the difficulties that all people face. Sustainable development goals (SDGs) are one example: they include most common difficulties facing human society. From the perspective of global warming, the power generation industry is influential. Globally, 25% of greenhouse gases derive from the electricity and heat production sector [1]. Clean energy promotion is necessary for this industry.

However, people who respect clean energy sometimes exaggerate the efficiency of renewable energy resources. Sometimes, they ignore important shortcomings of clean energy such as vulnerability to drought, flood, and poor wind resources. Moreover, despite their low initial cost, their climate performance is weak. One can argue that shutting down all fossil fueled power plants by social consensus is necessary, thereby downgrading our quality of life. Nevertheless, no country to date has realized any such initiative.

C. Harteveld et al. (Eds.): ISAGA 2022, LNCS 13622, pp. 149–162, 2023.
https://doi.org/10.1007/978-3-031-37171-4_10

Electricity as a product received from a wall outlet shows no differences based on the resources from which it derives. Therefore, most consumers devote little attention to the origin and delivery of electricity. The source is invisible. For that reason, it is quite difficult to consider, imagine, and learn the best mix of power sources. Human society shall not depend on a single resource. Rather, it is necessary to establish a balanced power supply plan while considering safety, price, greenhouse gas (GHG) emissions, redundancy, and other characteristics. Letting students learn the best mix of power sources without using numbers is therefore an extremely difficult task.

To resolve that difficulty, we developed the "Power Mix Game" (PMG). For the game, players form a group and choose a CEO of an electrical utility: a power plant operating company. They invest in huge amounts of infrastructure, prepare for any circumstances, deliver sufficient electricity stably, and devote attention to costs and to the environment. In doing so, the game is intended to help students increase their understanding of the best mix of power sources: a necessary idea to ensure sustainability from the perspective of electricity consumers and policy planners.

2   Literature Review

Various methods have been used to teach students about electrical generation mixes. Complicated issues are involved, related to business, environment, international politics, and national energy policy. Instead of traditional, conventional lectures, Gaming Simulation (GS) might be easier and more effective for learners. Many GSs incorporate various perspectives. The roots can be found in the 1980s. Robinson and Ausbel demonstrated, in 1983, the idea of gaming based on the relation of CO_2 and fossil fuels [2]. Therefore, research into gamification of power generation has been conducted since the 1980s. "Future Voltage", a gaming simulation developed by Benders and Vries in 1989, specifically addressed three points of view: economic systems, energy supply, and the environment [3].

Recently, environmental issues have been recognized as affecting people worldwide. Global warming is accelerating. Scales of natural disasters are increasing. While maintaining humanity's current quality of life, how can global warming be avoided? Crookall argued in 2013 that taking actions against global warming presents an urgent issue for human beings. He addressed the roles of simulation, gaming, and debriefing as particularly important [4].

Rooney-Varga et al. recently introduced a computer model for energy policy and learning called "En-ROADS". It covered three sectors: energy supply, transport, and building industry. Players act in roles of different sectors in different countries to achieve global solutions [5]. Agusdinata and Lukosch proposed a transdisciplinary (TD) approach and introduced a "HOME-RUN Game" to raise awareness of food, energy, and water consumption behavior at the home level [6]. Tribaldos and Schneider expanded on Agusdinata and Lukosch's approach. To facilitate learning about various aspects of sustainable development, they invented the "Theory of Change Game", which uses a board and cards [7]. Fjællingsdal and Klöckner held gaming nights to assess environmental issues using four existing board games [8].

Numerous scholars have promoted environmental education in diverse ways, but few games teach students about the power mix chosen by power generation companies as a business activity.

3   Design of the Power Mix Game

To provide opportunities to learn the power mix correctly and effectively, along with providing great fun, the authors chose to design a new business game in 2019: PMG. The PMG has four major characteristics.

(1) It is a tangible board and card game.
(2) It is a business game.
(3) Participants mutually share many competitions, negotiations, and discussions.
(4) All situations are open to other players.

The players purchase power facilities, procure resources, and combine them to generate power to receive rewards three times. Before purchasing facilities, various random events occur. To mitigate event effects and to give some players advantages over others, the right to make investments can be purchased by players through bidding. In doing so, students learn about facilities, fuels, and diversification strategies to manage power supply businesses. Various events add reality. The authors repeated many trials to balance prices, quantity, efficiency, income, debt, and contents of cards. To seek the best way to let students stimulate motivation to learn the best mix of power sources, the authors have continued tuning those settings. Yusa and Hamada summarized the concept briefly in 2021 [9].

3.1   Purpose

The game purpose is to supply stable electricity necessary for national development by choosing proper power sources. Each player becomes the chief executive officer of an electric power company that is entrusted with the responsibility of supplying power supply to a certain country. Each must purchase power generation facilities and procure resources to generate electricity. If the required electricity is satisfied, then the country will develop; otherwise, the development will stagnate.

Although the electricity requirements can be expected to increase along with national development, the available resources are limited. The amounts of permitted greenhouse gas emissions are also limited. Consequently, the characteristics of each power source and adoption of appropriate strategies must be evaluated in light of resource markets, other players' intentions, the domestic and international situation, and other considerations.

3.2   Target

Fundamentally, the game is designed for four teams. Each team can have up to three players. If some teams have played the game and can give specific instructions to the others, then the game finish can be reached in approximately one hour. An earlier study by the authors evaluated a preliminary version of the game. Results confirmed that the game is enjoyable as a commercial board game and that it is effective for understanding some general characteristics of power sources.

3.3 Time Scale (Term)

Figure 1 shows the GDP growth per person of Japan in the left panel and electric power consumption per person in the right panel during 1960–2010 [10]. The charts show clear relations between GDP and power. Stated differently, improvements in quality of life required more power. The authors constructed PMG while following the implications of that story. The gaming simulation covers the history of Japan after World War II to recent times. The timeline is divided into three "Terms" in PMG.

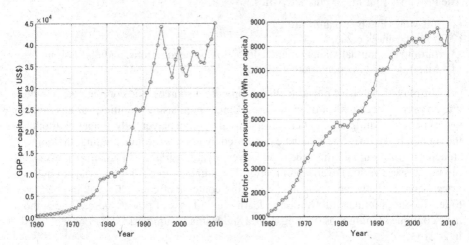

Fig. 1. Long-term comparison of GDP and Electric Power consumption in Japan. (World Bank Open Data)

3.4 Timeline (Phase)

As mentioned in 3.3, The term is repeated three times, and each is separated into nine events and decision makings. Figure 2 shows its flow at a glance. It covers fundamental ideas of power business, including unique characteristics that do not exist in other businesses. The authors introduce adequate competition and interactions among the teams while devoting maximum attention to keeping a balance of parameters.

3.5 Winner

When a player who achieves the highest GDP level at the third stage successfully completes the duties of power generation, the player is declared a winner. If there are more than two winners, then the winner with most cash is the winner.

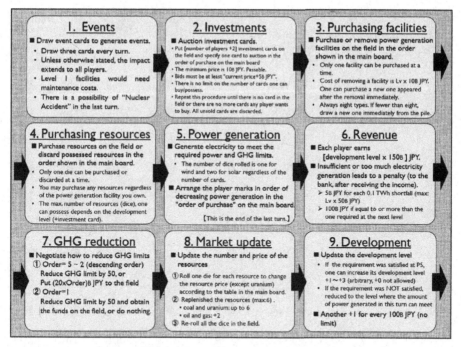

Fig. 2. Flow of PMG game in a Term

4 Ideas of the Power Mix Game

In this paragraph, the authors introduce unique ideas, concepts, and charts.

4.1 GDP Level Indicator

Figure 3 shows an image of the GDP Level indicator. The game has four companies: Red, Green, Blue, and Yellow. Within three terms, four companies compete the power generation quantity which reflects the country's economic growth. Depend on the GDP level, GHG cap and prices of fossil fuel are defined. They are indicated in the center and on the right side of the chart.

4.2 Resource Market

Most power generation companies procure fossil fuels from the world market (Fig. 4). However, the fuel quantity and quality are not stable. To reflect those ideas, a fossil fuels market exists on the right side of the gaming board. For the other resources, quality and quantities are decided using dice at every term. Both the quantity and quality fluctuate to reflect the changing nature of fossil fuels markets. The other three prices and numbers are defined during phase 8 in Fig. 2, in the prior term. The spots on the dice represent the quality of resources.

GDP Level	Power needed	GHG Limit	Coal (6@Phase8)	Oil (+2@P8)	Gas (+2@Phase8)	Uranium (6@Phase8)
1	6.5 TWh	300	15B	30B	20B	10B
2	10.0 TWh	350	20B	40B	25B	15B
3	12.0 TWh	400	20B	40B	25B	15B
4	15.5 TWh	450	25B	60B	35B	10B
5	20.0 TWh	500	15B	50B	30B	15B
6	23.0 TWh	550	30B	80B	40B	10B
7	30.0 TWh	600	25B	100B	50B	20B
8	34.0 TWh	650	30B	120B	60B	15B
9	37.0 TWh	700	35B	140B	70B	20B
10	40.0 TWh	750	40B	80B	80B	15B
11	46.0 TWh	800	60B	300B	120B	20B

Fig. 3. GDP Indicator, GHG cap, and Fossil fuel price list

In this example. The column in the far left shows GDP level that follows power supply level. The second column is the required power in each stage. Third column means the GHG upper limit which player must keep. If the company generate GHG more than indicated number, the company must pay huge compensation. The right-side numbers show a price of fossil fuels. It is unstable, sometimes goes up, sometimes goes down.

Not only the price but the quantity and quality of fossil fuels are unstable, too. In PMG, the number of dice means quantity and spot means the quality of resources. In this example, there are five resources in the coal market. Quality is low in three pieces (only two spots). In the gas market, quality and quantity are well-balanced. In Uranium market, the first comer can gain five-spot resources, but the second comer can access to the lowest quality resources only.

4.3 Power Generation Facilities

Each type of power plant has a different level: Level 1 to Level 3. At a higher level of generation, more power can be generated, but to do so, it is more expensive. The prices of resources which the fossil-fired facilities require for electricity generation increase as the game time passes. The price of uranium remains constant. Although coal and uranium have plentiful supplies in the market, the amounts of oil and gas are constrained. It is noteworthy that the prices of the power generation facilities and how the prices of

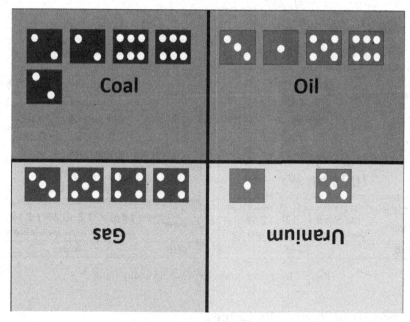

Fig. 4. Fossil Fuel Market

resources fluctuate are based respectively on the levelized costs of electricity in Japan and the prices of the resources on international markets during the last several decades. Table 1 presents the seven types of power generation facilities used in the game. Figure 5 shows some ideas for power generation facility cards.

Table 1. Types of Power Generation Facilities in PMG

	Resource needed	GHG emission	Output
Hydro	None	None	Controllable
Coal-fired	Coal	Large	Controllable; proportional to the amount of
Oil-fired	Oil	Medium	resource input
Gas-fired	Gas	Small	
Wind	None	None	Greatly fluctuates
Solar	None	None	Fluctuates
Nuclear	Uranium	None	Constant but 100% operation only

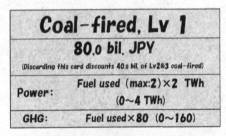

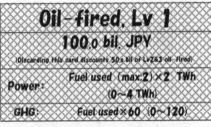

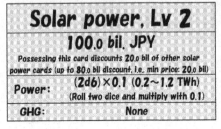

Fig. 5. Images of Power Generation Facility Cards.

5   Processes of Power Mix Game

5.1   Initial

Players launch a power plant company. The government provides 500 million JPY as shared capital. The government constructs a Level-1 dam and a coal plant and delivers them to the player.

5.2   Individual Works

Let us review PMG process from the player (Ken)'s viewpoint. The authors summarized the whole stories in Fig. 6.

(1) Ken became the president of the Power Supply Company called "Blue". His appointment is for three terms. There are three rival companies in the same country: Red, Green, and Yellow.

(2) Blue company already held two power plants at the beginning of the game: Coal-level 1 (Max. 4 Twh) and Dam-level 1 (Max. 2 Twh). He can generate 6 Twh at most. His company lacks the minimum requirement in Level 2 (10 Twh), so he needs to increase the facility.

(3) The facilitator drew the event card. The card said, "New Coalmine developed". The facilitator increased the number of coal dice, and their quality was indicated by the number of spots.

(4) The Facilitator drew some investment cards and show the contents to the players. He applied to the card called "GHG Quota + 100", but the Red Company president also applied to the same card. So, Ken and Red company president match bidding managed by the facilitator.

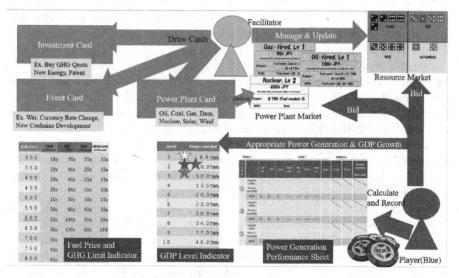

Fig. 6. Flow of PMG game from Player's side

(5) The facilitator opened some facility cards and opens them in the power plant market. He purchased gas level-2 plant by bidding.
(6) Ken needed coal and gas. By winning against other rivals, he procured enough fuel.
(7) Ken calculated the result. He carried out the requirement in terms of demand and GHG cap.
(8) Ken received sales revenue.
(9) Ken decided to try GDP level 4 (15.5Twh) in the next term.
(10) Those processes are recorded on power generation performance sheet.

6   Experiments

The author demonstrated the Power Mix Game at two schools. The KOSEN education system in Japan extends for five years, enrolling 15–20-year-old students, particularly for teaching students practical engineering.

(1) National Institute of Technology, Asahikawa College, Hokkaido, Japan (Asahikawa Kosen).
(2) National Institute of Technology, Tomakomai College, Hokkaido, Japan (Tomakomai Kosen).

6.1   Trial at Asahikawa Kosen

The game was assigned as part of a lecture called "Management of Environment" in the advanced course of the National Institute of Technology, Asahikawa College, From April to June 2021. Students had attained education equivalent to third year students of university undergraduate courses.

The 29 students were separated into 10 groups, designated as companies. Two independent games exist: the first is easier; the second is more complex. Each game consists of three terms to make decisions.

Because of the time table, the authors were unable to make a long session. All opportunities are limited to 90 min. Every week, the sessions were restarted and closed. The authors also had to wait if some teams were late. Huge time losses had to be accepted. Therefore, operations were only one term per week. Thereby, one game was completed every three weeks. The total play time was 540 min.

During April-June, we continued the games, including three weeks of cancellations because of the Covid-19 outbreak between the two games. After students returned to school, they forgot even the basic rules. Consequently, the author decided to start the game again.

Students' reactions were mostly positive; they used aggressive styles. Once they found ways to block other teams' business strategies, most of the bidding became more active and challenging. For example, Buy "GHG Regulation -100 to all" let coal-based rivals reduce fossil fuel usage while preparing nuclear power plants and sufficient stocks of uranium. Although a player has no coal-fueled plant, procuring coal would halt a rival's coal plant. The authors also saw many scenes in which companies discussed matters together and cooperated to produce mutually satisfactory outcomes. Consequently, PMG performed well for students to learn the nature of power supply business, to provide opportunities to learn the best mix of power sources, and to encourage learning motivation.

6.2 Trial at Tomakomai Kosen

The author applied PMG for a class called "Advanced Cold Weather Environmental Engineering" in the advanced engineering course of Tomakomai Kosen in 2022. Students are regarded as third and fourth grade students in university undergraduate courses. The school, undertaking the nature of game learning, provided a one-day quota so that the author conducted a full-day workshop for four days by changing the formation and setting. In all, 21 students participated in the class (Fig. 7).

Outline of the four-day session is the following.

Day 1: Individual.

Day 2: Individual (with the same opponent for Round 1).

Day 3: Pairs of students.

Day 4: Pairs of students (with different partners and opponents for Round 3).

At the end of the session, the author, as a facilitator, had few actions. Most rules and facilitation were automated at each table. They teach the rules together, manage the bidding, and calculate correctly.

7   Results

7.1   Results Obtained at Asahikawa Kosen

At the beginning of the session, we had a "Before" questionnaire and "After" at the end. The authors let students demonstrate their understanding about ten important key ideas with responses given on a five-point Likert scale. Comparison of the results can

Fig. 7. Students Playing PMG at Tomakokami KOSEN (Day 1, Term 1, Phase 5, Power Generation Performance Recording).

demonstrate the game effectiveness. At Asahikawa Kosen, the authors administered questionnaires before and after the session. Ten key ideas are presented below.

1. Power mix meanings
2. Greenhouse gas regulation meanings
3. Thermal power generation is a flexible resource.
4. Nuclear facilities provide good baseload power if risks can be ignored.
5. Fossil resource prices fluctuate.
6. Power generation facilities are expensive.
7. Solar and wind power depend on unpredictable factors.
8. GHG regulations affect power generation companies.
9. Exchanging GHG rights is demanded.
10. Power companies must address redundancy.

Table 2 presents the results. Differences between pre-questionnaire and post-questionnaire results were evaluated using one-sided Wilcoxon signed-rank tests. The null hypothesis of the test is "playing the game did not improve the understanding of the participants." The table indicates that the differences are statistically significant except that of Question 2.

All scores increased, on average, Question 1 represents PMG's teaching purpose. One can see the greatest improvement for this question. The average score for Question 2 is high. We can infer that participants at Asahikawa Kosen recognize the word "GHG" more than other people do. Applied ideas for GHG, indicated typically on Questions 8 and 9, show remarkable progress. A similar tendency can be inferred for Question 4. Most students had experienced the aftermath of the severe accident which occurred at the Fukushima nuclear power plant on March 11, 2011.

Table 2. Growth of understanding attributable to PMG (Asahikawa Kosen).

No.	1	2	3	4	5	6	7	8	9	10	Average
Question	Meanings of Power Mix	Meanings of Green House Gus Regulation	Thermal Power Generation is flexible power resource.	Nuclear is good base-load power if we ignore the risk of accident.	Price of Fossil resources swings.	Power Generation Facility is very expensive.	Solar or Wind power depends on luck.	GHG regulation affects power generation company a lot.	There is a demand to exchange /purchase GHG rights.	Power plant company must keep redundancy.	
After	3.05	3.95	3.71	4.38	4.05	4.19	4.52	3.95	3.43	4.19	3.94
Before	1.90	3.48	2.90	3.81	3.38	3.10	3.81	3.10	2.33	3.33	3.11
A−B	1.14	0.48	0.81	0.57	0.67	1.10	0.71	0.86	1.10	0.86	0.83
p	0.0002	0.0714	0.0054	0.0137	0.0071	0.0004	0.0029	0.0035	0.0007	0.0049	

n=20

One can infer that PMG is a useful invention to learn about the best mix of power sources.

7.2 Results Obtained at Tomakomai KOSEN

Every student played PMG four times in the class. After the game, the authors conducted a questionnaire survey, which yielded responses from five students. The following are responses to the question "What did you think of the Power Management Game?".

* "At the beginning, I was wondering if an optimal strategy existed, but as the game progressed, I realized that it was not possible to make a decision based on the situation alone. For example, an accident will invariably halt nuclear power generation; even thermal power generation can be stopped in some domestic problems. We did not know when or what would happen, so we tried to choose a stable option. However, I felt that it was necessary to take a certain amount of risk because we would lose the game if our power generation was lower than that of other countries and the participants could not improve our developing level. We were able to experience schematically and simply the power generation and energy supremacy battles among nations through the game. I think we understood the difficulty of fully tackling energy issues."

* "I felt that there was a high degree of luck in this game. I think it was exciting and I would like to play it about ten times more. However, the hydroelectric power was very strong; the debt was set up simply so as not to break the game's flow, but I think it would be more complicated in real life. This game is a simple way to make a country's power generation policy. I think this game is helpful for expanding thinking about energy."

* "This game was exciting. I enjoyed playing it repeatedly while learning about power generation facilities and their GHG emissions. It was easy to understand and fun to participate in the game because it was based on reality, such as the fact that oil prices

tend to increase and uranium remains cheap. However, I thought that the game was 70% luck and 30% skill and thinking. Therefore, it was frustrating to lose because of luck."

* "It was a valuable opportunity to think about the best mix of power sources because I had fun and used my head to formulate strategies. Even though I wanted to purchase power generation equipment, there were many times when I could not proceed as I wished to because I did not have insufficient funds or other people blocked me. I felt that it is necessary for policymakers to think about these issues properly and to find a certain compromise level."

* "The rules were so complicated: it took me a long time to learn them. However, the restrictions on greenhouse gas emissions are pretty strict. The more developed a country is, the more it is adversely affected, which explains why developed countries are apparently suffering in reality. In addition, I somehow understood why Japan wants to use nuclear power plants. If you have a certain amount of money, uranium is cheap, generates great amounts of electricity, does not emit GHG, and has a slight possibility of an accident. It seems to me that it is a very excellent type of power generation facility."

Comments were mostly positive. One can infer that PMG-based learning stimulated their consideration and learning from various perspectives.

8 Discussion

Throughout the descriptions presented so far, the authors designed the Power Mix Game. Its teaching effectiveness was proved to a certain extent. What is the next step?

First, both cases took too long, even though they are not amateurs of engineering. If the target is common people, kids, or foreign students, then PMG might take more time. We must examine PMG in many schools as soon as possible. We shall cut off some ideas without hesitation if the current setting is too complex. Heavy games lead students to hurry and reduce their motivation to learn [11].

Second, it is necessary to pursue reconciliation between power plant companies and residents. It is true that the sector produces many GHGs. Actually, residents' groups, which often emphasize their global warming concerns, criticize power plant businesses. They request impossible missions from the industry: shut down thermal and nuclear power plants but maintain a stable power supply. Given this phenomenon, it is impossible to achieve progress. By understanding the concept of a best mix of power sources, then within a friendly game workshop, a closed door might open. Indeed, the authors intend that PMG be adopted to work toward compromise and practical discussion between power plant businesses and residents. To contribute to this fundamentally important issue, the authors intend to continue their efforts. The authors look forward to support and suggestions.

Acknowledgments. This Research was supported by the Foundation for the Fusion of Science and Technology (FOST), Yokohama, Kanagawa, Japan.

References

1. Intergovernmental Panel on Climate Change (2014). https://www.ipcc.ch/site/assets/uploads/2018/02/ipcc_wg3_ar5_full.pdf. Accessed 20 March 2022

2. Robinson, J., Ausubel, J.H.: A game framework for scenario generation for the Co_2 issue. Simul. Gaming **14**(3), 317–344 (1983). https://doi.org/10.1177/104687818301400306
3. Benders, R., de Vries, B.: Electric power planning in a gaming context. Simul. Gaming **20**(3), 227–244 (1989). https://doi.org/10.1177/104687818902000301
4. Crookall, D.: Climate change and simulation/gaming: learning for survival. Simul. Gaming **44**(2–3), 195–228 (2013). https://doi.org/10.1177/1046878113497781
5. Rooney-Varga, J.N., Kapmeier, F., Sterman, J.D., Jones, A.P., Putko, M., Rath, K.: The climate action simulation. Simul. Gaming **51**(2), 114-140 (2020).https://doi.org/10.1177/104687811 9890643
6. Agusdinata, D.B., Lukosch, H.: Supporting interventions to reduce household greenhouse gas emissions: a transdisciplinary role-playing game development. Simul. Gaming **50**(3), 359–376 (2019). https://doi.org/10.1177/104687811984813
7. Tribaldos, T., Schneider, F.: Enabling players to develop theories of change for sustainable development: a severe game. Simul. Gaming **52**(5), 664–678 (2021). https://doi.org/10.1177/10468781211022399
8. Fjællingsdal, K.S., Klöckner, C.A.: Green across the board: board games as tools for dialogue and simplified environmental communication. Simul. Gaming **51**(5), 632–652 (2020)
9. Yusa, N., Hamada, R.: Development of a board game for studying energy mix. J. Ener. Environ. Educ. **15**, 21–28 (2021)
10. The World Bank Open Data. https://data.worldbank.org/. Accessed 20 March 2022
11. Hamada, R., Hiji, M., Kaneko, T.: BASE business game creation charter. Proc. JASAG Nat. Conf. **2015**(Autumn), 56–61 (2015)

Health

Reducept VR: The Importance of a Design Rationale for the Immersiveness of a Virtual Reality Game to Support Chronic Pain Treatment Effectively

D. A. Kuipers[1]([✉]) [iD], F. Kleiman[1] [iD], L. Zantema[2], and I. Wenzler[1]

[1] NHL-Stenden University of Applied Sciences, Rengerslaan 8-10, 8917 DD Leeuwarden, The Netherlands
derek.kuipers@nhlstenden.com
[2] Reducept, Hilversum, North Holland, The Netherlands

Abstract. Virtual reality games are widely renowned for their inherent immersive experiences. However, the challenge of a successful serious virtual reality (SVR) game in terms of effectiveness, is found in the degree of meaningfulness of the immersive experience itself. This requires a theoretically grounded design rationale and a diligent design process. In this paper we explain what the game Reducept aims to do, how design research led to successful prototypes, and what the underlying design rationale was.

We conclude that there is a natural fit between the known therapies for unexplained chronic pain, which relied heavily on patients' imagination, and the inherent properties of a VR experience using a mental model of reality. Accordingly, the use of a metaphorical recontextualization was essential in the design process of Reducept. We argue that it resulted in the appropriate form of transfer between the SVR game and the state of chronic pain of the participants. Further research is needed not only on the effects of these and many other VR artifacts, but also on the supporting design process which gets them to succeed.

Keywords: Design for transfer · Games for Health · Chronic pain · Serious gaming · Virtual reality

1 Introduction

In this article, we highlight Reducept VR. Studies have shown promising results from trials with patients, demonstrating the effectiveness of Reducept VR in chronic disease treatment. Our goal is to explain the success of this SVR from a properly conducted design research perspective and the choices made therein.

A common uptake on games for health is emulating the world as it is, by faithfully mimicking the target context. From a design for transfer perspective, the design rationale thereby follows the idea that common stimulus properties lead to a transfer effect, and transfer conditions are optimized by a recognizable similarity between the simulated and the known reality.

C. Harteveld et al. (Eds.): ISAGA 2022, LNCS 13622, pp. 165–170, 2023.
https://doi.org/10.1007/978-3-031-37171-4_11

Interesting about VR games is that, inherent to the medium itself, it opens up possibilities for a different design rationale for certain types of serious games for health [1]. The use of virtual reality technologies in the context of treating unexplained chronic pain is appealing because of its immersive properties. By creating a metaphor in which the patient does experience and influence one's own pain, treatment options are created that were previously only possible by using imagination. VR artifacts can be presented as a metaphorical environment in which emotional problems in particular can be addressed. Often these emotional aspects have no real-world connections, which makes faithful mimicking undesirable or even impossible, and therefore a good match with the possibilities that a VSR offers. This evoked immersivity creates a highly desirable state of suspension of disbelief in a way that we also see in the exercises applied in known treatments aimed at pain management [2]. Maintaining and maximizing these inherent features of VR gaming lies at the heart of Reducept's design.

The immersion of VR provides the unique ability to better influence the cognitions, attention and emotions of patients with chronic pain [3]. Being able to direct the patient's experience makes it possible for patients to always achieve success in their training. For patients who have had many painful, ineffective and invasive treatment experiences, this is of great importance for obtaining a positive growth mindset [4].

Reducept VR has been showing many positive results to enable patients to manage their chronic pain state. Each day, hundreds of patients already log on into Reducept VR. Over more than 10 thousand Reducept VR sessions, patients report decreases in pain scores 75% of these sessions. While researchers are focusing on proving these effects [5, 6], we take another perspective on the case. The main question for us is to explore the reasons for such a positive result in using this SVR game to fight chronic pain.

2 Foundations of Reducept: A Grounded Understanding of Chronic Pain

In recent years, the number of Virtual Reality (VR) applications developed to reduce pain in patients has increased dramatically [7]. Much of this research related to this emerging technology is conducted in universities in a clinical setting, and focuses purely on distraction from acute pain. Rarely is a solution sought to increase the quality of life (QOL) of people experiencing chronic pain [3, 8]. There is a growing use of SVR games for immersive experiences as the technology is becoming more accessible and easy to use [9]. The specific use of this media for chronic pain treatments is also on the rise, though there is still a lot to learn on how to use it effectively and about the impact of virtual reality on chronic pain [10].

In the Netherlands alone, over 3 million people suffer from chronic pain [11]. For these patients, chronic pain has a considerable impact on their daily functioning, well-being and their direct environment. Chronic pain can also lead to absenteeism from work and, in 75% of the cases, to work disability [11]. The care consumption of this group of patients is high and long-term. The chronic pain patient often sees 10, up to sometimes 25 specialists and often experiences the organization of pain care as a pinball [12]. Diagnostics and triage are not unambiguous, treatment pathways are fragmented and often do not lead to sustainable recovery or relief of pain. The social and economic costs (of care and absenteeism) in The Netherlands are estimated at more than 20 billion euros per year for all chronic pain patients and 4 billion euros for patients with pain related to the spine [13]. The Regieraad Kwaliteit van Zorg outlined these issues in the report on chronic pain [11].

From the perspective of positive health [14], it is important that the patient is enabled to adapt to the physical, emotional and social challenges associated with the chronic pain condition. The International Association for the Study of Pain (IASP) defines pain as an unpleasant sensory and emotional sensation. It is usually associated with actual or potential tissue damage or described in terms of damage [15], or in short, pain that can be pointed to and explained. But pain also exists that is less clearly identifiable. Physiologically, physical stimuli lead to electrical impulses that travel through nerve pathways towards the brain. Within the brain, it is decided if and how much pain should be produced, based on the perceived threat within the current context. This pain system is not like a telephone connection that transmits a signal, but it is a self-regulating system that can amplify, attenuate, or transmit impulses one to one depending on the circumstances. This ensures that patients with similar conditions can experience great differences in pain perception.

From a growing focus on biopsychosocial-focused care, it is emphasized that chronic pain is a multi-dimensional psychological form of care that extends beyond medical care alone [16, 17]. Therefore, influencing pain experiences in daily life-before and during, or even replacing medical treatment of persistent chronic pain (e.g., through surgery or pharmaceuticals) it offers opportunities to explore a new way of pain management.

3 Reducept Design Process: Figural Transfer at Play

We want to draw focus in this article on the design process of Reducept VR, focusing on using the immersive qualities of VR to advance and enhance existing treatments. Also, we focused on supporting and enhancing the required use of a patient's imagination in existing pain management. (Fig. 1). We hypothesize that the main reason for a successful outcome is related to the foundation of the design process which was based on the idea of figural transfer. According to Royer [18], figural transfer (belonging to the second transfer class) involves situations where a known complex of ideas, concepts, and knowledge is juxtaposed against some new problem or situation. Figural transfer uses existing world knowledge to think or learn about a particular issue. Clear examples of the usage of figural transfer can be found in figural language such as metaphor or simile. Transfer occurs because of a successful memory search triggered by a figural learning context, assisting in understanding the transfer context.

For the Reducept VR, virtual reality was conceived as a metaphorical recontextualization of what might be called a mental model [19–21] of one's own pain. Various activities were developed in the design space through iterations, incrementally building the metaphor [4]. Through a meticulous translation of pain-related elements into a playable world, the pain patient is challenged to engage in meaningful operations and interactions with their own pain. From modern pain theory, this is referred to as retraining the pain center.

The above means that much of the demonstrable positive effects of playing Reducept VR can be attributed to reflection in action [7, 22], but also to a form of in-game transfer,

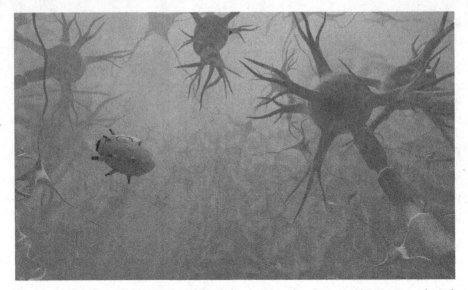

Fig. 1. A screenshot of pain representation in Reducept – the player needs to prevent the pain impulses from connecting to the brain receptors.

as reductions in pain scores in real life are reported. If we follow the definition of figural transfer, our position is that Reducept VR works through this form of transfer, but also that these are unique properties for SVR games in general.

By understanding the experience of pain as the result of the (emotional) brain assigning a certain degree of danger to the context in which the pain arises, it becomes possible to address this emotional sense of danger as such. In the design research process, we developed through a series of prototypes, a visual and interactive representation, in which pain could be recognized and made influenced by the players. This was an iterative and incremental design process in which there was a continuous search with pain patients for appropriate forms of interacting with their 'own' pain. Finding and calibrating an appropriate metaphor which serves as a carrier of a mental model of reality for a broader group of patients was intensive, delicate and time-consuming. In addition to the pain patients themselves, practitioners formed their own target group.

The recontextualization of pain theory in a game metaphor is more difficult for this group to embrace than for the pain patients themselves. Known medical interventions for unexplained chronic pain control are used differently within Reducept VR. The success of Reducept VR's acceptance as it stands is related to the iterative design process in which pain specialists have been part of. As mentioned, this approach resulted from combining immersive characteristics found in VR with the required use of a patient's imagination in existing pain treatment, as found in modern pain theory, the strict adherence of the design for transfer rationale and introducing pain education and mindfulness exercises to maximize the therapeutic effect.

For both user groups, adherence to a metaphorical design approach to the game had to be a starting point for design. We emphasize that this fact has been an essential component to the success of Reducept VR: a design rationale in which the choice of

VR, combined with targeted elements from pain management theory and a pre-intended transfer type, has provided a design framework from which each design decision has emerged.

Figural transfer as a design rationale for designing SVR games should strengthen the delivery of such gaming interventions, especially in situations where the problem cannot be directly mimicked. This can include issues related to depression, anxiety, burnout and trauma, all of which have no direct physical or functional manifestation. The Reducept VR case provides us with evidence for such discussion. The application of figural transfer in other contexts and towards other topics, as well as the extent to which the Reducept design process is generalizable to other SVR game development is to be further researched.

4   Conclusions

This paper reflects on the Reducept VR design process, indicating the importance of a strong grounded theory to design a successful SVR game intervention. Modern pain theory, which is incorporated as a key ingredient within Reducept, offers a natural match between immersive properties of a VR game and required imagination of the chronic pain patient. But that's not enough: designing a metaphor that large groups of users can relate to and want to interact with, is no easy task. It is important to design transfer conditions very conscientiously and rigorously that enable in-game individual pain experiences to be addressed..

We conclude that the grounding on patients' imagination, which is heavily used by common therapies and treatments for unexplained chronic pain, tends to underuse the potential of VR technologies for this type of intervention. Though they are based on a logical match of inherent properties from VR experiences, they tend not to be as effective as Reducept.

The appropriate iterative design process, including a design for transfer rationale, was the one which unleashed the potential of the Reducept VR game. We learned that many kinds of chronic pain can be addressed by SVR games, having the game being played in pain clinics, by specialised physiotherapists and hospitals, all in a therapeutical setting under guidance of a trained care professional. Further research is needed to progress with the application of figural transfer in other contexts. Also, it is recommended that the method is discussed when used in SVR gaming interventions aiming at other topics.

Lastly, new insights should come by checking the generalization of the findings and discussions related to the Reducept VR design process to other SVR game development. To this day, a vital activity of the Reducept team is to get its SVR and the metaphorical approach therein, accepted by practitioners, hospitals and health insurance companies, which stresses that this line of thinking and designing serious games is not yet common practice.

References

1. Kuipers, D.A., Terlouw, G., Wartena, B.O., Job Tb van 't Veer, Prins, J.T., En Pierie, J.P.: The role of transfer in designing games and simulations for health: systematic review. JMIR Ser. Games **5**(4), e23 (2017)

2. Jensen, M.P., et al.: Effects of hypnosis, cognitive therapy, hypnotic cognitive therapy, and pain education in adults with chronic pain: a randomized clinical trial. Pain **161**(10), 2284–2298 (2020)
3. Jin, W., Choo, A., Gromala, D., Shaw, C., Squire, P.: A virtual reality game for chronic pain management: a randomized, controlled clinical study. Stud. Health Technol. Inform. **220**, 154–160 (2016)
4. Fennema, M., Zantema, L.: Reducept Guidelines for the Treatment of Chronic Pain (Version 1.0). Medical Centre Leeuwarden (2019)
5. Hippert, T.A.: (tessa): "The applicability of virtual reality in patients with rheumatoid arthritis and chronic pain complaints: a mixed methods pilot study." umcg.studenttheses.ub.rug.nl. https://umcg.studenttheses.ub.rug.nl/id/eprint/2988
6. Smits, M., van Goor, H., n.d. "PijnVRij: a qualitative study into the lived experiences of patients with non-specific chronic low-back pain using virtual reality." vr4rehab.org. https://vr4rehab.org/vr4rehab-08/
7. Millan, M.J.: The induction of pain: an integrative review. Prog. Neurobiol. **57**(1), 1–164 (1999)
8. Wiederhold, B.K., Gao, K., Sulea, C., Wiederhold, M.D.: Virtual reality as a distraction technique in chronic pain patients. Cyberpsychol. Behav. Soc. Netw. **17**(6), 346–352 (2014)
9. Maggio, M.G., et al.: The growing use of virtual reality in cognitive rehabilitation: fact, fake or vision? a scoping review. J. Natl Med. Assoc. **111**(4), 457–463 (2019)
10. Jones, T., Moore, T., Choo, J.: The impact of virtual reality on chronic pain. PLoS ONE **11**(12), e0167523 (2016)
11. Bekkering, G.E., et al.: Epidemiology of chronic pain and its treatment in The Netherlands. Neth. J. Med. **69**(3), 141–153 (2011)
12. Rombout, B.: Niet steeds hetzelfde verhaal. Zorgvisie ICT **19**(1), 32–33 (2018). https://doi.org/10.1007/s41186-018-0012-8
13. Boonen, A.: Large differences in cost of illness and wellbeing between patients with fibromyalgia, chronic low back pain, or ankylosing spondylitis. Ann. Rheum. Dis. (2004). https://doi.org/10.1136/ard.2003.019711
14. Huber, M., et al.: How should we define health? BMJ **343:d4163**, 26 July 2011
15. Merskey, H., Bogduk, N.: International Association for the Study of Pain. Task Force on Taxonomy. Classification of Chronic Pain: Descriptions of Chronic Pain Syndromes and Definitions of Pain Terms. IASP Press, Seattle (1994)
16. Davey, E.S.: Psychology and Chronic Pain. Anaesthesia Intensive Care Med. **17**(11), 568–570 (2016)
17. Moseley, G.L., Butler, D.S.: Fifteen years of explaining pain: the past, present, and future. J. Pain Official J. Am. Pain Soc. **16**(9), 807–813 (2015)
18. Royer, J.M.: Theories of the Transfer of Learning. Educational Psychologist **14**(1), 53–69 (1979)
19. Bogost, I.: Unit Operations: An Approach to Videogame Criticism. The MIT Press, Cambridge (2006)
20. Frasca, G.: "Videogames of the Oppressed: Videogames as a Means for Critical Thinking and Debate." School of Literature, communication, and culture, Georgia Institute of http://ludology.org/articles/thesis/FrascaThesisVideogames.pdf (2001)
21. Laurel, B.: SimSmarts, an interview with will wright. Des. Res. Methods Perspect. 253–259 (2003)
22. Schön, D.A.: The Reflective Practitioner: How Professionals Think in Action. Routledge (2017)

How Playfulness Can Enable Greater Understanding of Game-Based Adult Mental Health Interventions

Leland Masek[✉]

Tampere University, Tampere, Finland
leland.masek@tuni.fi

Abstract. Playfulness is a critical term for the study of games, simulations, mental health. In addition to formal characteristics of games, how players perceive, experience those games has shown effect on the outcomes of interventions. One experience that is critically connected to games is playfulness. Simultaneously playfulness has recently been studied in psychology for its benefits on adult mental health, as a state of mind and a personality trait. This makes playfulness a highly valuable term to study in the context of game-based interventions that aim to affect mental health symptoms. Addresses empirical literature connecting playfulness and mental health using a new model of playfulness as engagement seeking. By analyzing past works two primary pathways for how playfulness affects mental health emerge. Based upon these pathways and how past studies have methodologically used them.

Keywords: Mental Health · Playfulness · Literature Review

1 Introduction

Playfulness is a critical term for the study of games, simulations, and game related phenomena. In addition to the structure of a game, scholars have also identified that how players engage with a game, including perceived frames (Tomasino et al. 2013) and hedonic states (Cassotti et al. 2012), is essential for understanding perception and emergent behavior in games. Recent work in game studies has framed playfulness as a useful term for addressing internal experiences often generated within play and games (Stenros 2015). This difference between game, the perception of game, and the experience of that game is a longstanding topic of interest in the field of game studies (Möring 2013). In simulations, past works have shown promising qualitative results by analyzing how participants expressed subjective playfulness (Goutx et al. 2019). This tension has been especially essential to unpack as the concept of game has been applied outside of its traditional social context for gamification. Playfulness has been highlighted as a key term for design efforts and gamification intending to create the experiences of play or games outside of traditional social contexts (Sicart 2014, Deterding et al. 2011). One such promising application for games and gamification has been in mental health interventions (Mcgonigal 2015). However, the study of playfulness as a key term has yet

© The Author(s), under exclusive license to Springer Nature Switzerland AG 2023
C. Harteveld et al. (Eds.): ISAGA 2022, LNCS 13622, pp. 171–184, 2023.
https://doi.org/10.1007/978-3-031-37171-4_12

to be applied to its fullest extent in game-based interventions. It is common instead to describe concepts very similar to what would be called playfulness by some fields using terms such as "likability" or "game experience". These slightly different terms leave a fruitful union between disciplines under-explored. For example, in a recent work in the ISAGA community justified their approach in part by arguing "play activities in Collaborative Virtual Environments (CVEs) [23] are thought to be particularly promising and to provide a context for investigating new therapeutic practices" (Vona et al. 2020, p. 50). The essence of play in an experience is a major topic of study in psychology (Shen 2020), occupational therapy (Bundy et al. 2001), and digital design (Moon and Kim 2001) under the concept of playfulness. In this way, it is valuable for the game and simulation studies community to spend time investigating playfulness and how it relates, and could relate, to designing game-based interventions for mental health.

Playfulness has shown to have robust correlations with mental health. Studies in psychology have correlated playfulness as a personality trait with coping with stress, (Hess and Bundy 2003; Magnuson and Barnett 2013; Staempfli 2007) subjective happiness, (Proyer 2014; Yue et al. 2016) and general well-being (Staempfli and Mannell 2005). Playfulness in parents has been shown to correlate with mental health in young children (Menashe-Grinberg and Atzaba-Poria 2017; Cabrera et al. 2017). Participation in a playful community was correlated to progressive increases in resilience in the elderly (Chang, Yarnal and Chick, 2016) and increased positive emotions in elderly individuals with subthreshold depression (Li, Theng and Foo 2016). Playfulness has shown such numerous health benefits that past research argues it reduces population-wide psychopathology (Gray 2011) and that "playful adults live an average of ten years longer than their less playful peers" (Gordon 2014 p. 249). In this way, playfulness has a consistent history of being associated with mental health benefits.

This work aims to bring greater awareness of how playfulness has been analyzed in mental health interventions to communities that study game-based interventions. This work goes over the historical tensions with defining playfulness both in psychology and game studies. Using a recent literature review, a re-framing of playfulness as seeking engagement is explained. The work then analyzes past mental health interventions that include playfulness through the new framework of engagement. Two pathways for how playfulness is said to affect mental health through engagement are described: *Participation* and *Personality*. Finally, new studies that would contribute to the field are discussed.

2   Background

Playfulness is a rapidly growing term of importance in both psychology and the study of games. Playfulness has been described as essential to a healthy mindset since the beginning of positive psychology. Maslow defined it as one of the characteristics of peak experience (Maslow 1971). Winnicott viewed playfulness in his psychotherapeutic work as required for a healthy lifestyle (Winnicott 1971). Csikszentmihalyi studied the attitudes of players in various types of games when he constructed the concept of flow (Beard and Csikszentmihalyi 2015). Self Determination Theory (Deci and Ryan 2000) and the concept of intrinsic motivation therein has been used as a defining feature of playfulness (Moon and Kim 2001). Psychological studies have since shown consistent correlation between playfulness and mental health (Gordon 2014). However there have also been problematic theoretical factors slowing the progress of this promising line of inquiry. Play has had a variety of definitions, often focusing on children, without a clear consensus of its essential characteristics that can apply across age groups (Shen, Chick and Zinn 2014). Recent scholars have put in greater work investigating how playfulness affects adult life (Proyer 2017). In order to address these more general characteristics, modern psychology has shifted focus away from behavioral features of play and games towards internal conceptions of the state of mind or a personality trait called playfulness (Barnett 1991 pp. 52–54).

Game studies has seen a similar turn in interest toward analyzing internal characteristics that may be called playful. A desire to find an essence inside of games and play outside of their normal social context is also a primary design challenge of gamification (Deterding et al. 2011). Recent game studies literature has identified playfulness as a key term for broadening the object of study beyond normally identifiable "games" (Sicart 2014; Stenros 2015). Considering the long history of game studies to use analytic tools on cultural constructs not normally identified as play or game, such as a court room and its theatrical elements (Huizinga 1938), playfulness is an essential term to bring to the forefront. Game studies has however lacked consistent definitions to bring the discussion under the same umbrella, especially for empirical applications on the potential effects of games.

Considering the promising outcomes that are associated with the internal, essential characteristic of playfulness, it is of value to explicitly bring together theoretical work on playfulness with empirical research on its consequences. This article takes a step in that direction by highlighting the theoretical pathways whereby playfulness is predicted to improve mental health. This work is building upon a recent literature review (Masek 2020; Masek and Stenros 2021). This review concluded that that playfulness is most essentially defined as an experiential frame that prioritizes engagement. Constructs that enable the seeking of engagement, in any of its diverse forms, above other priorities have been defined as playful. The focus on organizing engagement creates a coherent umbrella to place internal events of games and play that can be brought outside of the traditionally understood social contexts. This theory has recently seen empirical testing and support (Vahlo et al. 2022). This also aligns with a recent review on gamified mental health applications which concluded the number one justification for using gamification was "promoting engagement" (Cheng et al. 2019 abstract). This new framework will be applied to unpack new insight on how games and play can be integrated into mental health interventions through playfulness and enable the full potential of being human. By analyzing past psychological interventions involving playfulness, two themes for playful engagement emerge: 1. Playfulness increases engagement with unrelated mentally healthy occupations 2. Playfulness is a primary target of intervention because it is defined as a mentally healthy personality trait that desires to engage with life in general.

3 Methods

The literature discussed in this paper is not an exhaustive review, but rather a subset from a previously conducted systematic review (Masek and Stenros 2021) and other literature subsequently read by the author. This review is non-systematic, rather sources are selected by the author to demonstrate an analytic perspective on how mental health is predicted to be affected by playfulness in empirical studies, from the perspective of engagement. The playfulness in these works is playfulness in adults, though some of the studies correlate parental adult playfulness with child mental health. Adults are the primary target mostly for ease, as the literature on playfulness and mental health in children is vast especially in Occupational Therapy (Bundy et al. 2001) and Play Therapy (Bratton and Ray 2000).

The work selected focuses on conducted interventions, or empirical correlations, rather than purely theoretical predictions. There are several excellent works unpacking potential theoretical predictions of playfulness on mental health (e.g. Tonkin and Whitaker 2016; Tonkin and Whitaker 2019). The nature of the empiricism is rather broad though, examples are taken from programs that measure outcomes quantitatively, qualitatively, or through observation by program runners. While there are more definitive steps to be done in this regard, it is the author's belief that this method brings together a valuable and diverse set of studies for scholars interested in this critical topic.

This article is not going to rigorously criticize any of the entries discussed. So, the position of this paper is one of ontological trust: If they describe themselves as talking about playfulness and mental health, they are believed. The word playfulness and playful are the guiding features of the discussed phenomenon. This means the results are likely highly under-inclusive of playfulness. Works in the sample define certain things as playful, such as passionate engagement with games (Abós et al. 2019), that are used in other works, yet not called playfulness (Fleming et al. 2017). This speaks to the value of this contribution and a need for additional work identifying past literature that may be relevant to discussions of playfulness, even if they do not use that word.

4 Two Pathways for How Playfulness Affects Mental Health

All of the analyzed works in the following section describe playfulness in adults as an essential concept affecting mental health. The context of the studies mentioned vary considerably from positive psychological interventions (Proyer et al. 2021) to traditional psycho-dynamic therapy (Yonatan-Leus et al. 2018) to game-based workplace interventions (Abós et al. 2019) to psychological correlation studies (Farley et al. 2021). The definition of what is mentally healthy includes various perspectives including quantitative measures of wellbeing or reduced depression (Proyer et al. 2021), and less clearly defined concepts like perceived creativity (West et al. 2017). While there is great diversity in the specifics of how playfulness, wellbeing, and the empiricism are conducted, there are two general pathways by which playfulness is connected to mental health through engagement.

4.1 Pathway One: Playfulness Increases Engagement with an Independently Healthy Activity

The first pathway describes the perception of playfulness as causing participants to engage more willingly in a mentally healthy activity. In this pathway, playfulness itself is not described as the source of the benefit but is considered to increase willingness to do a theoretically beneficial act. This framework is common for studies that are based in theatrical interventions, as well as other creative disciplines.

Theatrical based mental health interventions often present playfulness in this manner. One such program that applies this style of thinking is the *Geriatrics and Friends Intergenerational Theater Company.* They view their theatrical intervention as at "G&F's core is a focus on playfulness… Playfulness is able to help members of G&F build scenes. Directors of the company use games that utilize the playfulness of the group in order to find themes and structures for scenes. This works well with a community theatre group because members do not feel pressure – they only have to play the game." (Gusul 2015, p. 88). Critical to this perspective is the idea that playfulness is a short-term experience of the current intervention. The playfulness creates a reduction in normal resistance that participants would have in participating, thus playful experience increases the willingness to engage in the independently healthy theatrical endeavors. Other theatrical interventions similarly describe the playfulness of the theatrical environment as improving willingness to participate (Balyasnikova et al. 2018; West et al. 2017). The findings on well-being in these studies are also similar to results on the effects of theater interventions that do not study the term playfulness (Yuen et al. 2011). In this way, participants experiencing playfulness is an important characteristic to study in theatrical interventions on mental health.

Other creativity-based interventions present a similar pathway for how playfulness affects mental health. Other studied forms of creativity include dance therapy (Mills and Daniluk 2002; Margariti et al. 2012). As one form of dance therapy described "play, rhythm, dance and song work on a symbolic level. The aim is to alert the participants to act and express themselves, while orienting their drives in a positive way." (Margariti et al. 2012, Abstract). In this quotation we can see the characteristic quality of this pathway: Playfulness allows greater engagement in the mentally healthy activity, in this case expressing oneself and orienting drives in a positive way.

This view of playfulness is also used for certain studies on exercise programs (Abós et al. 2019; Li, Theng and Foo 2016). The playfulness in these works is not very clearly defined and is based upon the program activities that are known as a "game", such as the Wii sports programs (Li, Theng, and Foo 2016). Both of these works describe playfulness as causing positive experience, which is then associated with ongoing mental health. In this way we can see a pathway for how playfulness is theoretically predicted to affect mental health: Playfulness increases participatory engagement with mentally healthy activities.

Pathway 1: Participation

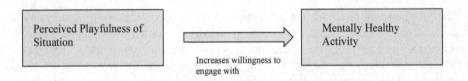

4.2 Pathway Two: Playfulness Increases Engagement with Life in General

The second pathway for how playfulness was predicted to affect mental health describes the personality trait of playfulness as a key feature of mental health. When playful experiences are repeated this causes an increase in playfulness as a personality trait, often as a target outcome. Playfulness as a personality trait is then furthermore correlated with other measures of mental health especially a general desire to engage with important relationships, positive experiences, and life in general.

There are several intervention programs that focus upon increasing playfulness. The Red Hat Society is a leisure society for older adults that has a few studies on its effectiveness (see Yarnal 2006). Other programs have targeted playfulness to affect wellbeing without clear findings such as the "funshop" workshop (Killick and Kenning 2015) that targets playfulness in adults with dementia. The Nursing Angels Institute similarly aims to bring more playfulness into hospital settings (Rodrigues et al. 2017). There are also several established theoretical frameworks that have been used to test this model of how playfulness connects to mental health.

Winnicott's (1971) *theory of playing* is an influential theoretical framework used in psychotherapy. This framework views therapy as a form of playing between a patient and the therapist. Through the playful interaction, a patient's ability to play is predicted to increase. This playfulness is the primary tool for how a person integrates their internal experience creatively with the external events that occur and enables a desire to live. As Winnicott (1971) describes.

> This gives us our indication for therapeutic procedure- to afford opportunity for formless experience, and for creative impulses, motor and sensory, which are the stuff of playing. And on the basis of playing is built the whole of man's experiential existence. No longer are we either introvert or extrovert. We experience life in the area of transitional phenomena, in the exciting interweave of subjectivity and objective observation, and in an area that is intermediate between the inner reality of the individual' and the share reality of the world that is external to individuals (Winnicott 1971, p. 64).

Winnicott's theory of playing has been test by a few psycho-therapeutic interventions. Yonatan-Leus et al. for example have studied how playful therapists have more therapeutic influence on participants (Yonatan Leus et al. 2018) the more sessions of successful therapy they have received (Yonatan Leus et al. 2020). In Winnicott's work playfulness can be seen as a target outcome of a mental health intervention. For example, Yonatan-Leus et al. (2018) wrote "Winnicott (1971) defined play as a significant component of a person's mental health and psychological development. He associated playfulness with an experience of authenticity, spontaneity, and vitality. He defined the increase in a clients' ability to play and being playful as one of the goals of therapy." (p. 2). Herrick (2018) uses a similar framework without citing Winnicott, and found an inverse relationship between playfulness in adult romantic relationships and depressive symptoms. Herrick similarly depicted playfulness as an outcome measure of successful family therapy.

Positive Psychology also presents several frameworks for playful experience increasing playfulness as a personality trait which subsequently improves mental health. Positive Psychological Interventions (PPI) are one source of empirical findings on this topic. PPIs are typified by short and self-guided interventions, where individuals focus upon and intentionally enact parts of their life that they consider to be positive. As described by Seligman et al. 2005.

Positive psychology is an umbrella term for the study of positive emotions, positive character traits, and enabling institutions. Research findings from positive psychology are intended to supplement, not remotely to replace, what is known about human suffering, weakness, and disorder. The intent is to have a more complete and balanced scientific understanding of the human experience – the peaks, the valleys, and everything in between. (p. 874)

In positive psychology, playfulness is viewed as a personality trait and is empirically connected to well-being and fewer depressive symptoms. In intervention, Wellenzohn et al. (2016; 2018) used this framework to study the effects of several humor-based interventions, which they define as a form of playfulness. For example, they tested *the three funny things task* on participants' well-being. In this intervention, participants were asked to reflect on humorous things from their day for seven consecutive days. Their work tested several of these types of playful interventions and found "All of the five one-week interventions enhanced happiness, three for up to six months" (Wellenzohn et al. 2016, abstract). In subsequent works they connected this happiness increase with general increases in sense of humor finding "changes in sense of humor from pretest to the 1-month follow-up predicted changes in happiness and depressive symptoms" (Wellenzohn et al. 2018, p. 1). Other positive psychologists have studied other models of playfulness in a similar intervention format. Proyer et al. (2021) conducted a PPI that focused upon the recollection of "playful things" (p. 6) in daily life and found similar beneficial results on wellbeing also moderated by changes in the participants' playful personality traits.

Another positive psychological theoretical framework used to integrate playfulness into empirical studies of mental health is the broaden-and-build theory which predicts playful experiences as "building physical, intellectual, psychological and social resources" (Fredrickson 2003, p. 333). Playfulness is a foundational component of the broaden-and-build theory where interventions are supposed "to create the urge to play, push the limits and be creative" (Fredrickson 2004, p. 1369). These studies describe a mutual relationship between playful activity and playful personality traits. Playful reflection and situations cause a general change in personality trait towards playfulness, and playful personalities are more likely to engage in acts of play. This cycle is then correlated with improving general engagement with other people and one's own life. This framework has also guided empirical findings that playfulness is correlated to resilience (see Chang, Yarnal and Chick 2016).

There are also several studies that predict a similar relationship between playfulness as a personality trait and mental health through correlational comparison. Harlinger and Blazina (2016) applied a PPI style intervention and found correlation between state of playfulness, playfulness as a personality trait, and a secure attachment style between participants and canine companions. This secure attachment was then seen as predictive of general attachment ability. Saliba (2018) found general correlation between personality trait playfulness and quality of life in older adults, a finding they have found in subsequent studies as well (Saliba and Barden 2021). Farley et al. (2021) found that adult playfulness exhibited "robust positive relations with positive emotion, engagement while with others and during activities, relationships, finding meaning in one's life, and overall well-being" (abstract). Similar studies have correlated playful personalities with subjective happiness in adulthood (Proyer 2014; Yue et al. 2016). During the coronavirus pandemic, Li et al. (2021) found that for college students "playfulness positively relates to life satisfaction and negatively correlates to school burnout" (abstract). Other works have found predictive relationships between humor and playfulness with subjective happiness and reduced depression for university students (Leung 2014). Brauer et al. (2021) has found playfulness to improve relationship satisfaction in older couples. Demir (2021) found playfulness in friendships to predict subjective happiness. Cabrera et al. (2017) correlated playfulness in parent interactions to greater wellbeing in children. Other works have found playfulness of parents as predictive of better mental health in 1–3 year-old children (Menashe-Grinberg and Atzaba-Poria 2017). For children with ASD, Roy and Kumar (2021) found that "more playful parents have better parent–child relationships and are competent in parenting" (Abstract).

In this way we see several renditions of similar theoretical frameworks. Winnicott's theory of playing, PPIs, Broaden-and-Build theory and correlational studies all view playful interactions as inspiring greater playfulness as a personality trait. Playful personalities are happier, have less depression, seek greater engagement in life and have more skill at coping with negative events in a way that does not reduce desire to engage. It is common to depict playfulness as a target of an intervention, and also view playful personalities as more willing to engage in playful interventions, creating a positive feedback loop. In this way, we see a general second pathway for how playfulness is connected to mental health: Playfulness as a personality trait is directly connected with definitions of mental health and general desire to engage with life.

Pathway 2: Personality

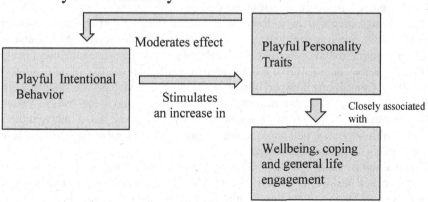

5 Conclusion and Discussion

By analyzing past empirical works connecting playfulness and mental health, two pathways emerged for how engagement is a critically mediating term: Pathway 1: Participation- Playfulness increases engagement with unrelated mentally healthy occupations. Pathway 2: Personality- Playful interactions increase playfulness as a personality trait which is mentally healthy because it increases capacity to engage with life in general. The first recommendation from this work is that mental health interventions involving serious games, or other game-based interventions should analyze the mediating concept of playfulness in their studies. Furthermore, studies can gain deeper insight by understanding playfulness as a way of re-organizing context to enable engagement, a claim that has seen recent empirical support in the context of player motivations in games (Vahlo et al. 2022). This is also a critical choice as improving engagement is also the most common explanation for why games are applied to improve mental health (Cheng et al. 2019). In this way, game based mental health interventions and playfulness based mental health interventions have very similar goals.

There are two major ways playfulness can be integrated as a mediating term into game based mental health interventions. The first way is as an ongoing experience. Many game-based interventions do not measure the player's experience of a game (Fleming et al. 2017). When playful experience is measured in gamification studies it is found that experiencing an intervention as playful has "a positive direct association with continued use" (Hamari and Koivisto 2015, abstract) as would be expected from pathway 1. However, this work and most like it present playfulness as a part of other constructs in this case "hedonic motivation" (p. 421). This placement of playfulness as inside other constructs, rather than its own construct, makes it more difficult to connect studies that analyze its effects. Other studies that have studied playful experience of an intervention have similarly found it to be a revealing concept in their conclusions (Codish and Ravid 2014). Considering how playfulness predicts desire to engage in an intervention, it is valuable for game-based interventions to measure ongoing playful experience as a mediator.

Secondly, playfulness as a personality trait is a valuable target outcome to be considered in game based mental health interventions. It is generally rare for gamification or game-based interventions to look at personality traits of participants (Bevins and Howard 2018). Some studies have looked at personality traits in game-based interventions for example, extraversion (Codish and Ravid 2014) or game personalities (Tu et al. 2015). When they are analyzed, it is found to be partially predictive of motivation (Tu et al. 2015). Considering how playfulness as a personality trait has been studied in other works as mediating the effects of mental health interventions, it seems that is a valuable outcome measure to analyze in games and gamification. Game based interventions on mental health may very well have clearer results if playful personality traits are tested before, during and after an intervention.

In addition to these two ways playfulness can be integrated into game-based and gamified mental health interventions, there is also a procedural difference that may prove useful in future studies. Playfulness pathway one often uses an expert facilitator whose primary goal is maintaining a playful experience for a participant. Most game-based interventions do not use an expert facilitator to apply an intervention and that expert even more rarely is described as attempting to enable a playful experience (Fleming et al. 2017). Past work in simulation and game studies has seen benefits from facilitators especially in education (Leigh et al. 2019; Sugiura 2021). In this way, it seems promising that an expert facilitator may enable greater playfulness in participants and thus improve results of mental health interventions.

Another valuable result of this endeavor is also the extension of playful engagement beyond a simplistic binary of playful and gameful. As seen in Wellenzohn et al. (2018), humor is also a commonly defined as a playful frame. The inclusion of humor directly confronts the long standing paidia vs. ludus conceptualization started by Caillois (2001) and continued into modern gamification (Deterding et al. 2011). While there is almost certainly benefits to understanding engagement caused by following rules and engagement unrestricted by rules, it is valuable to note that both have been defined, numerous times, as playfulness (Masek and Stenros 2021). In addition, outside of rules, there are other characteristics that are defined as playful in these works, such as imaginary performance (West et al. 2017). This also inspires the important question of whether humor and imagination are generally understood as playful by most people. This is a part of the broader question of what are the social contexts that are generally typified as playful?

This work aims to bring to light how important playfulness has been and should be to both mental health interventions and to the study of games. Considering how numerous fields have great interest in designing engaging interventions that improve players lives, it seems important for them to be brought into conversation with each other. They do have very different uses of similar terms, so it is also critical that further work is done on how to connect playful engagement to these diverse scholastic pursuits.

References

Abós, Á., Sevil-Serrano, J., Haerens, L., Aelterman, N., García-González, L.: Towards a more refined understanding of the interplay between burnout and engagement among secondary school teachers: a person-centered perspective. Learn. Individ. Differ. **72**, 69–79 (2019)

Balyasnikova, N., Higgins, S., Hume, M.: Enhancing teaching english as an additional language through playfulness: seniors (Ethno) drama club in Vancouver's downtown eastside. TESOL J. 9(3), 481–497 (2018)

Barnett, L.A.: The playful child: measurement of a disposition to play. Play Cult. 4(1), 51–74 (1991)

Beard, K.S.: Theoretically speaking: an interview with Mihaly Csikszentmihalyi on flow theory development and its usefulness in addressing contemporary challenges in education. Educ. Psychol. Rev. 27(2), 353–364 (2014). https://doi.org/10.1007/s10648-014-9291-1

Bevins, K.L., Howard, C.D.: Game mechanics and why they are employed: what we know about gamification so far. Issues Trends Learn. Technol. 6(1) (2018)

Bundy, A.C., Nelson, L., Metzger, M., Bingaman, K.: Validity and reliability of a test of playfulness. Occup. Therapy J. Res. 21(4), 276–292 (2001)

Brauer, K., Sendatzki, R., Scherrer, T., Chick, G., Proyer, R.T.: Revisiting adult playfulness and relationship satisfaction: APIM analyses of middle-aged and older couples. Int. J. Appl. Positive Psychol. 1-29 (2021)

Bratton, S., Ray, D.: What the research shows about play therapy. Int. J. Play Therapy 9(1), 47 (2000)

Cabrera, N.J., Karberg, E., Malin, J.L., Aldoney, D.: The magic of play: low-income Mothers' and Fathers' playfulness and children's emotion regulation and vocabulary skills: Mothers' and fathers' playfulness. Infant Ment. Health J. 38(6), 757–771 (2017). https://doi.org/10.1002/imhj.21682

Caillois, R.: Man, Play, and Games. University of Illinois Press (2001)

Cassotti, M., Habib, M., Poirel, N., Aïte, A., Houdé, O., Moutier, S.: Positive emotional context eliminates the framing effect in decision-making. Emotion 12(5), 926 (2012)

Chang, P., Yarnal, C., Chick, G.: The longitudinal association between playfulness and resilience in older women engaged in the red hat society. J. Leis. Res. 48(3), 210–227 (2016). https://doi.org/10.18666/jlr-2016-v48-i3-6256

Cheng, V.W.S., Davenport, T., Johnson, D., Vella, K., Hickie, I.B.: Gamification in apps and technologies for improving mental health and well-being: systematic review. JMIR Mental Health 6(6), e13717 (2019)

Codish, D., Ravid, G.: Personality based gamification-Educational gamification for extroverts and introverts. In: Proceedings of the 9th CHAIS Conference for the Study of Innovation and Learning Technologies: Learning in the Technological Era, vol. 1, pp. 36–44. The Open University of Israel, Ra'anana (2014)

Deci, E.L., Ryan, R.M.: The, "what" and "why" of goal pursuits: human needs and the self-determination of behavior. Psychol. Inq. 11(4), 227–268 (2000). https://doi.org/10.1207/S15327965PLI1104_01

Deterding, S., Dixon, D., Khaled, R., Nacke, L.: From game design elements to gamefulness: defining "gamification". In: Proceedings of the 15th International Academic MindTrek Conference: Envisioning Future Media Environments, pp. 9–15, September 2011

Demir, M.: Perceived playfulness in same-sex friendships and happiness. Curr. Psychol. 40(5), 2052–2066 (2019). https://doi.org/10.1007/s12144-018-0099-x

Farley, A., Kennedy-Behr, A., Brown, T.: An investigation into the relationship between playfulness and well-being in Australian adults: an exploratory study. OTJR: Occup. Participation Health 41(1), 56–64 (2021)

Fleming, T.M., Bavin, L., Stasiak, K., Hermansson-Webb, E., Merry, S.N., Cheek, C., Hetrick, S.: Serious games and gamification for mental health: current status and promising directions. Front. Psychiatry 7, 215 (2017)

Fredrickson, B.L.: The broaden–and–build theory of positive emotions. Philos. Trans. Royal Soc. London Ser. B Biol. Sci. 359(1449), 1367–1377 (2004)

Fredrickson, B.L.: The value of positive emotions: the emerging science of positive psychology is coming to understand why it's good to feel good. Am. Sci. **91**(4), 330–335 (2003)

Gordon, G.: Well played: the origins and future of playfulness. Am. J. Play **6**(2), 234 (2014)

Goutx, D., Sauvagnargues, S., Mermet, L.: Playing (in) a crisis simulation. In: Wardaszko, M., Meijer, S., Lukosch, H., Kanegae, H., Kriz, W.C., Grzybowska-Brzezińska, M. (eds.) ISAGA 2019. LNCS, vol. 11988, pp. 50–60. Springer, Cham (2021). https://doi.org/10.1007/978-3-030-72132-9_5

Gray, P.: The decline of play and the rise of psychopathology in children and adolescents. Am. J. Play **3**(4), 443–463 (2011). https://files.eric.ed.gov/fulltext/EJ985541.pdf

Gusul, M.: Knowing how to play or being playful? the playful/ontic approach and intergenerational theatre in Canada and India. Appl. Theatre Res. **3**(1), 85–100 (2015)

Harlinger, M., Blazina, C.: Exploring the role of playfulness with canine companions in coping with stress: how men are impacted by human–animal interaction through calling on a memory of play. In: Blazina, C., Kogan, L. (eds.) Men and Their Dogs. Springer, Cham (2016). https://doi.org/10.1007/978-3-319-30097-9_8

Hamari, J., Koivisto, J.: Why do people use gamification services? Int. J. Inf. Manag. **35**(4), 419–431 (2015)

Herrick, P.: The Presence of Playfulness in the Context of Couple Relationship, Relationship Satisfaction and its Associations With Symptoms of Depression. Doctoral dissertation (2018)

Hess, L.M., Bundy, A.C.: The association between playfulness and coping in adolescents. Phys. Occup. Ther. Pediatr. **23**(2), 5–17 (2003). https://doi.org/10.1080/j006v23n02_02

Huizinga, J.: Homo ludens: proeve fleener bepaling van het spel-element der cultuur. Tjeenk Willink, Haarlem (1938)

Killick, J., Kenning, G., Hand i pockets: creativity, playfulness and fun. J. Dement. Care (2015)

Leigh, E., Tipton, E., de Wijse-van Heeswijk, M.: A journey to the role of facilitator: personal stories unfolding alongside world trends. In: Wardaszko, M., Meijer, S., Lukosch, H., Kanegae, H., Kriz, W.C., Grzybowska-Brzezińska, M. (eds.) ISAGA 2019. LNCS, vol. 11988, pp. 3–13. Springer, Cham (2021). https://doi.org/10.1007/978-3-030-72132-9_1

Leung, C.L.R.: Adult playfulness and its relationship with humor, subjective happiness and depression: a comparative study of Hong Kong and mainland China (2014)

Li, Y., Hu, F., He, X.: How to make students happy during periods of online learning: the effect of playfulness on university students' study outcomes. Front. Psychol. **12** (2021)

Li, J., Theng, Y.L., Foo, S.: Exergames for older adults with subthreshold depression: does higher playfulness lead to better improvement in depression? Games Health J. **5**(3), 175–182 (2016)

Magnuson, C.D., Barnett, L.A.: The playful advantage: how playfulness enhances coping with stress. Leisure Sci. **35**(2), 129–144 (2013). https://www.ideals.illinois.edu/bitstream/handle/2142/29611/Magnuson_Cale.pdf?sequence=1

Margariti, A., Ktonas, P., Hondraki, P., Daskalopoulou, E., Kyriakopoulos, G., Economou, N.T., Vaslamatzis, G.: An application of the primitive expression form of dance therapy in a psychiatric population. Arts Psychother. **39**(2), 95–101 (2012)

Masek, L.: Playfulness as an Organization of Experience: Prioritizing Engagement over Realness, Relevance, or Consequence (Master's thesis) (2020)

Masek, L., Stenros, J.: The meaning of playfulness: a review of the contemporary definitions of the concept across disciplines. Eludamos J. Comput. Game Cult. **12**(1), 13–37 (2021)

Maslow, A.H.: The Farther Reaches of Human Nature, vol. 19711. Viking Press, New York (1971)

McGonigal, J., SuperBetter: The Power of Living Gamefully. Penguin (2015)

Menashe-Grinberg, A., Atzaba-Poria, N.: Mother-child and father-child interaction: the importance of parental playfulness as a moderator of the links between parental behavior and child negativity: parental playfulness and child negativity. Infant Ment. Health J. **38**(6), 772–784 (2017). https://doi.org/10.1002/imhj.21678

Mills, L.J., Daniluk, J.C.: Her body speaks: the experience of dance therapy for women survivors of child sexual abuse. J. Couns. Dev. **80**(1), 77–85 (2002)

Moon, J., Kim, Y.: Extending the TAM for a world-wide-web context. Inf. Manag. **38**(4), 217–230 (2001). https://doi.org/10.1016/S0378-7206(00)00061-6

Möring, S.: Games and Metaphor–A Critical Analysis of the Metaphor Discourse in Game Studies. IT University of Copenhagen (2013)

Proyer, R.T.: Z. Gerontol. Geriatr. **47**(6), 508–512 (2013). https://doi.org/10.1007/s00391-013-0539-z

Proyer, R.T.: A new structural model for the study of adult playfulness: assessment and exploration of an understudied individual differences variable. Personality Individ. Differ. **108**, 113–122 (2017)

Proyer, R.T., Gander, F., Brauer, K., Chick, G.: Can playfulness be stimulated? a randomised placebo-controlled online playfulness intervention study on effects on trait playfulness, well-being, and depression. Appl. Psychol. Health Well Being **13**(1), 129–151 (2021)

Rodrigues da Silva, L.S., da Silva Correia, N., Lessa Cordeiro, E., Tavares da Silva, T., Oliveira da Costa, L.T., de Véras Souza Maia, P.C.: Nursing angels: the playfulness as an instrument of citizenship and humanization in health. J. Nurs. UFPE/Revista de Enfermagem UFPE, **11**(6) (2017)

Roy, R.G., Kumar, A.: The mediating role of parental playfulness on parent–child relationship and competence among parents of children with ASD. Adv. Autism (2021)

Saliba El Habre, Y.: Aging well: How subjective age, playfulness, and depression influence quality of life among older adults (2018)

Saliba, Y.C., Barden, S.M.: Playfulness and older adults: implications for quality of life. J. Ment. Health Couns. **43**(2), 157–171 (2021)

Shen, X.: Constructing an interactionist framework for playfulness research: adding psychological situations and playful states. J. Leis. Res. **51**(5), 536–558 (2020)

Shen, X.S., Chick, G., Zinn, H.: Playfulness in adulthood as a personality trait: a reconceptualization and a new measurement. J. Leis. Res. **46**(1), 58–83 (2014)

Sicart, M.: Play Matters. MIT Press (2014)

Staempfli, M.B.: Adolescent playfulness, stress perception, coping and well being. J. Leis. Res. **39**(3), 393–412 (2007)

Staempfli, M., Mannell, R.C.: Adolescent playfulness and well-being. In: Eleventh Canadian Congress on Leisure Research, pp. 17–20, May 2005. https://pdfs.semanticscholar.org/3ab4/6301253342d52b0cb7c3b3cc2814c7904cd8.pdf

Stenros, J.: Playfulness, Play, and Games: A Constructionist Ludology Approach. Tampere University (2015)

Kikkawa, T., Kriz, W.C., Sugiura, J.: Differences between facilitator-guided and self-guided debriefing on the attitudes of university students. In: Wardaszko, M., Meijer, S., Lukosch, H., Kanegae, H., Kriz, W.C., Grzybowska-Brzezińska, M. (eds.) ISAGA 2019. LNCS, vol. 11988, pp. 14–22. Springer, Cham (2021). https://doi.org/10.1007/978-3-030-72132-9_2

Tomasino, B., Lotto, L., Sarlo, M., Civai, C., Rumiati, R., Rumiati, R.I.: Framing the ultimatum game: the contribution of simulation. Front. Hum. Neurosci. **7**, 337 (2013)

Tonkin, A., Whitaker, J. (eds.) Play in Healthcare for Adults: Using Play to Promote Health and Wellbeing Across the Adult Lifespan. Routledge (2016)

Tonkin, A., Whitaker, J. (eds.) Play and Playfulness for Public Health and Wellbeing. Routledge (2019)

Tu, C.H., Yen, C.J., Sujo-Montes, L., Roberts, G.A.: Gaming personality and game dynamics in online discussion instructions. Educ. Media Int. **52**(3), 155–172 (2015)

Vahlo, J., Tuuri, K., Välisalo, T.: Exploring gameful motivation of autonomous learners. Front. Psychol. **13** (2022)

Vona, F., Silleresi, S., Beccaluva, E., Garzotto, F.: Social MatchUP: collaborative games in wearable virtual reality for persons with neurodevelopmental disorders. In: Ma, M., Fletcher, B., Göbel, S., Baalsrud Hauge, J., Marsh, T. (eds.) Serious Games. JCSG 2020. Lecture Notes in Computer Science(), vol. 12434. Springer, Cham (2020). https://doi.org/10.1007/978-3-030-61814-8_4

Wellenzohn, S., Proyer, R.T., Ruch, W.: Humor-based online positive psychology interventions: a randomized placebo-controlled long-term trial. J. Posit. Psychol. 11(6), 584–594 (2016)

Wellenzohn, S., Proyer, R.T., Ruch, W.: Who benefits from humor-based positive psychology interventions? the moderating effects of personality traits and sense of humor. Front. Psychol. 9, 821 (2018)

West, S., Hoff, E., Carlsson, I.: Enhancing team creativity with playful improvisation theater: a controlled intervention field study. Int. J. Play 6(3), 283–293 (2017)

Winnicott, D.W.: Playing and Reality. Psychology Press (1971)

Yarnal, C.M.: The Red Hat Society®: exploring the role of play, liminality, and communitas in older women's lives. J. Women Aging 18(3), 51–73 (2006)

Yonatan-Leus, R., Tishby, O., Shefler, G., Wiseman, H.: Therapists' honesty, humor styles, playfulness, and creativity as outcome predictors: a retrospective study of the therapist effect. Psychother. Res. 28(5), 793–802 (2018)

Yonatan-Leus, R., Shefler, G., Tishby, O.: Changes in playfulness, creativity and honesty as possible outcomes of psychotherapy. Psychother. Res. 30(6), 788–799 (2020)

Yue, X.D., Leung, C.L., Hiranandani, N.A.: Adult playfulness, humor styles, and subjective happiness. Psychol. Rep. 119(3), 630–640 (2016)

Yuen, H.K., Mueller, K., Mayor, E., Azuero, A.: Impact of participation in a theatre programme on quality of life among older adults with chronic conditions: a pilot study. Occup. Ther. Int. 18(4), 201–208 (2011)

Measuring the Interaction of Conflict-Minimizing and Goal-Seeking Motor Imperatives in Autism Spectrum Disorder

Sundararaman Rengarajan[1](✉), Jonathan Cannon[2], Brendan Baron[3], Naren Mohan[4], and Leanne Chukoskie[1,5]

[1] Department of Physical Therapy, Movement and Rehabilitation Sciences, Northeastern University, Boston, USA
rengarajan.s@northeastern.edu
[2] Department of Brain and Cognitive Sciences, Massachusetts Institute of Technology, Cambridge, USA
[3] Khoury College of Computer Sciences, Northeastern University, Boston, USA
[4] Department of Mechanical and Industrial Engineering, College of Engineering, Northeastern University, Boston, USA
[5] Art + Design, College of Arts, Media and Design, Northeastern University, Boston, USA

Abstract. When subjected to sensory conflict, our bodies respond spontaneously and unconsciously to reduce or resolve it. We developed a Virtual Reality (VR) phase-matching task to establish a framework for explaining behaviors under conflict using hand-tracking, eye-tracking and pupillometry. We also describe a computational model of this behavior that was designed to help us understand differences in observed behavior from autistic individuals and non-autistic peers. We expect that known differences in prediction and attention mechanisms in autism will be important for accounting for behavioral differences observed in the task, highlighting these mechanisms as targets for future intervention.

Keywords: Autism · Virtual Reality · Active Inference · Modeling · Eye-tracking

1 Introduction

According to a classical control-theoretic perspective on self-movement, our brains pilot our bodies to achieve goals, sometimes using open-loop predictive models and sometimes with closed-loop feedback. From this perspective, synchronization of self-motion with a moving target is a simple control problem, where error between body and target is minimized by some combination of responsive and predictive control.

However, not all self-movement can be described in terms of goals. A second, more subtle, driver of movement is the reconciliation of multisensory prediction

© The Author(s), under exclusive license to Springer Nature Switzerland AG 2023
C. Harteveld et al. (Eds.): ISAGA 2022, LNCS 13622, pp. 185–198, 2023.
https://doi.org/10.1007/978-3-031-37171-4_13

errors (prediction error is the difference between what an individual expects from a circumstance based on one's internal model and what actually happens) (Friston et al., 2016). When subjected to, for example, visual/proprioceptive conflict, our bodies respond spontaneously and unconsciously to reduce or resolve it (Botvinick & Cohen, 1998; Pavani et al., 2000; Holmes et al., 2004; Holmes et al., 2006; Tsakiris & Haggard, 2005; Makin et al., 2008; Heed et al., 2011; Limanowski & Blankenburg, 2016). This phenomenon has been demonstrated in a small but growing collection of experiments, initially drawing on clever use of rubber hands (Asai 2015) but more recently taking advantage of virtual reality technology (Burin et al., 2019; Lanillos et al., 2021).

These two drivers of movement are unified within the theoretical framework of Active Inference (Maselli et al., 2021). This theory proposes that self-movement is always in service of resolving or avoiding prediction error (Friston et al., 2010), and that the intent to move is best understood as a prediction of a certain proprioceptive experience that is spontaneously fulfilled through self-motion (Adams et al., 2013). Active Inference offers an elegant model of synchronization of, for example, a hand movement with a visual target: we predict that our experienced hand motion will align with the target and also with the image of our own hand, and our resulting movement unfolds in order to minimize a weighted sum of the prediction errors from these two sources (Kilner et al., 2007; Grafton & Hamilton, 2007). In this model, the proprioceptive/visual prediction error between our body and the target is hardly different from the proprioceptive/visual prediction error that would drive our movement if our hand and its image were misaligned. In other words, we synchronize by identifying with - or embodying - the moving target.

This active inference model of synchronization has been formalized in Limanowski & Friston (2020). Their hierarchical generative model continuously estimates the velocities and positions of the oscillating target and the participant's hand based on two visual streams of information (the target hand image and the own hand image), one proprioceptive stream, and an internal model of the dynamics of the system and the noisiness of each stream. Their estimation was done through a sinusoidal mapping of the states of the hand and the states of the target, where both the target and hand state vary linearly with time and become sinusoidal via the respective sensory mapping of causes to sensory data. We propose a simpler formulation. The estimation can be done via Kalman filtering, a method that continuously estimates a multivariate Gaussian distribution over possible system states, i.e., a set of mean estimated positions and velocities and a set of covariances between these quantities representing the uncertainty about the estimates. As prescribed by Active Inference, movement is created by self-fulfilling prediction: the hand sets its actual velocity based on its estimated velocity. Estimates of hand velocity are made with a strong prior that the velocity will change to align the hand and the target, causing the agent to pursue the goal of synchronization.

The weight of each sensory stream in the estimation process depends on the inverse of the noisiness of each sensory stream in the internal model, or its "precision". Precision of each stream may vary by participant and may depend on eye gaze (Feldman & Friston, 2010; Edwards et al., 2012; Brown et al., 2013), causing either the target tracking error or visual/proprioceptive conflict to take priority in actuating movement.

This perspective on movement may offer us new insights into movement-related neurodiversity. For example, it has been suggested that people with autism make proprioceptive judgments that are less affected by visual- proprioceptive conflict (Paton et al., 2012). Separately, it has been demonstrated that people with autism are less responsive to timing perturbations during finger-tapping synchronization to an auditory pacing sequence (Vishne et al., 2021). Similarly, other studies suggest that autistic individuals might adjust minimally to movement initiation under uncertain circumstances (Arthur et al., 2021), have greater reliance on proprioception (Hirai et al., 2021), have greater reliance on proprioception while avoiding visual consequences during motor learning (Mostofsky & Ewen, 2011), overestimate the volatility of sensory environments (Arthur et al., 2021), demonstrate context-specific differences in Active Inference (Arthur et al., 2021), and weigh perceptual prediction errors highly (Allenmark et al., 2021). According to our model of synchronization, these observations may represent different parts of the same elephant: they could follow from reduced sensitivity to sensory/proprioceptive prediction errors.

We aim to explore this hypothesis using a visual synchronization task in VR. Participants will synchronize a cyclic opening and closing hand movement with an opening and closing target hand. We will introduce two types of perturbation: a transient delay of the target hand, and a transient delay of the image of their own hand. We predict that delays in the target hand image will cause participants to delay their own motion, just like delays in the target hand, demonstrating the multisensory-conflict-reducing driver of self-motion. We also predict that delays in the virtual hand image will cause participants to delay their own motion, as an attempt to sync their virtual hand with the target hand, demonstrating the multisensory-conflict-reducing driver of self-motion. We further predict that responsiveness to the two types of perturbation will covary between individuals (after controlling for attention to one hand or the other based on eye gaze), and that autistic participants will show similarly reduced responsiveness to the perturbation of target hand and no difference in their responsiveness for their virtual hand perturbation when controlled for attention.

2   Methods

2.1   Participants for the Pilot

For our pilot, a total of 11 healthy participants (non-autistic) (7 men, 4 women) took part in this study. They were between 18 and 28 years old, with an average of 22 years. All participants completed all the experiment conditions successfully. The experiment and the procedure were approved by the Northeastern University

Human Subjects Research Protection committee and conducted in accordance with the usual guidelines.

2.2   Design and Stimuli

This experiment is a $2 \times 2 \times 2$ mixed factorial experimental design with experiment (control and condition), attending object (virtual hand and target hand) and participants groups (autistic, non-autistic) as the factors where participants are randomly assigned to each group with Dynamic Time Warping distance as the response variable. The conditions are randomized and are counterbalanced across participants with the control task as a control for condition task, and non-autistic serving as controls for autistic individuals. Participants are asked to perform a phase-matching task in VR where they are instructed to perform a repetitive hand grasping movement whose speed is determined by a target hand opening and closing. This is intended to reduce bias towards the visual modality for its abstractness. The virtual hand is controlled through the hand tracking feature of Leap Motion sensor attached to the front of the VR headset of their real hand that's not visible to them, which decouples vision from proprioception. In the control trials, virtual hand and the real hand are in sync with each other and in the condition trials, the virtual hand is transiently delayed by 500 ms with respective to real hand for 6 s and the target hand is transiently delayed by 500 ms for 6 s. To control for attention, participants are asked to focus on the target hand for the entire task (both control and condition) and focus on their virtual hand for the entire task (both control and condition) and the data are collected (Fig. 1 and 2).

Control Target Hand: Participants are asked to sync their real hand with the target hand with no transient delays in either of the hands while looking at the target hand.

Condition Target Hand: Participants are asked to sync their real hand with the target hand with transient delays in both their virtual hand and target while looking at the target hand.

Control Virtual Hand: Participants are asked to sync their real hand with the target hand with no transient delays in either of the hands while looking at their virtual hand.

Condition Virtual Hand: Participants are asked to sync their real hand with the target hand with transient delays in both their virtual hand and target while looking at their virtual hand.

2.3   Task Design in Unity

The task was designed using the Unity Game Engine and currently runs within Unity. To run the task, we are using an HTC Vive Pro Eye, which has built-in Tobii Eye Tracking to gain information about eye gaze patterns. We also use a Leap Motion sensor attached to the front of the Vive to track the hand motion

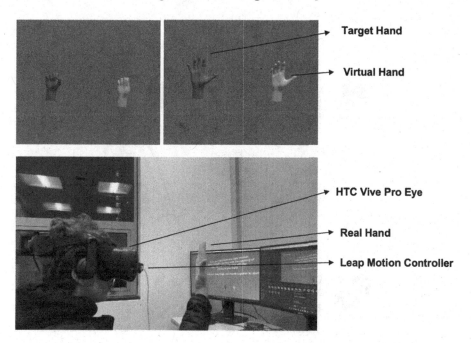

Fig. 1. Snippet from the VR task designed in the HTC Vive Pro Eye with Leap Motion sensor attached. Participants synchronize a cyclic opening and closing hand movement with an opening and closing of target hand.

of the participants. By using the Ultraleap SDK in Unity, we gain access to the Ultraleap tracking service within Unity, allowing us to track the location of the fingers in space and their current orientations. The control task has no perturbations and is run without changes to the data being gathered from the Leap Motion tracking (own hand and target hand). However, the condition task which has two perturbations (the target and own hands are transiently delayed independently for 6 s) varies because the Leap Motion tracking data is put into a queue that is not accessed for the desired delay time. For example, if you want to make the virtual hand (own hand and target hand) lag behind your real hand for 500 ms, you introduce a timer that does not allow you to access the hand data for 500 ms, then the queue remains full of data that is 500 ms behind what your real hand is doing. The eye data does not undergo changes per task. The SRanipal SDK outputs where the participant is looking and their current pupil sizes for each task. The task runs at 90 frames per second and outputs data at the same frequency $+/-$ 3 frames.

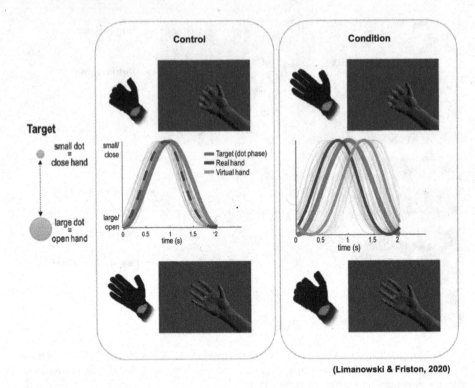

(Limanowski & Friston, 2020)

Fig. 2. Participants synchronize a cyclic opening and closing hand movement with an opening and closing target hand. In the condition task, we introduce two types of perturbation: a transient delay of the target hand, and a transient delay of the image of their own hand. We predict that delays in the target hand image will cause participants to delay their own motion, just like delays in the target hand, demonstrating the multisensory-conflict-reducing driver of self-motion. We also predict that delays in the virtual hand image will cause participants to delay their own motion, as an attempt to sync their virtual hand with the target hand, demonstrating the multisensory-conflict-reducing driver of self-motion. We further predict that responsiveness to the two types of perturbation will covary between individuals (after controlling for attention to one hand or the other based on eye gaze), and that autistic participants will show similarly reduced responsiveness to both types of perturbation.

2.4   Data Collection

Participants are asked to sit in an upright position that's comfortable for them in front of a desktop. They're then mounted with the VR headset that has the Leap Motion sensor attached to it. The VR headset and the built-in eye-tracker is sanitized using Cleanbox (UVC disinfecting machine) and calibrated before each participant's experiment. Each participant is asked to complete the two sets of tasks (control and condition) two times controlling for their attention (gaze at the target hand vs gaze at their virtual hand). Each task's duration is 120 s. This block is repeated 3 times. The tasks restarts if the participant's hand is not detected by the Leap Motion sensor (hand falls out of the field of view) and the data from that trial is not recorded. After successful completion of all the trials (4×3 trials), the raw data (grab angles of the real hand and the virtual hand, eye gaze location, and left and right pupil size at each frame) is exported into a CSV file.

2.5 Data Analysis

The output data file has grab angles of the real hand and the virtual hand at each frame which is Leap Motion sensor attribute that gives a value from 0 (open hand) to π (closed hand). The Vive Pro eye-tracker gives the x-, y- and z-coordinates of the eye-gaze location and the pupil size at each frame. The output data from the CSV file is noisy and is not ideal for analysis. Hence, the data collected is pre-processed with Butterworth low pass filter 1 Hz cut off frequency to filter the noise. The filtered data is then min-max normalized using

$$x^{'} = a + \frac{(x - \min(x))(b - a)}{\max(x) - \min(x)} \tag{1}$$

where (a, b) are the new range of data. We set the new range of data to (−1, 1) as the range of the input data of the target hand varies sinusoidally between −1 to 1.

For the response analysis, we used Dynamic Time Warping (DTW) algorithm to analyze the synchronization of the real hand with the target hand by computing the time difference at each frame from the two time-warped signals (real hand and target hand) using the below algorithm (Fig. 3).

In our case, the series 'u' is the grab angles of the target hand at each frame and the series 'v' is the grab angles of the real hand. To compute the mapping between two series, matrix 'g' is calculated by using the step 2 and 3 in a recursive manner to obtain the optimal mapping between both the series where T is the time series. The function 'd' in the above algorithm is the Euclidean distance. And the overall DTW distance 'D' between the two series is calculated as the sum of the Euclidean distances of the two series at the optimal mapping points. The time difference (lag) between these mapped points quantifies the synchronization between the real hand and the virtual hand.

Eye gaze data is used to validate where the participant is looking, specifically, if they are looking at the target hand, virtual hand or elsewhere. For this, we define a bounding box for both the target hand and the virtual hand of 120% of their original size and examine if the eye gaze point falls in either of these bounding boxes. Eye gaze at target hand, virtual hand or elsewhere are represented as color-coded highlighted regions in the plots. The eye gaze when looked at the target hand is highlighted in red, when looked at the virtual hand is highlighted in blue and when looked elsewhere is highlighted grey.

1. *Input*:
series $u = \{u_1, u_2, \ldots, u_{T_u}\}$
series $v = \{v_1, v_2, \ldots, v_{T_v}\}$

2. *Base conditions*:
$g(0,0) = 0$
$g(1,1) = d(u_1, v_1) \cdot w_D$
$g(i,0) = \infty$ for $1 \le i \le T_u$
$g(0,j) = \infty$ for $1 \le j \le T_v$

3. *Recursive relation*:
$$g(i,j) = \min \begin{cases} g(i, j-1) + d(u_i, v_j) \cdot w_V \\ g(i-1, j-1) + d(u_i, v_j) \cdot w_D \\ g(i-1, j) + d(u_i, v_j) \cdot w_H \end{cases}$$
for $1 \le i \le T_u$ and $1 \le j \le T_v$

4. *Output*:
DTW-distance $D(u,v) = k(w) \cdot g(T_u, T_v)$

Fig. 3. DTW algorithm

The pupillometry data is also preprocessed to remove the blinks by forward filling the blink data points and then plotted as a measure of arousal.

2.6   Results

The preliminary results (Figs. 4 and 5) suggest that the non-autistic individuals were able to follow the target hand's movement and adapt to the perturbations by delaying their real hand movements. DTW analysis reiterates the same. In the control task, the DTW and reference line almost overlap each other. Whereas in the condition task, there is an increase in time difference during the perturbation thereby confirming the adaptation.

2.7   Discussion

When subjected to visual/proprioceptive conflict, our bodies respond spontaneously and unconsciously to reduce or resolve it. This phenomenon has been

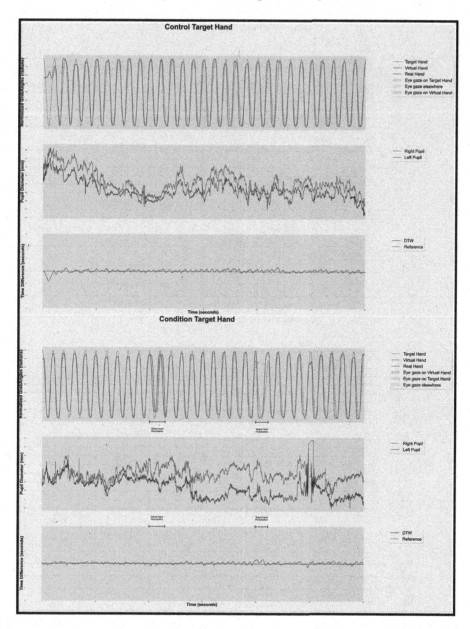

Fig. 4. This is a representative data from one non-autistic participant from the 11 participants data collected. There are two sets of plots - One for the control and other for the condition tasks while looking at the target hand. The top graph in all the tasks visualizes the participant's synchronization response to the target hand. Red dashed line shows the target hand's movement, blue line the participant's hand and green line their virtual hand. The red highlighted region shows the time the participant was looking at the target, blue region is the time looking at their virtual hand and grey region is the time looking elsewhere. The middle graph shows the left and right pupil sizes serving as a measure of arousal. The bottom graph shows the DTW analysis of the participant's real hand synchronization with the target hand. (Color figure online)

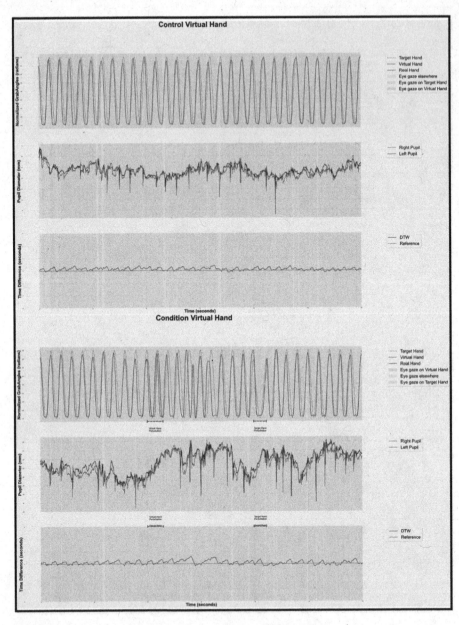

Fig. 5. This is a representative data from one non-autistic participant from the 11 participants data collected. There are two sets of plots - One for the control and other for the condition tasks while looking at their virtual hand. The top graph in all the tasks visualizes the participant's synchronization response to the target hand. Red dashed line shows the target hand's movement, blue line the participant's hand and green line their virtual hand. The red highlighted region shows the time the participant was looking at the target, blue region is the time looking at their virtual hand and grey region is the time looking elsewhere. The middle graph shows the left and right pupil sizes serving as a measure of arousal. The bottom graph shows the DTW analysis of the participant's real hand synchronization with the target hand. (Color figure online)

demonstrated in a growing collection of experiments, initially drawing on clever use of rubber hands (Asai 2015) but more recently taking advantage of virtual reality technology (Yuan & Steed 2010). It has recently been suggested that this motor phenomenon can be unified with the goal-oriented function of self-motion within the theory of Active Inference (Perrinet et al., 2014). This theory proposes that self-movement is always in service of resolving or avoiding prediction error, and that the intent to move is best understood as a prediction of a certain proprioceptive experience that is spontaneously fulfilled through self-motion (Shipp 2016).

The theory of active inference emerges from the theory of predictive processing, which models cognition as a process of approximate Bayesian inference about the hierarchical structure and state of the world (Friston & Kiebel 2009). In this modeling framework, different sources of sensory input are assigned different levels of "precision" that vary with "attention" and between individuals. In the context of Bayesian inference, precision corresponds with the inverse of the noisiness expected from each sensory stream; functionally, it assigns a weight to each source of information so that multiple potentially conflicting sources can be weighed against each other.

The predictive processing modeling framework offers the opportunity to model conflict-resolving movement in terms of underlying precision parameters (Maselli et al., 2021). Thus, measurements of conflict-resolving movement can be used to study variation in these parameters with attention and between individuals. Individual-by-individual variation in sensory precision, and in contextual adjustment of sensory precision, are especially interesting in the context of predictive processing theories of neurodiversity and disorder. For example, one account of autism proposes that many characteristics of autism arise from inflexible precision-weighting (Van de Cruys et al., 2014), and it has been suggested that people with autism are less responsive to visual-proprioceptive conflict (Paton et al., 2012).

To study the dynamic interaction of goal-oriented and conflict-resolving motor imperatives, we designed a virtual reality task [adapted from Limanowski & Friston (2020)]. The participant was able to see a VR image of their hand in the same relative position and state as their real hand, creating a sense of identification with the hand image. They were then instructed to synchronize the opening and closing of their real hand with the opening and closing of a target hand that is shown near the image of their own hand. We introduced visual-proprioceptive conflict during the performance of the task by transiently delaying the image of their virtual hand relative to their actual hand and transiently delaying the image of the target hand. We collected data from each of these tasks after controlling for attention.

According to the theory of Active Inference, a participant's response to the introduction of the delay perturbation will reflect their current balance of precision assigned to their proprioceptive sensation of their hand, the image of their hand, and the image of the target hand. If they assign high precision to the target hand and to their proprioception, they should be insensitive to this perturbation.

If they assign high precision to their virtual hand and to their proprioception, they should slow the advance of their hand movement to better align their virtual hand with their proprioceptive hand. And if they assign high precision to the target hand and the virtual hand, they should speed up their hand movement to better align the virtual hand to the target. We further expect that the baseline precision weighting will vary consistently among individuals, across the autism spectrum, etc. This task should offer us sufficient flexibility to fit a full active inference model of task performance on an individual-by-individual basis. To explore a higher dimensional behavior space, we introduce delays in the target hand and/or instruct participants to foveate one hand or the other.

Preliminary results in non-autistic individuals indicate that delays in visual self-motion cause participants to delay their own motion, demonstrating the multisensory-conflict-reducing behavior. In this context, we aim to study inter-individual differences in active inference processes.

Certain sensorimotor differences reported in autism, including differences in the weighting of proprioceptive relative to visual input and weaker error correction during entrained finger tapping, could follow from reduced sensitivity to sensory/proprioceptive prediction errors in the context of active inference. We are currently recruiting autistic individuals for this task. Our model suggests that reduced sensitivity to sensory/proprioceptive prediction errors should make autistic individuals less responsive to both types of perturbation compared to non-autistic peers (after controlling for visual attention). This result would establish a link among several sensorimotor differences in autism that can be explained in terms of active inference and would help to identify targets for future interventions.

References

Adams, R.A., Shipp, S., Friston, K.J.: Predictions not commands: active inference in the motor system. Brain Struct. Funct. **218**(3), 611–643 (2013). https://doi.org/10.1007/s00429-012-0475-5

Allenmark, F., Shi, Z., Pistorius, R.L., et al.: Acquisition and use of 'priors' in autism: typical in deciding where to look, atypical in deciding what is there. J. Autism Dev. Disord. **51**, 3744–3758 (2021). https://doi.org/10.1007/s10803-020-04828-2

Arthur, T., Harris, D., Buckingham, G., et al.: An examination of active inference in autistic adults using immersive virtual reality. Sci. Rep. **11**, 20377 (2021). https://doi.org/10.1038/s41598-021-99864-y

Asai, T.: Illusory body-ownership entails automatic compensatory movement: for the unified representation between body and action. Exp. Brain Res. **233**(3), 777–785 (2015). https://doi.org/10.1007/s00221-014-4153-0

Botvinick, M., Cohen, J.: Rubber hands "feel" touch that eyes see. Nature **391**(6669), 756 (1998). https://doi.org/10.1038/35784

Brown, H., Adams, R.A., Parees, I., Edwards, M., Friston, K.: Active inference, sensory attenuation and illusions. Cogn. Process. **14**(4), 411–427 (2013). https://doi.org/10.1007/s10339-013-0571-3

Burin, D., Kilteni, K., Rabuffetti, M., Slater, M., Pia, L.: Body ownership increases the interference between observed and executed movements. PLoS ONE **14**(1), e0209899 (2019). https://doi.org/10.1371/journal.pone.0209899

Edwards, M.J., Adams, R.A., Brown, H., Pareés, I., Friston, K.J.: A Bayesian account of "hysteria." Brain J. Neurol. **135**(Pt 11), 3495–3512 (2012). https://doi.org/10.1093/brain/aws129

Feldman, H., Friston, K.J.: Attention, uncertainty, and free-energy. Front. Hum. Neurosci. **4**, 215 (2010). https://doi.org/10.3389/fnhum.2010.00215

Friston, K.J., Daunizeau, J., Kilner, J., Kiebel, S.J.: Action and behavior: a free-energy formulation. Biol. Cybern. **102**(3), 227–260 (2010). https://doi.org/10.1007/s00422-010-0364-z

Friston, K., Kiebel, S. Predictive coding under the free-energy principle. Philos.Ttrans. R. Soc Lond. Ser B Biol. Sci. **364**(1521), 1211–1221 (2009). https://doi.org/10.1098/rstb.2008.0300

Friston, K., FitzGerald, T., Rigoli, F., Schwartenbeck, P., O Doherty, J., Pezzulo, G.: Active inference and learning. Neurosci. Biobehav. Rev. **68**, 862–879 (2016). https://doi.org/10.1016/j.neubiorev.2016.06.022

Grafton, S.T., Hamilton, A.F.: Evidence for a distributed hierarchy of action representation in the brain. Hum. Mov. Sci. **26**(4), 590–616 (2007). https://doi.org/10.1016/j.humov.2007.05.009

Heed, R., et al.: Visual information and rubber hand embodiment differentially affect reach-to-grasp actions. Acta Physiol. (Oxf) **138**(1), 263–271 (2011). https://doi.org/10.1016/j.actpsy.2011.07.003

Hirai, M., Sakurada, T., Izawa, J., et al.: Greater reliance on proprioceptive information during a reaching task with perspective manipulation among children with autism spectrum disorders. Sci. Rep. **11**, 15974 (2021). https://doi.org/10.1038/s41598-021-95349-0

Holmes, N.P., Crozier, G., Spence, C.: When mirrors lie: "Visual capture" of arm position impairs reaching performance. Cogn. Affect. Behav. Neurosci. **4**, 193–200 (2004). https://doi.org/10.3758/CABN.4.2.193

Holmes, N.P., Snijders, H.J., Spence, C.: Reaching with alien limbs: visual exposure to prosthetic hands in a mirror biases proprioception without accompanying illusions of ownership. Percept. Psychophys. **68**, 685–701 (2006). https://doi.org/10.3758/BF03208768

Kilner, J.M., Friston, K.J., Frith, C.D.: Predictive coding: an account of the mirror neuron system. Cogn. Process. **8**(3), 159–166 (2007). https://doi.org/10.1007/s10339-007-0170-2

Lanillos, P., Franklin, S., Maselli, A., et al.: Active strategies for multisensory conflict suppression in the virtual hand illusion. Sci. Rep. **11**, 22844 (2021). https://doi.org/10.1038/s41598-021-02200-7

Limanowski, J., Blankenburg, F.: Integration of Visual and proprioceptive limb position information in human posterior parietal, premotor, and extrastriate cortex. J. Neurosci. **36**(9), 2582–2589 (2016). https://doi.org/10.1523/JNEUROSCI.3987-15.2016

Limanowski, J., Friston, K.: Active inference under visuo-proprioceptive conflict: simulation and empirical results. Sci. Rep. **10**(1), 1–14 (2020). https://doi.org/10.1038/s41598-020-61097-w

Makin, T.R., Holmes, N.P., Ehrsson, H.H.: On the other hand: dummy hands and peripersonal space. Behav. Brain Res. **191**(1), 1–10 (2008). https://doi.org/10.1016/j.bbr.2008.02.041

Maselli, A., Lanillos, P., Pezzulo, G.: Active inference unifies intentional and conflict-resolution imperatives of motor control. PsyArXiv 2021. Retrieved from psyarxiv.com/9chs2

Mostofsky, S.H., Ewen, J.B.: Altered connectivity and action model formation in autism is autism. Neurosci. Rev. J. Bring. Neurobiol. Neurol. Psychiatry **17**(4), 437–448 (2011). https://doi.org/10.1177/1073858410392381

Paton, B., Hohwy, J., Enticott, P.G.: The rubber hand illusion reveals proprioceptive and sensorimotor differences in autism spectrum disorders. J. Autism Dev. Disord. **42**(9), 1870–1883 (2012). https://doi.org/10.1007/s10803-011-1430-7

Pavani, F., Spence, C., Driver, J.: Visual capture of touch: out-of-the-body experiences with rubber gloves. Psychol. Sci. **11**(5), 353–359 (2000). https://doi.org/10.1111/1467-9280.00270

Perrinet, L.U., Adams, R.A., Friston, K.J.: Active inference, eye movements and oculomotor delays. Biol. Cybern. **108**(6), 777–801 (2014). https://doi.org/10.1007/s00422-014-0620-8

Shipp, S.: Neural elements for predictive coding. Front. Psychol. **7**, 1792 (2016). https://doi.org/10.3389/fpsyg.2016.01792

Tsakiris, M., Haggard, P.: The rubber hand illusion revisited: visuotactile integration and self-attribution. J. Exp. Psychol. Hum. Percept. Perform. **31**(1), 80–91 (2005). https://doi.org/10.1037/0096-1523.31.1.80

Van de Cruys, S., et al.: Precise minds in uncertain worlds: predictive coding in autism. Psychol. Rev. **121**(4), 649–675 (2014). https://doi.org/10.1037/a0037665

Vishne, G., Jacoby, N., Malinovitch, T., Epstein, T., Frenkel, O., Ahissar, M.: Slow update of internal representations impedes synchronization in autism. Nat. Commun. **12**(1), 1–15 (2021). https://doi.org/10.1038/s41467-021-25740-y

Yuan, Y., Steed, A.: Is the rubber hand illusion induced by immersive virtual reality? In: 2010 IEEE Virtual Reality Conference (VR), pp. 95–102 (2010)

Resto Quest – A Serious Game on the Restorative Effects of Immersive Virtual Environments

Weilun Chen[1], Conchita Martin Hoogerwaard[1], Jeffrey Lim[1], Tim Polderdijk[1], Tom Saveur[1], Asror Wali[1], Suzanne Brinkman[2], Ineke J. M. van der Ham[2], and Rafael Bidarra[1(✉)]

[1] Delft University of Technology, Delft, The Netherlands
r.bidarra@tudelft.nl
[2] Leiden University, Leiden, The Netherlands
c.j.m.van.der.ham@fsw.leidenuniv.nl

Abstract. Mostly, restorative environments, like parks and forests, are only thought of in the real world. However, one can wonder whether their restorative effects translate to a virtual world; and whether the environment itself makes any difference. In order to assess the possible translation of restorative properties from the real world to a virtual setting, we developed *Resto Quest*, a single-player, first-person exploration game, designed to investigate the possible restorative effects of both natural and urban virtual environments. *Resto Quest* is playable on a normal personal computer, and its main game play loop consists of exploring the environment, locating in it a task to accomplish, and completing a simple minigame. After completion of each minigame, a positive change in the scenery takes place. Evaluation of *Resto Quest* has shown that players found its game mechanics relaxing, and that the minigames offer balanced difficulty between two interchangeable environments.

Keywords: Restorative Environments · Attention Restoration Theory · Serious Games · Virtual environments

1 Introduction

Mental stress and fatigue can stem from a variety of sources, and most people are affected by some kind of mental stress or fatigue throughout the day. One can reduce stress by participating in certain activities, such as yoga [30], or placing oneself in a restorative environment. Restorative environments are studied within the research area of environmental psychology. Environments are considered restorative when they provide positive influence on cognitive capacities, experience of stress and mental fatigue, and positive affect of an individual [1,9]. While restorative environments can vary for different individuals, a majority indicates that natural environments are considered restorative [14,27,35].

Travelling to natural environments is not always an option for everyone, due to such factors as money, time, or the lack of knowledge. A possible solution could

C. Harteveld et al. (Eds.): ISAGA 2022, LNCS 13622, pp. 199–213, 2023.
https://doi.org/10.1007/978-3-031-37171-4_14

be to develop a virtual environment that mimics the corresponding real world natural environment. Such a virtual environment, e.g. in the form of a digital serious game, could prove beneficial, as it would make restorative environments more accessible to the public at large. Moreover, research has shown that gaming can de-stress individuals [22]. However, while a serious game can provide a safe setting for individuals to play in, it is also possible that its natural elements get inadequately translated from reality into the virtual domain [8]. A good simulation of an environment should convey to players the notion that they 'are taken away' from their current surroundings. Findings from research suggest that natural environments are usually experienced as restorative [11]. In contrast, there has not been much research done on the possible restorative effects of urban environments.

A considerable part of the current studies on restorative environments employ virtual exposure methods such as pictures or videos. Using a video-game as a virtual exposure method offers a different research opportunity. Video-games require from an individual inherently more engagement with the environment than a photo or video. This engagement with the environment increases the opportunity of a restorative experience, as is shown in studies by Duvall [5] and Pasanen et al. [21]. The application opportunities for restorative video-games could also be more prevalent, since it is a popular pastime for large groups in the population. Although there have been some virtual restoring examples proposed [2–4,15,24,38,40], to the best of our knowledge, there has been no *serious game* proposed to research the restorative properties of interactive virtual environments, including the comparison of restorative differences of disparate virtual environments.

In this paper, we use exploration to assess how restorative properties can be well translated from the real world into different virtual environments. For this, we designed and developed the serious game *Resto Quest*, aimed at supporting research on the restorative effects of such virtual environments. For psychological comparative research, game environments can be considered balanced when they are fully similar on key characteristics, and the same game mechanics can be equally applied to either of them. We can then say that these environments are interchangeable.

In its current form, *Resto Quest* offers comparable gameplay within two very different virtual environments: one is a natural world, and the other an urban world. In this paper, we describe the main game design aspects of *Resto Quest*, its basic game mechanics, as well as our comparative evaluation of its virtual environments. Actual use of *Resto Quest* in a clinical setting is currently underway, and will be reported elsewhere.

2   Related Work

Prior research has been done in the fields of restorative environments, psychology regarding human attention, and use of virtual worlds. This research supports the underlying design choices of *Resto Quest*.

2.1   Theories on Attention Restoration

A person's attention capacity is important because many daily activities require sustained cognitive demand. Such activities are stressful and will eventually lead to a decrease in performance. Stress can also be a triggering or aggravating factor for many diseases and pathological conditions [39].

In cognitive psychology, focusing on a task that requires effort is called *voluntary attention*. One cause of attention fatigue is the activity of focusing on a specific task or stimulus with minimal motivational draw, while suppressing distractions which seem more interesting [12]. This fatigue causes a person's actions to be delayed, perception to be impaired, plan making abilities to decrease and irritability to increase.

In contrast to voluntary attention, which requires effort, there is *involuntary attention*, defined as attention that is not elicited by conscious decisions, but by certain outside events that are either intriguing or important stimuli. Fan et al. [6] clearly distinguish between voluntary attention and involuntary attention. More importantly, it has been shown that when involuntary attention is triggered, voluntary attention capacities can recover [12,31].

2.2   Natural Environment Theories

Involuntary attention is attention captured by intriguing stimuli, as e.g. those elements in natural environments, which are fascinating to humans. There are multiple theories that imply that exposure to nature enhances psychological well-being. For this research, three theories were considered: the Biophilia hypothesis, Attention Restoration Theory (ART), and Stress Reduction Theory (SRT).

The Biophilia hypothesis [13] states that humans have an innate need to affiliate with other living things, because of the humans' close relation with nature throughout evolution. Lin et al. [16] explores this and shows that even trees that are unconsciously noticed in an urban environment may restore the individual.

The Attention Restoration Theory [11] claims that urban living taxes attentional capacities and leads to mental fatigue. In contrast to urban environments, natural environments are suggested to contain elements that are inherently fascinating. ART states that for an environment to be restorative, e.g. natural environments, it needs four attributes: (1) it has to encourage involuntary attention. (2) the person experiencing the environment must have a feeling of *being away*. (3) the environment must be adequately rich to make up a whole other world. (4) the environment must meet the characteristics and the goals of the person.

The Stress Reduction Theory [18] states that exposure to natural environments with water, vegetation, and other elements that accompanied human evolution produce a response characterised as decreased physiological arousal, decreased negative affect, and increased positive affect.

All three theories highlight the impact of the natural environment on the human well-being, but research has also been done on urban environments. Ulrich et al. [33] and Reetz et al. [23] compare psychological effects of urban environments against that of natural environments, in which nature consistently performed better than the urban scenes. Ulrich et al. [33] additionally show that the complexity of an environment, the number of perceived elements and their dissimilarity, is less important than the content.

2.3 Restoration Through Leisure Activities

Not all activities are equivalent in restorative properties. Rupp et al. [25] show that playing games and reading are both more restorative than doing nothing. They distinguish between affective restoration (feeling better) and cognitive restoration (performing better), and show that playing games causes affective restoration.

An experience does not need to be complex to carry restorative properties. Valtchanov et al. [34] show that a person can benefit from the restorative properties of an environment just by looking at images of that environment using an VR headset.

Casual games have more benefits than just the possible restorative property. Whitbourne et al. [37] look at adult players ranging from 18 to 80 years old who casually play the popular free online game, *Bejeweled Blitz*. All players show an improvement in memory, in quicker perception, in recognising patterns, as well as a clever resourcefulness and a boost in confidence.

2.4 Challenges of Using Virtual Worlds in Game Design

A crowded environment can induce anxiety in a person, therefore it is important to be aware of the number of humans in the environment. In theory, the fewer humans, the more restorative it becomes [36], but this does not mean that the environment should feel lonely [19].

The geography of an environment also affects the restorative properties. Schebella et al. [26] show that a hilly environment is more restorative than one that is flat. This corresponds with the notion that natural environments could be more restorative than urban environments, since hills are often more perceptible in natural environments.

Ulrich et al. [33] discuss the colours and patterns that are often found in the different environments. Nature consists largely of blue and green colours, while urban environments contain more grey, black, and white colours.

Much research has been done on methods to generate virtual worlds [29], both natural [10,20] and urban [28,32], so the creation of a virtual environment can be largely facilitated by employing a variety of procedural methods. In any case, when developing a virtual world for a serious game, one should always take into account its purpose, to keep a good balance among gameplay, meaning, and realism [8].

3 Game Design

Resto Quest is a 3D first-person exploration game in which the player can explore one of two virtual environments: urban and natural. The two environments are interchangeable by design, featuring similar game mechanics, story, and goals,

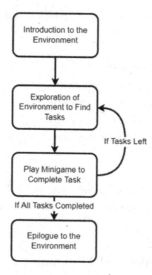

Fig. 1. Main game loop, iterating between exploration and each minigame.

in order to compare their psychological effects, as done by Ulricht et al. [33] and Reetz et al. [23].

Another essential design feature of *Resto Quest* is that it presents a set of low-cognitive-load minigames that simply keep you busy and relaxed while in the environment. In this way, researchers using *Resto Quest* can more easily focus on the relation between restorative elements in real life and in the particular virtual environment of the game.

3.1 Game Synopsis

Resto Quest is an exploration game with interchangeable environments, in which the player is encouraged to walk around, searching for minigames. In both environments, the minigames will only differ in theme, the gameplay will be basically the same. At the game introduction, players are told they are either a park ranger preparing for the next camping season, in the natural environment, or the vice mayor preparing for the upcoming town festival, in the urban environment. The inclusion of this overarching story line helps to integrate the different minigames, as well as keeping the player's engagement, immersion, and motivation throughout the game, instead of relying just on players' curiosity to explore its environment.

3.2 Main Game Loop

The game starts with a brief introduction to the environment, after which the player iterates between exploring the environment while looking for the next task on their task list, and playing the respective minigame; see Fig. 1. After completing each minigame, the task is ticked off the list, and the environment will

Table 1. The five minigames: description and finish condition.

Minigame name	Activity	Finish Condition
Stacking blocks	Stack 10–15 objects	Stable for 10 s
Matching colours	Match object with right colour	10 times correct match
Connect the dots	Connect two dots without crossing	Complete 3 levels
Sweeping	Scrap the top layer to reveal text	Top layer is removed
Scavenger hunt	Collect items throughout the environment	All items collected

undergo some visible positive (rewarding) change. When all tasks are completed, the player transitions into the epilogue. The intended playtime of *Resto Quest* is around 15 min.

3.3 Key Game Mechanics and Minigames

Resto Quest comprises several game features. In the first place, basic navigation allows the player to explore the environment. Moreover, other features and game mechanics, such as the task list, minigames and the corresponding score, and rewards, contribute to the gameplay and immersion of the player.

3.3.1 Exploration

Navigation. As exploration of the environment is key in *Resto Quest*, it is necessary to be able to see the whole environment around the player. As usual in first-person games, players can look around using their mouse, and move using the directional keys. This gives them full control on motion and on where to look, reinforcing their immersion in the environment.

Directions. While exploration is encouraged in *Resto Quest*, players could possibly become frustrated when they cannot find a minigame location. Therefore, hints, such as signs or descriptions, are occasionally given, in order to help players locate their pending tasks.

3.3.2 Tasks and Minigames

Task List. When a minigame is completed, the task associated to it is ticked off the list. The use of a task list is consistent with the low-cognitive requirement desired for *Resto Quest*: the player does not have to remember which tasks are already completed nor which still have to be done.

Minigames. Currently, there are five different minigames in *Resto Quest*, of which a short generic description is provided in Table 1. Most of the minigames are based on games that parents play with their young children [7]. Again, the choice for these infant-themed games ties in with the desire for low-cognitive-load activities. While each minigame mechanics stays consistent between the urban and natural environments, their assets and story differ slightly to keep consistency with the respective main story-line, as described in Subsect. 3.1. Table 2 summarises the stories of the minigames in both environments.

Rewards. Upon completion of a minigame, the player receives a reward consisting of a visible change in the current scenery, e.g. when the player sweeps away dirt, ground will show up beneath. This is a permanent change to the environment, and it is meant to give a sense of satisfaction to the player.

Table 2. Stories associated to the minigames.

Mingame	Urban environment	Natural environment
Stacking blocks	Help the builders near the music stage with building the Ferris wheel	Help the camp by stacking firewood near the log cabins.
Matching colours	Help the valet service near the stadium	You have to help the butterflies reach the correct flowers in order for them to pollinate the other flowers. You can most likely find them at the big flower patch along the pathways.
Connect the dots	More electricity is needed for the party, please use the electricity box near the airport to rewire it	The fountain does not work, please try to find the issue and fix it. It can be found near the pathways.
Sweeping	There has been an oil spill near the refinery and at the church, please sweep it up	There are loads of leaves on the pathways, please sweep them up when you find them.
Scavenger hunt	Send 5 invitations to the party. The mailboxes are scattered around the city	Help the animals by finding them food; maybe you should start with the deer near the log cabins

3.4 Game Style

The game uses a low-poly art style, due to its non-distractive nature, as well as to the small effort required to make it look good. The low-poly art style is also low on hardware requirements, so most computers should be able to run *Resto Quest* without issues. The low-poly art assets used for the urban[1] and natural[2] environments can be found in the Unity Asset Store.

The ambience for both environments was desired to be neither stressful nor scary. The time of day is 3–4PM, which is a fitting time since both stories take

---

[1] https://assetstore.unity.com/packages/3d/props/low-poly-ultimate-pack-54733.
[2] https://assetstore.unity.com/packages/3d/environments/landscapes/lowpoly-style-ultra-pack-108275.

(a) Urban environment

(b) Natural environment

Fig. 2. Graphics style of *Resto Quest*. (Color figure online)

place during work time. This allows for some daylight and a good general visibility. *Resto Quest* uses only sounds that are expected on the respective environments, so that they are not distracting and only serve the purpose of increasing immersion. In the natural environment, these are mostly animal, water, and tree noises, while the urban environment mostly has people talking and cars in the background, such that ART [11], the Biophilia Hypothesis [13], and SRT [18] can apply. In both environments, there are some creatures or humans, enough to make sure that neither the player will feel lonely, which can cause stress, nor the environment will be too crowded [19,36]. The natural environment also has hills, in contrast to the urban environment, to align with restorative effects hills can provide [26]. The colour scheme of both environments has been chosen according to Ulrich et al. [33]: largely blue and green for natural environment and overall grey, black and white colours in the urban environment.

Figure 2 gives a good impression of the graphics style of *Resto Quest*. A short trailer with more footage on the game can be found elsewhere[3].

4   Evaluation

This evaluation is a preliminary exploration before full psychological research takes place. In order to properly evaluate *Resto Quest* and assess whether it is fit

---

[3] https://surfdrive.surf.nl/files/index.php/s/NfsmsNKViE4aJlx/download.

to be used for such research on the restorative effects of virtual environments, the gameplay should be equivalent in all regards, except for the actual environment. This would mean that the restorative aspects of the visual elements of the virtual environments can be separately evaluated. Furthermore, it is important that the various game elements are well perceived as such by the players, as intended by design.

4.1 Method

The participants played one of the environments, after which they answered the questionnaire in Table 3. To measure the time spent exploring the environment, a logging system was implemented that keeps track of: total playtime, time spent per task, and amount of clicks per minigame. These values are used to calculate an exploration rate as a ratio between time spent exploring the environment and time spent in minigames. These metrics contribute to answering whether *Resto Quest* is suitable for experimental research and, particularly, whether the environments are interchangeable.

Table 3. Interview protocol used.

Nr	Question	Question type
1	What is your age?	Open question
2	Do you game more than 10 h a week?	Closed question
3	On a scale from 1 to 5, how well were the game elements a translation from reality? (Feel free to further elaborate on your answer)	Likert scale Open question
4	Did you feel relaxed after playing this game? Why (not)?	Closed question Open question
5	What elements in the game could be changed to improve your experience?	Open question

The selection of the participants (n = 12) was done by asking acquaintances to play the game in one of the environments (urban and natural). For both environments one older, non-gamer person played the game. Urban and natural environments were equally distributed among the other participants, by our assignment, rather than by their choice. Most participants were students, with ages in the range 20–27.

4.2 Results

The average realism grade given (question 3) was 4.3 for the urban environment, and 3.9 for the natural environment, yielding an overall realism grade of 4.1.

With regard to relaxation effect (question 4), 50% of players in the urban environment report experiencing relaxation, and this figure went up to 66% for the natural environment. Overall, more than half of the players report they were in a relaxed mood after the game.

The logged data, summarised in the charts of Fig. 3, reveals that the exploration rate is higher for the natural environment than for the urban environment. Moreover, the average total playtime for the urban environment is slightly higher but has a much lower spreading.

Regarding the duration of the various minigames, except for the Matching game, their playtime is, on average, balanced between the two environments; see the charts in Fig. 4. All charts displayed feature the same error bars, which use the exclusive median, including inner and outlier points (Table 4).

Table 4. Participant answers to questions 1 and 2 from the interview in Table 3. ('Gamer' was defined as 'participant plays more than 10 h a week')

ID	Age	Gamer?	Environment
1	24	no	urban
2	23	no	natural
3	21	no	urban
4	21	yes	natural
5	27	no	natural
6	57	no	urban
7	20	no	urban
8	23	no	natural
9	23	no	urban
10	49	yes	urban
11	25	yes	urban
12	55	no	natural

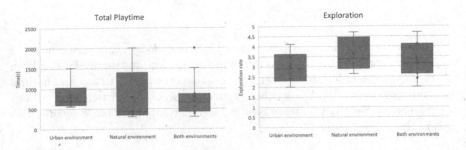

Fig. 3. Total playtime (in seconds) and exploration rate.

4.3   Discussion

From the results above we can conclude that the two environments in *Resto Quest* are perceived as relaxing by over 50% of the participants.

The playtime logged data depicted in Fig. 3 shows small differences between the minigames in the urban and natural environments. The data shows that, on average, players have a slightly higher average playtime in the urban environment compared to the natural environment. However, there is a much larger variance in the total playtime of participants in the natural environment than in the urban environment. We therefore conclude that participants did spend more time exploring the natural environment, while they seemed to move on quicker to the tasks in the urban environment.

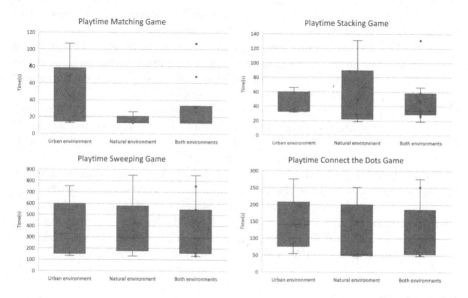

Fig. 4. Playtime (in seconds) for each of the minigames.

The average exploration rate was higher in the natural environment. A reason for that could be the irregular placement of its minigames, making it harder to figure out where to go next. In contrast, the grid layout of the city and its clear roads, might be making the navigation more intuitive.

Regarding the playtime data per minigame, in Fig. 4, we found out that the longer playtime for the Matching game in the urban environment was due to the unfortunate coincidence of one specific asset having white in it, becoming at times less distinguishable. For the rest, the data does not show a significant difference between environments in terms of minigame difficulty or average time taken to complete the game. Overall, the total time and effort taken is much more dependent on the players themselves than on which environment they played.

This is also a good result regarding the interchangeability of these two virtual environments within *Resto Quest*, as similar times indicate similar difficulty.

One limitation of the current sampling method is selection bias: due to non-probability sampling, the researchers chose the subjects and this may involve a certain bias. However, for testing whether the game is fit for psychological research, this evaluation is considered sufficient.

5   Conclusion

Real-world restorative environments are effective, but far from accessible to everyone. Virtual environments are a promising alternative, if only they properly translate the right restorative elements. We presented *Resto Quest*, a first-person exploration game designed to support psychological research on the restorative effects of both natural and urban virtual environments.

By design, the main game loop of *Resto Quest* casually leads the player to explore the environment, looking for tasks to accomplish towards an overarching goal. Each task involves a low-cognitive load minigame, that gently integrates into the main game story within each virtual environment.

Evaluation of the game mechanics of *Resto Quest* has confirmed its suitability and potential for experimental deployment by experienced psychologists. Research is currently underway, on the restorative effects of various virtual environments, including those in *Resto Quest*.

From the direct feedback received, we identified several directions for improving *Resto Quest*. Particularly the urban environment could be improved in terms of immersion and experience (e.g. accessible places, spread of objects). Moreover, most minigames could be made somewhat more challenging, possibly featuring some adaptive difficulty adjustment mechanism [17]. Finally, the graphics, textures, and animations could as well be enhanced, for improved realism.

References

1. Berto, R.: Exposure to restorative environments helps restore attentional capacity. J. Environ. Psychol. **25**(3), 249–259 (2005). https://doi.org/10.1016/j.jenvp.2005.07.001
2. Björling, E.A., Sonney, J., Rodriguez, S., Carr, N., Zade, H., Moon, S.H.: Exploring the effect of a nature-based virtual reality environment on stress in adolescents. Front. Virtual Reality **3** (2022). https://doi.org/10.3389/frvir.2022.831026. https://www.frontiersin.org/article/10.3389/frvir.2022.831026
3. Browning, M.H.E.M., Saeidi-Rizi, F., McAnirlin, O., Yoon, H., Pei, Y.: The role of methodological choices in the effects of experimental exposure to simulated natural landscapes on human health and cognitive performance: a systematic review. Environ. Behav. **53**(7), 687–731 (2021). https://doi.org/10.1177/0013916520906481
4. Depledge, M.H., Stone, R.J., Bird, W.J.: Can natural and virtual environments be used to promote improved human health and wellbeing? Environ. Sci. Technol. **45**(11), 4660–4665 (2011). https://doi.org/10.1021/es103907m. pMID: 21504154

5. Duvall, J.: Using engagement-based strategies to alter perceptions of the walking environment. Environ. Behav. **45**(3), 303–322 (2011). https://doi.org/10.1177/0013916511423808

6. Fan, J., McCandliss, B.D., Fossella, J., Flombaum, J.I., Posner, M.I.: The activation of attentional networks. Neuroimage **26**(2), 471–479 (2005). https://doi.org/10.1016/j.neuroimage.2005.02.004

7. Guyton, G.: Using toys to support infant-toddler learning and development. Young Child. **66**, 50 (2011)

8. Harteveld, C., Guimarães, R., Mayer, I.S., Bidarra, R.: Balancing play, meaning and reality: the design philosophy of LEVEE PATROLLER. Simul. Gaming **41**(3), 316–340 (2009). https://doi.org/10.1177/1046878108331237

9. Herzog, T.R., Black, A.M., Fountaine, K.A., Knotts, D.J.: Reflection and attentional recovery as distinctive benefits of restorative environments. J. Environ. Psychol. **17**(2), 165–170 (1997). https://doi.org/10.1006/jevp.1997.0051

10. Huijser, R., Dobbe, J., Bronsvoort, W.F., Bidarra, R.: Procedural natural systems for game level design. In: 2010 Brazilian Symposium on Games and Digital Entertainment (SBGAMES), pp. 189–198. IEEE (2010)

11. Kaplan, R., Kaplan, S.: The experience of nature: a psychological perspective. CUP Archive (1989)

12. Kaplan, S.: The restorative benefits of nature: toward an integrative framework. J. Environ. Psychol. **15**(3), 169–182 (1995). https://doi.org/10.1016/0272-4944(95)90001-2

13. Kellert, S.R., Wilson, E.O.: The biophilia hypothesis. Bull. Sci. Technol. Soc. **15**(1), 52–53 (1995). https://doi.org/10.1177/027046769501500125

14. Korpela, K., Staats, H.: The restorative qualities of being alone with nature, pp. 351–367. Wiley (2013). Chapter 20. https://doi.org/10.1002/9781118427378.ch20

15. Li, H., et al.: Effect of a virtual reality-based restorative environment on the emotional and cognitive recovery of individuals with mild-to-moderate anxiety and depression. Int. J. Environ. Res. Public Health **18**(17), 9053 (2021). https://doi.org/10.3390/ijerph18179053

16. Lin, Y.H., Tsai, C.C., Sullivan, W.C., Chang, P.J., Chang, C.Y.: Does awareness effect the restorative function and perception of street trees? Front. Psychol. **5** (2014). https://doi.org/10.3389/fpsyg.2014.00906

17. Lopes, R., Bidarra, R.: Adaptivity challenges in games and simulations: a survey. IEEE Trans. Comput. Intell. AI Games **3**(2), 85–99 (2011)

18. McMahan, E.A., Estes, D.: The effect of contact with natural environments on positive and negative affect: a meta-analysis. J. Posit. Psychol. **10**(6), 507–519 (2015). https://doi.org/10.1080/17439760.2014.994224

19. Nordh, H., Alalouch, C., Hartig, T.: Assessing restorative components of small urban parks using conjoint methodology. Urban For. Urban Greening **10**(2), 95–103 (2011). https://doi.org/10.1016/j.ufug.2010.12.003

20. Onrust, B., Bidarra, R., Rooseboom, R., van de Koppel, J.: Ecologically-sound procedural generation of natural environments. Int. J. Comput. Games Technol. **2017**, 7057141 (2017)

21. Pasanen, T.P., Neuvonen, M., Korpela, K.M.: The psychology of recent nature visits: (how) are motives and attentional focus related to post-visit restorative experiences, creativity, and emotional well-being? Environ. Behav. **50**(8), 913–944 (2017). https://doi.org/10.1177/0013916517720261

22. Pine, R., Fleming, T., McCallum, S., Sutcliffe, K.: The effects of casual videogames on anxiety, depression, stress, and low mood: a systematic review. Games Health J. **9**(4), 255–264 (2020). https://doi.org/10.1089/g4h.2019.0132

23. Reetz, A., Valtchanov, D., Barnett-Cowan, M., Hancock, M., Wallace, J.R.: Nature vs. stress. Proc. ACM Hum.-Comput. Interact. 5(CHI PLAY), 1–13 (2021). https://doi.org/10.1145/3474674

24. Rockstroh, C., Blum, J., Hardt, V., Göritz, A.S.: Design and evaluation of a virtual restorative walk with room-scale virtual reality and impossible spaces. Front. Virtual Reality 1 (2020). https://doi.org/10.3389/frvir.2020.598282. https://www.frontiersin.org/article/10.3389/frvir.2020.598282

25. Rupp, M.A., Sweetman, R., Sosa, A.E., Smither, J.A., McConnell, D.S.: Searching for affective and cognitive restoration: examining the restorative effects of casual video game play. Hum. Factors J. Hum. Factors Ergon. Soc. 59(7), 1096–1107 (2017). https://doi.org/10.1177/0018720817715360

26. Schebella, M.F., Weber, D., Lindsey, K., Daniels, C.B.: For the love of nature: exploring the importance of species diversity and micro-variables associated with favorite outdoor places. Front. Psychol. 8 (2017). https://doi.org/10.3389/fpsyg.2017.02094

27. Scopelliti, M., Carrus, G., Bonaiuto, M.: Is it really nature that restores people? A comparison with historical sites with high restorative potential. Front. Psychol. 9, 2742 (2019). https://doi.org/10.3389/fpsyg.2018.02742

28. Silva, P.B., Eisemann, E., Bidarra, R., Coelho, A.: Procedural content graphs for urban modeling. Int. J. Comput. Games Technol. 2015, 808904 (2015)

29. Smelik, R.M., Tutenel, T., Bidarra, R., Benes, B.: A survey on procedural modelling for virtual worlds. Comput. Graph. Forum 33(6), 31–50 (2014)

30. Smith, C., Hancock, H., Blake-Mortimer, J., Eckert, K.: A randomised comparative trial of yoga and relaxation to reduce stress and anxiety. Complement. Ther. Med. 15(2), 77–83 (2007). https://doi.org/10.1016/j.ctim.2006.05.001

31. Staats, H.: Restorative Environments. Oxford University Press, Oxford (2012). https://doi.org/10.1093/oxfordhb/9780199733026.013.0024

32. Taal, F., Bidarra, R.: Procedural generation of traffic signs. In: Eurographics Workshop on Urban Data Modelling and Visualisation. Eurographics (2016)

33. Ulrich, R.S.: Natural versus urban scenes: some psychophysiological effects. Environ. Behav. 13(5), 523–556 (1981). https://doi.org/10.1177/0013916581135001

34. Valtchanov, D., Barton, K.R., Ellard, C.: Restorative effects of virtual nature settings. Cyberpsychol. Behav. Soc. Netw. 13(5), 503–512 (2010). https://doi.org/10.1089/cyber.2009.0308

35. Van den Berg, A.E., Joye, Y., Koole, S.L.: Why viewing nature is more fascinating and restorative than viewing buildings: a closer look at perceived complexity. Urban For. Urban Greening 20, 397–401 (2016). https://doi.org/10.1016/j.ufug.2016.10.011

36. Wang, X., Rodiek, S., Chengzhao, W., Chen, Y., Li, Y.: Stress recovery and restorative effects of viewing different urban park scenes in Shanghai, China. Urban For. Urban Greening 15, 112–122 (2016). https://doi.org/10.1016/j.ufug.2015.12.003

37. Whitbourne, S.K., Ellenberg, S., Akimoto, K.: Reasons for playing casual video games and perceived benefits among adults 18 to 80 years old. Cyberpsychol. Behav. Soc. Netw. 16(12), 892–897 (2013). https://doi.org/10.1089/cyber.2012.0705

38. White, M.P., et al.: A prescription for 'nature' - the potential of using virtual nature in therapeutics. Neuropsychiatr. Dis. Treat. 14, 3001–3013 (2018). https://doi.org/10.2147/ndt.s179038

39. Yaribeygi, H., Panahi, Y., Sahraei, H., Johnston, T.P., Sahebkar, A.: The impact of stress on body function: a review. EXCLI J. **16**, 1057 (2017). ISSN: 1611-2156. https://doi.org/10.17179/EXCLI2017-480
40. Yu, C.P., Lee, H.Y., Lu, W.H., Huang, Y.C., Browning, M.H.: Restorative effects of virtual natural settings on middle-aged and elderly adults. Urban For. Urban Greening **56**, 126863 (2020). https://doi.org/10.1016/j.ufug.2020.126863. https://www.sciencedirect.com/science/article/pii/S1618866720306804

Social Justice

A Moderated Mediation Analysis of Meaningfulness and Positive Intergroup Outcomes Through Prosocial Gameplay

Valerie Yu[✉], Gabrielle C. Ibasco, Bingyu Chen, and Vivian Hsueh Hua Chen

Wee Kim Wee School of Communication and Information, Nanyang Technological University, Singapore, Singapore
valeriej001@e.ntu.edu.sg

Abstract. This study examines how the meaningfulness of a story influences empathy and attitudes towards racial or ethnic outgroups through a prosocial video game that features meaningful dialogic encounters with a fictional NPC outgroup character. Through a moderated mediation analysis, the role of outgroup identification in facilitating empathic feelings is also examined. An online pre-post user study was carried out with 206 participants aged from 20 to 61. Results showed meaningfulness was positively associated with attitudes towards racial or ethnic outgroups after playing the game. Empathic feelings mediated the link between meaningfulness and intergroup attitudes. Outgroup identification positively moderated the relationship between meaningfulness and empathy. Theoretical implications and limitations are discussed.

Keywords: Intergroup relationships · video games · meaningful play · outgroup attitudes · empathy

1 Introduction

Stories have, for decades in the field of communication, been examined for the wide variety of media effects that they can convey to audiences. Through consumption of narrative experiences, it is suggested that people can be influenced to undergo various forms of belief and behavior change [1]. As technology has improved over the years, narratives have also found a place in more interactive and immersive forms of media, such as video games and virtual reality experiences [2, 3]. Interactive narrative experiences allow people to see, hear, and control stories with a higher level of fidelity and feel more personally involved in the story [4].

Through interactive narratives, scholars also suggest that individuals experience not just entertainment, but may also derive meaningfulness from the storyline and their involvement in shaping it [5, 6]. Perceived meaningfulness of narratives has also been linked in prior studies to positive belief and behavior change in line with the subject of the story. In one example, Steinemann and colleagues [7] found a positive relationship between meaningfulness and prosocial donating behaviors after individuals played a

© The Author(s), under exclusive license to Springer Nature Switzerland AG 2023
C. Harteveld et al. (Eds.): ISAGA 2022, LNCS 13622, pp. 217–227, 2023.
https://doi.org/10.1007/978-3-031-37171-4_15

game highlighting the struggles of being homeless. In another, Grasse and colleagues [7] utilized interactive storytelling as an ethics learning tool, finding that players developed stronger moral reasoning skills through successful navigation of presented moral dilemmas in a game. If applied correctly, the use of game-based interactive storytelling may thus be applicable to achieve a wide range of intended outcomes.

In intergroup literature, meaningful dialogic encounters with outgroup members are proposed to be influential in promoting more positive intergroup relationships [8, 9]. Game-based interactive storytelling provides a platform for designing such encounters and allowing individuals to experience them more accessibly. With the use of non- player characters (NPC) in place of actual outgroup individuals, it also minimizes po- tential harm that can take place in the event of a negative encounter. Additionally, prior studies show evidence that vicarious intergroup contact experiences (e.g., media expe- riences) are a viable and effective alternative to actual intergroup contact [10]. Thus far, however, only a few studies have examined the mechanisms of NPC-based meaningful interac- tive narratives on improving intergroup relationships. Through a custom game- based interactive story, this study aims to bridge this gap by examining and providing prelimi- nary empirical evidence for how perceived meaningfulness of a prosocial narrative may be able to promote positive intergroup outcomes such as empathy and attitude change towards different others.

1.1 The Link Between Meaningfulness and Positive Outgroup Attitudes

In the current context, we conceptualize meaningfulness in media consumption as a unique connection and understanding that individuals develop which helps them relate the media content to real-life situations [11]. Viewing and interacting with meaning- ful media can affect a person's perception of others; notably, more favorable attitudes towards the people or groups of people involved in the media content [12]. This mech- anism is also expected to be similarly effective when the context involves outgroup rather than ingroup members, suggesting that it may be useful in improving outgroup attitudes. Interactive narrative experiences are also expected to reduce resistance to embedded messages (e.g., promoting prosocial behavior) through willful suspension of disbelief when they are immersed in the story [13], which may help achieve positive attitudinal outcomes more organically and effectively compared to non-narrative mes- sages. To our knowledge, no study has yet examined this direct relationship between meaningful experiences and positive outgroup attitudes, particularly in the context of interactive narratives. However, there is some prior evidence in intergroup literature link- ing meaning-making mechanisms to improved attitudes which may aid this theoretical discussion.

Positive experiences involving outgroup members can aid the development of a sense of other relatedness [14], other connectedness [15], and gratitude [16], which sub- sequently improves outgroup perceptions. Game-based interactive storytelling provides opportunities for these various meaning-making mechanisms to take place, as the narra- tive is supplemented by concrete gameplay that puts players in a position to be an active participant in the story [5]. More specifically, Daneels and colleagues [11] suggest that engagement with the themes of the narrative (in this case, prosocial attitudes), the char- acters in the story, and narrative-impacting choices all contribute to creating meaningful gaming experiences. In other contexts, such as watching online videos, experiencing eudaimonia has been found to improve prosocial attitudes, such as stereotype reduction [17]. Expecting cognitive consistency between positive attitudes and stereotype reduction, we propose that:

H1: Experienced meaningfulness will be positively associated with reported outgroup attitudes.

1.2 The Mediating Role of Empathy

While we expect H1 to hold true following the experience of a game-based interactive narrative promoting positive contact and prosocial behavior towards an outgroup member, we are also cognizant to the fact that game experiences can be complex, and players may derive their own meaning beyond what is designed and expected [18]. Hence, it is important to examine other paths in which meaningfulness may be linked with positive outgroup attitudes.

Raney and colleagues [12] suggest that feelings of empathy may provide another link between meaningfulness and positive outgroup attitudes. Involvement in an interactive story and the process of meaning-making can also heighten emotional arousal, putting individuals in a position to be more empathetic when the opportunity presents itself [19]. The subsequent positive relationship between empathy and positive outgroup attitudes is well established and has been empirically observed in a significant body of existing studies. For example, one study found that feelings of empathy experienced after watching Paralympic athletes compete was linked to de-stigmatization and more positive attitudes towards persons with disabilities [20]. The link between empathy and positive outgroup attitudes is also relatively robust, having been observed not just in adult populations, but also found to be useful in shaping positive outgroup attitudes among young children [21] and adolescent populations [22]. Seeking to explore this established link and provide empirical evidence for the link between meaningfulness and empathy in the current study, we propose that:

H2: The relationship between meaningfulness and outgroup attitudes will be positively mediated by empathy.

1.3 Moderated Mediation and the Role of Outgroup Identification

Developing empathy through meaningful experiences may, however, not be invariable. In a study by Batson and colleagues [23], inducing empathy was found to be more effective when stigmatization of the outgroup was at a malleable level, however, when stigmatization was high, the effects of induced empathy were diminished. As empathy involves an other-oriented emotional response [12], a greater disparity in being able to relate to others may impede this effect. Being able to identify with different others is one route examined by prior research that can moderate feelings of empathy towards outgroup members [24–26]. A greater sense of outgroup identification develops a connection between self and others, and facilitates the perspective taking process, which is crucial to empathic feelings [27]. Hence, it may also be prudent to examine this relationship in the current study; we expect that:

H3: Outgroup identification moderates the relationship between meaningfulness and empathy such that higher levels of outgroup identification result in a more positive relationship between meaningfulness and empathy.

2 Methods

2.1 Participants

206 participants between the ages of 20 to 61 were recruited (Male = 92, Female = 114) from an online sign-up process after invitations were sent through email. Each participant received a digital shopping voucher upon completion of the online study.

2.2 Procedures

This study included three stages: a pre-test, game play, and a post-test. After signing the consent form, the participants received a link to a survey containing pre-test questions, the game, and post-test questions. They were asked to complete the pre-test survey as the first stage. Upon completion of the pre-test survey, they played a custom 2D prosocial game. Following gameplay, participants were also asked to complete a series of post-test questions.

2.3 Stimulus

The stimulus for this study was an online serious game developed using Unity and embedded in Qualtrics. It involved a single player role-playing experience where the protagonist (main character) had to solve various puzzles in the game to advance the story. As the story advanced, the protagonist was introduced to an antagonist non-player character that was later revealed to be innocent and helpful. In the later parts of the game, players had to cooperate with the antagonist to solve puzzles and complete the game. The narrative was linear and designed to encourage positive feelings towards the antagonist as the story advanced.

2.4 Measures

The pre-test questionnaire included the measures for attitudes towards outgroup members, empathy towards outgroup members, and demographic information. The same measures of attitude and empathy are also measured in post-test questionnaire. In addition to these two variables, game meaningfulness and outgroup identification were also measured in the post-test questionnaire. Participants were asked to rate "people of a different race or ethnicity from your own" as outgroup members.

Meaningfulness. Meaningfulness refers to participants' evaluation of the story after completing the game, which was measured using three items on a 7-point Likert scale (e.g., I found the story of this game to be very meaningful; I was moved by the story of the game), $\alpha = .88$.

Attitudes. Attitude towards outgroups was measured using a feeling thermometer scale ranging from 0 to 100 [28]. This measurement includes three pairs of items ("very cold

= 0" to "very warm = 100"; "not favorable = 0" to "favorable = 100"; "negative = 0" to "positive = 100"). This was measured in both the pre- (α = .92) and post-test (α = .89).

Empathy. Based on the emotional response questionnaire [23], a 7-point Likert scale was used to measure empathy. The scale included 4 items, 'warm', 'soft-hearted', 'compassionate', and 'moved', and was included in both pre- (α = .89) and post-tests (α = .94).

Outgroup Identification. Outgroup identification was measured on a 5-point Likert scale comprising 5 statements asking participants about their ability to identify with the NPC character (e.g., I was able to understand events in the game similar to how the NPC understood them; While playing the game, I wanted the NPC to succeed in achieving his goals), α = .87.

3 Results

We first conducted a series of ordinary least squares (OLS) regressions to identify significant predictors of attitudes toward the outgroup following gameplay (see Table 1). Among our control variables, pre-test empathy (β = .329, p = .000) and attitudes (β = .300, p = .000) both had significant positive associations with post-test attitudes, while age was found to be negatively associated (β = -.162, p = .020). Gender did not significantly relate to attitudes toward the outgroup (β = .023, p = .714). Supporting H1, meaningfulness was positively associated with attitudes (β = .165, p = .014), as was post-test empathy (β = .314, p = .000). However, outgroup identification was not significantly related to attitudes (β = .087, p = .623), nor did we find evidence for an interaction between outgroup identification and meaningfulness (β = -.075, p = .817).

Next, we ran an equivalent series of OLS regressions predicting post-test empathy, our proposed mediator of the relationship between meaningfulness and attitudes toward the outgroup (see Table 1). Pre-test baseline empathy was positively related with post-test empathy (β = .619, p = .000). Women were also more likely than men to report higher empathy scores after playing the game (β = .153, p = .007). Falling in line with the possibility of mediation (H2), meaningfulness was positively associated with post-test empathy (β = .226, p = .000). Moreover, though the association between outgroup identification and empathy was not significant (β = -.072, p = .231), we found a significant positive interaction between outgroup identification and empathy (β = .739, p = .013), suggesting the possibility of moderation.

To test H2, we computed a bootstrapped mediation model using Model 4 on the PROCESS macro developed for SPSS [29], with 5,000 bootstraps and covariates including gender, age, pre-test empathy, and pre-test attitudes. Complementing the results of our standard OLS regression models, pathway coefficients indicate that meaningfulness was positively associated with empathy after playing the game (b = .184, SE = .052, p = .000); in turn, greater post-test empathy related to more positive attitudes toward the outgroup (b = 5.26, p = .000). Supporting H1, there was a significant direct effect of meaningfulness on attitudes post-gameplay (b = 3.14, SE = .975, p = .002). Moreover,

Table 1. Predictors of empathy (proposed mediator) and attitudes (primary dependent variable) toward the outgroup measured after participants played the 2D game.

Dependent variable	Post-test empathy	Post-test attitudes
	B	β
Controls		
Age	− .095	− .162*
Gender (1 = man)	.153**	.023
Pre-Test Empathy	.619**	.329**
Pre-Test Attitudes	− .037	.300**
Independent variables		
Post-Test Empathy	-	.311**
Outgroup Identification	− .072	.049
Meaningfulness	.226**	.165*
Meaningfulness x Outgroup Identification	.739*	− .075
R²	.487	.400

$N = 206$, β = standardized regression coefficient, $*p < .050$, $**p < .001$.

validating H2, the indirect effect of meaningfulness on attitudes via empathy was significant, as the confidence interval of the effect did not include zero (b = .970, SE = .444, [.243, 1.96]).

Next, we used Model 8 on the PROCESS Macro [29] with 5,000 bootstraps to test H3, which predicted that this indirect effect via empathy would be moderated by outgroup identification. Controlling for pre-test empathy, attitudes, age, and gender, the index of moderated mediation was found to be significant, as the bootstrapped confidence interval did not include zero (b = .714, SE = .324, [.129, 1.39]). Aligning with the patterns we predicted under H3, the indirect effect of meaningfulness via empathy was largest when outgroup identification was high (+1 SD; b = 1.82, SE = .715, [.546, 3.33]), and smallest when outgroup identification was low (−1 SD; b = .823, SE = .409, [.129, 1.72]). A pairwise contrast analysis reveals that that the indirect effect among high identifiers (+1 SD) was significantly greater than the indirect effect among low identifiers (−1 SD; bdiff = .999, SE = .453, [.180, 1.94]). The conditional indirect effects and moderated mediation indices are presented in Table 2. The final moderated mediation pathway model is illustrated in Fig. 1.

Table 2. Indirect effects of meaningfulness on post-test attitudes toward the outgroup via empathy at low (–1 SD), average (Mean), and high (+1 SD) levels of outgroup identification.

Outgroup identification	Indirect effect	SE	95% CI
2.95 (–1 SD)	.823	.409	.129, 1.72
3.65 (Mean)	1.32	.537	.393, 2.48
4.35 (+1 SD)	1.82	.715	.546, 3.33

Note. SD = Standard deviation; SE = Standard error; CI = bootstrapped confidence interval

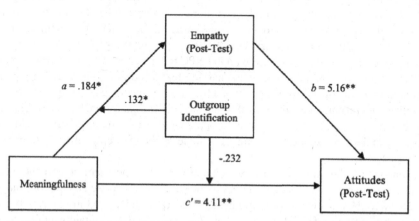

Fig. 1. Moderated mediation model with post-test empathy mediating the relationship between meaningfulness and attitudes toward the outgroup, and outgroup identification moderating the indirect effect. Statistical controls include age, gender, pre-test empathy, and pre-test attitudes.

4   Discussion

In this study, we tested whether a novel 2D game that features meaningful dialogic encounters with a fictional NPC outgroup could facilitate more positive attitudes toward racial or ethnic outgroups. We found evidence to support our predictions. Participants who derived greater meaning from the intergroup cooperation storyline endorsed more positive attitudes toward an unspecified ethnic outgroup after gameplay, even after controlling for baseline attitudes (H1). This finding enriches an existing body of research documenting how the perceived meaningfulness of gamified narratives could lead to positive moral cognitions [30] and intentions to engage in helping behavior [6]. Past research on interactive narratives has predominantly focused on perspective-taking, where players are made to embody the viewpoint of an outgroup or "othered" character [6, 31, 32]. To our knowledge, the present study is one of few to demonstrate how meaning derived from game narratives centered on a fictional inter- group contact scenario could relate to similar outcomes.

Interestingly, though the NPC characters and outgroup featured in the game narrative were entirely fictional, participants nonetheless reported improved empathy and attitudes toward an unspecific, generalized racial outgroup. Though we did not manipulate or test intergroup contact experimentally, it is possible that secondary transfer effects occurred, where the prosocial benefits of contact with one group (whether fictional or not) generalized to perceptions of analogous outgroups more broadly [33, 34]. Through the process of evaluative conditioning, the affective experience provided by the game scenario may have "spread" to related domains [35], particularly among players who resonated with the narrative's message. Similarly, our findings align with research on mediated intergroup contact, where media representations of contact between one's ingroup and an outgroup (even in fiction) could influence intergroup perceptions in the real world [36].

Moreover, as predicted, we found empathic feelings to constitute a significant mechanism underlying the association between perceived meaningfulness and intergroup attitudes (H2). In the intergroup relations literature, empathy has been identified as a mediator of strategies designed to reduce intergroup bias in both human-computer interactions [32, 37] and in the real world [38, 39]. In the present study, players who found the positive intergroup contact scenario with the NPC to be meaningful may have resonated with the storyline on an affective level, enabling feelings of other-directed warmth and compassion to manifest [19]. Being moved by the storyline may have thus related to an overall greater receptiveness to the egalitarian message the game tried to convey. Through storyline details that humanized the outgroup character over time, players could have indirectly undergone perspective-taking, a reliable predictor of empathy in past research [40, 41].

Nonetheless, the extent to which participants were able "put themselves in the shoes" of the outgroup NPC was not equal across participants—a moderated mediation analysis revealed that the association was strongest for those who identified most strongly with the fictional outgroup (H3). Past studies have likewise found that empathy inducement is most pronounced among people who see greater similarities or overlap between the 'self' and the 'other' [42, 43]. Our study thus lends support to the potential role of cognitive perspective-taking in the meaning-making process for gamified intergroup encounters. Indeed, interacting with an outgroup member has been found to facilitate a greater cognitive understanding of the outgroup's beliefs and motivations, and in turn, prosocial outcomes directed towards that outgroup [44]. Follow-up experimental research could unpack how identification with an outgroup character could be optimized through prosocial gameplay. Though players in the present study were able to embody the outgroup NPC at certain points, the experience of embodied perspective-taking was relatively brief and did not constitute a focal point of the game experience.

Even then, it should be noted that outgroup identification was generally high across participants in the current study. Low outgroup identifiers (-1 SD) in the sample re- ported an average of 2.95 units, which is above the midpoint of the 5-point identification scale. These generally high identification scores may explain why the association between meaningfulness and empathy was significant and positive at both low and high levels of outgroup identification. As such, to better capture how variance in outgroup identification influences intergroup outcomes, a follow-up study could systematically manipulate low vs. high levels of identification with the outgroup character to test for disparate effects.

This initial user study was not without its limitations, and certainly invites follow-up research to validate these associations. The within-subjects, correlational design of the study prevents us from making definite conclusions about whether causal relationships between meaningfulness, empathy, outgroup identification, and intergroup attitudes exist. Apart from manipulating identification with the outgroup character, it would also be fruitful to manipulate perceptions of meaningfulness, perhaps through active reflection exercises that require participants to document the key messages they gleaned from the game's storyline. It would also be worth investigating how gamified intergroup encounters with a fictional NPC outgroup compare against encounters with an outgroup designed to rep- resent a real-life racial outgroup. Would the effects we identified be more pronounced for narratives that address racial tensions relevant to the real world? Under what conditions would fictional NPC representations be more effective in generating meaning? Through such experimental investigations, scholars could have a deeper understanding of how narratives featuring fictional, NPC characters could be optimized to encourage social change in ecologically valid contexts.

Acknowledgements. This research is supported by the Ministry of Education, Singapore, under its Academic Research Fund Tier 1 Grant (RG41/20).

References

1. Green, M.C., Bilandzic, H., Fitzgerald, K., Paravati, E.: Narrative effects. Media Effects 130–145 (2019)
2. Ferguson, C., Broek, E.L.V.D., Oostendorp, H.V.: On the role of interaction mode and story structure in virtual reality serious games. Comput. Educ. **143**, 103671 (2020)
3. McGill, K.M.: The digital lineage of narrative: analyzing interactive fiction to further understand game narrative. In: Bostan, B. (ed.) Games and Narrative: Theory and Practice. ISCEMT, pp. 77–90. Springer, Cham (2022). https://doi.org/10.1007/978-3-030-81538-7_5
4. Sangalang, A., Johnson, J.M.Q., Ciancio, K.E.: Exploring audience involvement with an interactive narrative: implications for incorporating transmedia storytelling into entertainment-education campaigns. Crit. Arts **27**(1), 127–146 (2013)
5. Green, M.C., Jenkins, K.M.: Interactive narratives: processes and outcomes in user-directed stories. J. Commun. **64**(3), 479–500 (2014)
6. Iten, G.H., Steinemann, S.T., Opwis, K.: Choosing to help monsters: a mixed-method examination of meaningful choices in narrative-rich games and interactive narratives. In: Proceedings of the 2018 CHI Conference on Human Factors in Computing Systems, pp. 1–13 (2018)
7. Steinemann, S.T., Iten, G.H., Opwis, K., Forde, S.F., Frasseck, L., Mekler, E.D.: Interactive narratives affecting social change. J. Media Psychol. (2017)
8. Nagda, B.R.A.: Breaking barriers, crossing borders, building bridges: Communication processes in intergroup dialogues. J. Soc. Issues **62**(3), 553–576 (2006)
9. Nagda, B.R.A., Zuniga, X.: Fostering meaningful racial engagement through intergroup dialogues. Group Process. Intergroup Relat. **6**, 111–128 (2003)
10. Cadenas, G.A., Cisneros, J., Todd, N.R., Spanierman, L.B.: DREAMzone: testing two vicarious contact interventions to improve attitudes toward undocumented immigrants. J. Divers. Higher Educ. **11**(3), 295–208 (2018)
11. Daneels, R., Bowman, N.D., Possler, D., Mekler, E.D.: The 'eudaimonic experience': a scoping review of the concept in digital games research. Media Commun. **9**(2), 178–190 (2021)

12. Raney, A.A., Oliver, M.B., Bartsch, A.: Eudaimonia as media effect. Media Effects 258–274 (2019)
13. Murrar, S., Brauer, M.: Overcoming resistance to change: using narratives to create more positive intergroup attitudes. Curr. Dir. Psychol. Sci. **28**(2), 164–169 (2019)
14. Adachi, P.J., Willoughby, T.: The link between playing video games and positive youth outcomes. Child Dev. Perspect. **11**(3), 202–206 (2017)
15. Bobowik, M., Benet-Martínez, V., Repke, L.: United in diversity": the interplay of social network characteristics and personality in predicting outgroup attitudes. Group Process. Intergroup Relat. (2021)
16. Rambaud, S., Collange, J., Tavani, J.L., Zenasni, F.: Positive intergroup interdependence, prejudice, outgroup stereotype and helping behaviors: the role of group-based gratitude. Int. Rev. Soc. Psychol. **34**(1) (2021)
17. Krämer, N., Eimler, S.C., Neubaum, G., Winter, S., Rösner, L., Oliver, M.B.: Broadcasting one world: how watching online videos can elicit elevation and reduce stereotypes. New Media Soc. **19**(9), 1349–1368 (2017)
18. Cardoso, P., Carvalhais, M.: Breaking the game: the traversal of the emergent narrative in video games. J. Sci. Technol. Arts **5**(1), 25–31 (2013)
19. Bal, P.M., Veltkamp, M.: How does fiction reading influence empathy? an experimental investigation on the role of emotional transportation. PLoS ONE **8**(1), 55341 (2013)
20. Bartsch, A., Oliver, M.B., Nitsch, C., Scherr, S.: Inspired by the Paralympics: effects of empathy on audience interest in para-sports and on the destigmatization of persons with disabilities. Commun. Res. **45**(4), 525–553 (2018)
21. Taylor, L.K., Glen, C.: From empathy to action: can enhancing host-society children's empathy promote positive attitudes and prosocial behaviour toward refugees? J. Commun. Appl. Soc. Psychol. **30**(2), 214–226 (2020)
22. Miklikowska, M.: Empathy trumps prejudice: the longitudinal relation between empathy and anti-immigrant attitudes in adolescence. Dev. Psychol. **54**(4), 703 (2018)
23. Batson, C.D., Polycarpou, M.P., Harmon-Jones, E., Imhoff, H.J., Mitchener, E.C., Bednar, L.L., Highberger, L.: Empathy and attitudes: can feeling for a member of a stigmatized group improve feelings toward the group?. J. Pers. Soc. Psychol. **72**(1), 105 (1997)
24. Hinnant, J.B., Brien, M.: Cognitive and emotional control and perspective taking and their relations to empathy in 5-year-old children. J. Genet. Psychol. **168**(3), 301–322 (2007)
25. Valente, F.: Empathy and communication: a model of empathy development. J. New Media Mass Commun. **3**(1), 1–24 (2016)
26. McKeever, R.: Vicarious experience: experimentally testing the effects of empathy for media characters with severe depression and the intervening role of perceived similarity. Health Commun. **30**(11), 1122–1134 (2015)
27. Trautwein, M., Kanske, P., Böckler, A., Singer, T.: Training compassion and cognitive perspective taking separately: first evidence for differential mental training effects. In: European Summer Research Institute of the Mind and Life Institute, August 2014
28. Zavala-Rojas, D.: A procedure to prevent differences in translated survey items using SQP (2014)
29. Hayes, A.F.: Introduction to Mediation, Moderation, and Conditional Process Analysis: A Regression-Based Approach. Guilford Publications, Second Edition (2017)
30. Grasse, K.M., Melcer, E.F., Kreminski, M., Junius, N., Wardrip-Fruin, N.: Improving undergraduate attitudes towards responsible conduct of research through an interactive storytelling game. In: Extended Abstracts of the 2021 CHI Conference on Human Factors in Computing Systems, pp. 1–8 (2021)
31. Gutierrez, B., Kaatz, A., Chu, S., Ramirez, D., Samson-Samuel, C., Carnes, M.: Fair play: a videogame designed to address implicit race bias through active perspective taking. Games Health J. **3**(6), 371–378 (2014)

32. Herrera, F., Bailenson, J., Weisz, E., Ogle, E., Zaki, J.: Building long-term empathy: a large-scale comparison of traditional and virtual reality perspective-taking. PLoS ONE **13**(10), 204494 (2018)
33. Lolliot, S., Schmid, K., Hewstone, M., Ramiah, A.A., Tausch, N., Swart, H.: (2013)
34. Vezzali, L., Giovannini, D.: Secondary transfer effect of intergroup contact: the role of intergroup attitudes, intergroup anxiety and perspective taking. J. Commun. Appl. Soc. Psychol. **22**(2), 125–144 (2012)
35. Pettigrew, T.F.: Secondary transfer effect of contact: Do intergroup contact effects spread to noncontacted outgroups? Soc. Psychol. **40**(2), 55–65 (2009)
36. Joyce, N., Harwood, J.: Improving intergroup attitudes through televised vicarious intergroup contact: social cognitive processing of ingroup and outgroup information. Commun. Res. **41**(5), 627–643 (2014)
37. Chen, V.H.H., Ibasco, G.C., Leow, V.J.X., Lew, J.Y.Y.: The effect of VR avatar embodiment on improving attitudes and closeness toward immigrants. Front. Psychol. 4722– 4722 (2021)
38. Pettigrew, T.F., Tropp, L.R.: How does intergroup contact reduce prejudice? meta-analytic tests of three mediators. Eur. J. Soc. Psychol. **38**(6), 922–934 (2008)
39. Vescio, T.K., Sechrist, G.B., Paolucci, M.P.: Perspective taking and prejudice reduction: the mediational role of empathy arousal and situational attributions. Eur. J. Soc. Psychol. **33**(4), 455–472 (2003)
40. Batson, C.D., Polycarpou, M.P., Harmon-Jones, E., Imhoff, H.J., Mitchener, E.C., Bednar, L.L., Highberger, L.: Empathy and attitudes: can feeling for a member of a stigmatized group improve feelings toward the group? J. Pers. Soc. Psychol. **72**(1), 105–105 (1997)
41. Shih, M., Wang, E., Bucher, A.T., Stotzer, R.: Perspective taking: reducing prejudice to-wards general outgroups and specific individuals. Group Process. Intergroup Relat. **12**(5), 565–577 (2009)
42. Cooke, A.N., Bazzini, D.G., Curtin, L.A., Emery, L.J.: Empathic understanding: benefits of perspective-taking and facial mimicry instructions are mediated by self-other overlap. Motiv. Emot. **42**(3), 446–457 (2018). https://doi.org/10.1007/s11031-018-9671-9
43. Hinnant, J.B., O'Brien, M.: Cognitive and emotional control and perspective taking and their relations to empathy in 5-year-old children. J. Genet. Psychol. **168**(3), 301–322 (2007)
44. Heinke, M.S., Louis, W.R.: Cultural background and individualistic–collectivistic values in relation to similarity, perspective taking, and empathy. J. Appl. Soc. Psychol. **39**(11), 2570–2590 (2009)

Author Index

C. Harteveld et al. (Eds.): ISAGA 2022, LNCS 13622, p. 229, 2023.
https://doi.org/10.1007/978-3-031-37171-4

Printed in the United States
by Baker & Taylor Publisher Services